Shaikh Muhyiddeen Abdul-Qādir Gilāni

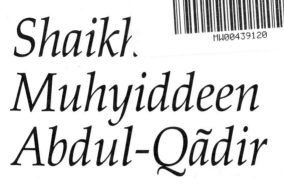

VOLUME 1

THE ENDOWMENT OF DIVINE GRACE
& THE SPREAD OF DIVINE MERCY
(Al-Fathu Rabbāni)

Translated by
Muhammad M. Al-Akili

PEARL PUBLISHING HOUSE
Philadelphia, Pennsylvania, U.S.A.

Title: **The Endowment of Divine Grace
and The Spread of Divine Mercy**
Subtitle: (Al-Fathu Rabbānï)
Volume 1

Translated by: Muhammad M. Al-Akili

Published in the United States of America by
Pearl Publishing House
P. O. Box 28870 Philadelphia, PA 19151 U.S.A.

Library of Congress Card Number 90-63799

ISBN 1-879405-01-6

Printed and bound in the U.S.A.

Table of Contents

The Endowment of Divine Grace
& the Spread of Divine Mercy
(Al-Fathu Rabbāni wal-Faidhu Rahmāni)

Volume 1

Shaikh
Muhyiddeen Abdul-Qādir Gilāni

PREFACE

In the Name of God, the Merciful, the Compassionate

Shaikh Muhyiddeen Abdul-Qādir Gilāni (1077-1166), God bless his soul, was the luminary of Baghdād whose enormous spiritual attainments and contributions to Islāmic spiritual science are well renowned .

Since the divine revelations were completed in the Holy Qur'ān and the coming of the Prophet Muhammad, upon whom be peace, each era has produced luminaries who testified to the message and gave explanations and guidance to thirsty seekers of knowledge. Among such luminaries came Shaikh Muhyiddeen Abdul-Qādir Gilāni, whose attainments triumph above all as they collectively attest to his exalted station and spiritual role.

Among his recorded and most renowned exhortations are his "Al-Fathu Rabbāni" (i.e., The Endowment of Divine Grace), which is a collection of sixty-eight sermons delivered in the year 1251-1252 in Baghdād. This volume represents the first thirty - five discourses, and what better way to introduce them than with the Shaikh's own words taken from a letter:

"Dear friend:

Your heart is a polished mirror. You must wipe it clean of the veils of dust which have gathered upon it, because it is destined to reflect the light of divine secrets... which will fall upon it if you wish for Him, from Him, and with Him... If only the lamp of divine secrets is kindled within your inner self, the rest will come, either all at once or little by little... Then you will see the sun of inner knowledge rising from the horizon of divine reason..."

"Some you already know, some we will tell you here. Read, listen and try to understand."

In an age of self-help books, this compilation of spoken talks addresses the questions of life and existence in clear, practical terms that are both timely and timeless. The concise explanations reverberate like the single, sweet note of a reed flute penetrating the noise and confusion of today's world.

To the reader who is not familiar with Islāmic traditions, this book brings a clear explanation of the essence of faith and how to deal with our human existence.

During the 12th century, sufi orders spread throughout the Muslim world, and many people claimed to have reached the state of ultimate truth (**haqïqa**) and illumination, to have been in communion with their Lord, and claimed that the divine laws of **sharï'a** and its precepts (**farā'idh**) were no longer applicable to them. Refuting their claims, Shaikh Abdul-Qādir stated in one of his discourses:

*"Omitting any of the prescribed duties of worship (**farā'idh**) is atheism, and to commit wrongdoing is a sin, because the prescribed laws of worship (**sharï'a**) are never abrogated in any person's case or under any circumstances."* (Al-Fathu Rabbanï, Chapter 11)

Chaos, confusion and innovation spread throughout some of the sufi orders. To such people, Shaikh Abdul-Qādir's words [رَضِيَ ٱللّٰهُ عَنْهُ] were miraculously effective in transforming the hearts of the of people who heard them, and those who later read them.

The eleventh and the twelfth centuries of Islāmic history were known for their extensive research and studies in religious knowledge and science. Theology, religious law, prophetic traditions, and Qur'ānic commentaries were some of the major branches of studies at the universities of Baghdād. Some of the renowned masters were Imām Al-Ghazāli (d. 1112), Ibn 'Aqïl (d. 1120), Qādi 'Iyadh Al-Māliki (d. 1115), Abdul-Qādir Girjanï (d. 1178), Jār-Allāh Zamakhshari (d. 1145), Abu Zakariya Tabrïzi (d. 1109) and many more who became the men of letters and doctors of religious interpretation in the Muslim world for generations to come.

When the essence and true meaning of the Islāmic caliphate was lost, many deputies of God's Messenger, upon whom be peace, and preachers of the truth stood to renew the call to the people. They reminded them of their covenant with God Almighty and His Messenger, upon whom be peace, drawing the beauty and sweetness of Islām into the hearts of the believers, calling them to devotion and obedience to God's command, and spreading the message and encouraging them to preserve their faith. Among these blessed servants of God Almighty were Al-Hassan Al-Basri,

Al-Fadhil Bin 'Iyād, Ma'rouf Al-Karkhi and others, may God Almighty be pleased with them forever.

Shaikh Abu Muhammad Muhyiddeen Abdul-Qādir Gilāni was born in the city of Jilān, in the northwestern part of Persia, in the year 1077. Guided by the hand of providence, he entered the city of Baghdad in 1095 at the age of eighteen to seek knowledge. Incidentally, this was the year in which Imām Al-Ghazāli left Baghdad in his quest for greater spiritual knowledge.

To satisfy his thirst for knowledge, Shaikh Abdul-Qādir went to nearly every renowned shaikh of the time including, Shaikh Abul Wafā' Ibn 'Aqïl, Shaikh Muhammad Bin Al-Hassan Al-Baqlāni and Abu Zakariya Tabrïzi. He learned the tariqa at the hands of Shaikh Hammad Bin Muslim Al-Dabbas, then completed his initiation at the hands of Shaikh Qādi Abi Sa'ïd Al-Mukhrami (d. 1127), a renowned shaikh who was the headmaster and teacher of seekers on the path, under whom many of the renowned shaikhs of Baghdād had studied. Also known as Shaikh Al-Mubarak Sa'ïd bin Al-Hassan, he was the one who handed down the order's traditional cloak (**sijjāda**) to Shaikh Abdul-Qādir Gilāni who was then over fifty years old. Shaikh Sa'ïd also commissioned him to head his then modest fellowship and school in Baghdad. Shaikh Abi Sa'ïd once said: "Shaikh Abdul Qadir received the cloak at my hand, but in fact, I also received my cloak at his hand." The school became known as the fellowship, also known as the Madrasa of Shaikh Muhyiddeen Abdul Qadir Gilāni.

He once related: *"At the beginning only two or three people came to hear me, then others heard about me and the place was soon crowded. After that, I used to sit in the mosque at bāb al-hilba, which became too small to handle the large crowds of people who would to come even at night, carrying candles and torches to see their way. My chair then was carried to the main street, then to the outskirts of the city, which became the new gathering place. People would come on foot, on horses, mules, mares, and camels. You could see them standing in a huge circle numbering nearly seventy thousand at some meetings."*

His regular meetings gathered more than four hundred scribes. Shaikh Al-Sha'rāni described Shaikh Abdul Qādir's fellowship (**tarïqa**) as follows: "His practice was based on the foundation of God Almighty's Oneness (**tawhïd**) in description, jurisdiction, and performance." He used to address his companions saying: *"Follow and do not invent; obey and do not pervert."* (Futüh Al-Ghaib, Chapter 1). *"If you find in yourself a failure to comply with an obligatory precept of the **shari'a**, then you should realize that satan has played a trick on you and allured you."* (Al-Tabaqāt Al-Kubrā, page 129). He firmly stated: *"Any 'truth' (**haqïqa**) which is not supported by the active testimony of the divine laws (**shari'a**) is atheism"* (Al-Fathu Rabbāni, p. 152).

Shaikh Abdul-Qādir spoke in thirteen different religious sciences, including Qur'ānic commentaries, prophetic traditions, theology, religious laws, the science of hadïth, sïra (the leading example and history of the Prophet's life), grammar and philology, among other branches of religious science. In the afternoons, he would read the Holy Qur'ān in the seven different recitation forms. He also would deliver legal opinions in religious matters (**fatwā**) including interpretation of the Shāfi'i and Hanbali schools of thought. He himself followed the school of Imām Ahmad Ibn Hanbal.

Describing his tarïqa, Ibn Rajab once related: "He strictly followed the precepts of the Prophetic sunnah in any commentaries concerning the divine attributes (**sifāt**), the divine decree (**qadar**) and other related subjects, and he was vehement in responding to those who followed other interpretations."

In his greatness, he stood humbly with children and servants and spoke kindly to them. He frequently sat in the company of poor people and befriended them, stroking their shoulders. He never knocked at the door of any minister or sultan. When the Caliph or his ministers visited him, he would leave the room before their arrival, then afterwards reenter to avoid standing up for them.

In his book *Qalā'idul Jawāhir*, Harāda described him as follows: "I have never seen anyone of better character, more magnanimous, more generous, kinder at heart, more trustworthy or loyal to his promise and friendships than our master, Shaikh Abdul-Qādir. Despite his revered status, profound knowledge and exalted station, he would stand and converse with the common people, honor the elders, initiate greetings, sit with the meek and humble himself to the poor."

Imām Al-Hāfiz Abu Abdullāh Al-Birzālï described him as follows: "His prayers were always answered. He was easily inclined to shed tears, contemplative, and continually invoking God's remembrance. He was cheerful, generous, and magnanimous. He possessed vast knowledge, honorable character, and maintained an ever increasing devotion and steadfastness in his studies."

The grand mufti of Baghdād, Abu Abdullāh Al-Baghdādi, described him saying: "He was the furthest person from wrong-doing and the closest to righteousness. He was the bravest in standing for the truth in regard to God's rights on us. He never got angry for himself and never took the side of anyone except his Lord."

Ibn Kathïr described the admonitions of Shaikh Abdul-Qādir saying: "He enjoined the people to do what is good and to abstain from what is evil. His admonitions addressed caliphs, ministers, people in authority, judges, companions and the masses. Standing in the pulpits of the mosques, he reprimanded them in the presence of witnesses, as well as during his public addresses. He disavowed the civil appointment of any unjust person, chose God's blessings over anyone else's wrath, and was not affected by any reproach."

In the book *Qalā'idul Jawāhir*, it is related: "When the Caliph Al-Muqtadï li-Amrillāh appointed Judge Abil-Wafā', Yahyā Bin Sa'ïd Al-Muzaffar, who was known to be an unjust person to fill the position of chief justice, Shaikh Abdul-Qādir stood on the pulpit of the grand mosque in Baghdād during his Friday sermon (**khutba**), and addressed the Caliph saying:

"You have appointed the worst of the unjust ones to judge over the Muslims! What will be your answer tomorrow before the Lord of the universes, the most merciful of the merciful ones?" The Caliph shook in fear at hearing that, cried, and immediately dismissed the aforementioned judge.

As the Shaikh of Baghdād, then the capital of the caliphate, he was distressed by the degenerating moral behavior of society. He fought in every way to vanquish hypocrisy and wickedness and called upon the people to return to the judgment of the Book and the leading example of the Prophet, upon whom be peace. He was an Imām who was able to bind the Muslim society back together and help it to cleanse itself from evil. In fact, it was God Almighty's design, work and mercy that made it all possible, for what comes from God will remain and what comes from anyone else will vanish. As the teachings of Shaikh Abdul-Qādir spred over the land, he taught and appointed many deputies to carry the work from the East to the West.

He reopened the door for the renewal of one's covenant with God Almighty, and Muslims came forward in crowds to repent, agreeing not to associate partners with God Almighty, not to deny God's favors, not to reject the faith, not to create divisiveness, not to invent new ways of life, not to introduce new ideas into God's perfect religion, not to be unjust, not to neglect what God Almighty enjoined upon them, not to sacrifice their lives for the sake of the world, and not to forget the hereafter.

His students were among the poor and the rich, the ruler and the subject, and after their repentance and renewing their faith, they followed his teachings with great love, sincerity and devotion, and thus regained their dignity and integrity as human beings. For over half a century, Shaikh Abdul-Qādir was able by God's leave to revive an entire generation, and the repercussions of such work are still being felt.

Shaikh Abdul-Qādir [رَضِيَ ٱللّٰهُ عَنْهُ] called upon the people to correct themselves, to cleanse their hearts, to dispel the love of the world from their hearts and instead to fill them with the love of God Almighty. He exhort them to follow the Messenger, upon whom be peace, to abstain from affectation, to dispel arrogance, hatred, jealousy, envy, perfidy, hypocrisy and falsehood. He called upon them to break their attachments to the world and dependence on its patrons, and instead turn to God Almighty for all their needs, for He is the Sustainer and Cherisher of the universes.

Shaikh Abdul-Qādir stated in one of his talks: *"The walls of the religion of Muhammad, upon whom be peace, are falling and its foundation is cracking. Let us come together, O people of the earth, and rebuild what was ruined, reestablish what fell! This is not acceptable! O Sun! O Moon! O Day! All of you come! O ye people! Islām is crying for help, holding its hands over its head in distress from these profligates and insolent ones, from those inventors, perverts and heedless ones, the unjust ones, the tyrants, those who wear forged garments of theologians and claim to have knowledge which they do not possess!"*

O Man! How hardened is your heart! Even a dog serves his master! He guards him, accompanies him in the fields and hunts for him, guards his herd and looks up to him with loyalty and hope that his master may give him a couple of bites from his dinner or put something aside for later. Ponder on that and compare it with your fattening yourself on God's favors and fully satisfying your desires in them, but never doing what He asks you to do! You do not pay Him what you owe, you neglect His orders and do not guard the limits which He ordained for you!" (Al-Fathu Rabbāni, p. 661)

He objected strongly to people who did not care to work to earn their livelihood, who lived dependent on others' donations, and encouraged people to earn their livelihood with their own sweat.

In his book *Zail Tabaqāt Al-Hanābila,* Ibn Rajab quoted Shaikh Muwaffaq Al-Deen, author of the book *Al-Maghni,* saying: "I have never heard of anyone having as many noble deeds and miraculous blessings **(karāmāt)** as those attributed to Shaikh Abdul Qādir."

This book will bring about a clear understanding of true Islām for Muslims, the average reader, as well as for scholars in the domain of comparative religious studies. It will open the reader's eyes to a higher vision and explain in clear terms the path of success on this spiritual journey.

❀ ❀ ❀ ❀ ❀

In the Name of God,
The Merciful, The Compassionate

All praises be to God Who has closed to us the door of need except for needing Him. Praise be to Him for His countless favors upon us, praises to equal the number of His creations and the number of all things encompassed in His knowledge.

O Lord, I ask You by him who praised You with the best of praises, to whom Thou revealed the innermost meanings of Thy beautiful names and attributes, and whom Thou raised to the highest rank in paradise, so that his station may never be surpassed, his prestige may never be rivalled, and no angel nigh unto Thee and no apostle sent by Thee may equal him in Thy sight. Lord, fulfill Thy promise of his intercession on the day of judgment for his family, descendents, and followers.

Lord, bless our Master Muhammad, who as the bearer of the most noble lineage proclaimed that God is the very truth, that His Book and revelations are the manifest proof, and that His path is the infallible road to salvation. Lord, bless him, the pure and chaste one, the immaculate, the one gifted with glorious miracles and confounding impact, and the one endowed with the virtues of absolute exaltedness. Lord, bless him and his followers as many times as there are manifestations of Thy perfection, and honor him, Lord, with a blessing worthy of his perfection.

Lord, bless our Master Muhammad and his followers as deserving his beauty, reverence and perfection. Make us taste, through these invocations of blessings upon him, the pure pleasure of our relationship to him, Lord, and endow his followers and companions with the same bounty and grace.

Lord, bless our unlettered Prophet, the beloved, the exalted, the possessor of the uppermost honor and keeper of the most revered rank. Lord, shower Thy peace and blessings upon his followers and companions. Let Thy subtle and secret bliss touch our lives and secure our welfare and that of all the believers.

Lord, bless our master Muhammad, along with his wives, the blessed mothers of the believers. Lord, grant us a heart filled with gratitude, shed over us a light of beauty and blissful joy, cast over us the garment of Thy love and effulgence, and endow us with a secret from Thine own presence.

Lord, shower Thy eternal blessings upon our master Muhammad, all the prophets, the angels, the celestial beings, and Thy blessed righteous servants among the dwellers of the heavens and the earth. Grant us, Our Lord, through Thy blessings to be among the sincere ones in their love for Thee, among the righteous ones, and the safeguarded ones in Thy Peace, O Lord and Cherisher of the universes.

The Endowment of Divine Grace
& the Spread of Divine Mercy
(Al-Fat<u>h</u>u Rabbāni wal-Fai<u>d</u>hu Ra<u>h</u>māni)

786

Chapter 1

Never Object to God's Will

Objecting to the will of God Almighty when His divine decree
(**qadar**) befalls you spells death to your religious life (**deen**), your
belief in God's Oneness, your trust in Him, and your sincerity. The
heart of a true believer does not know the question of: "How?" or
"Why?" Instead, it says: "Yes." The nature of the carnal self, mind
and desire (**nafs**) is made of open quarrels, remonstrations and
disagreements. Thus, when one wants to treat this illness, he
must oppose his mind, desire, and carnal self. He must teach
them true submission to the will of God Almighty in order for him
to escape from their evils. The carnal self is an evil within evil.
However, once opposed, defeated and brought to the state of
contentment, peace and clarity, it turns into a pure spring of
goodness within goodness. The carnal self then becomes obedient
to all of God's commands and abandons any objection to His will.
Only then will God Almighty say: "**O peaceful soul, return to Thy
Lord to be content in His Pleasure.**"

"يَا أَيَّتُهَا النَّفْسُ الْمُطْمَئِنَّةُ ارْجِعِي إِلَى رَبِّكِ رَاضِيَةً مَرْضِيَّةً"

Only then will it be right for the soul to yearn for its Lord
[عَزَّ وَجَلَّ]. Its evil nature will have dissipated and it will have
attachment to nothing in this world. At that point, it is fitting to
trace its lineage to its father Abraham, upon whom be peace. He
showed the leading example by freeing himself from his own
carnal self, mind and desire. He remained free from passion and
was able to journey with his heart at rest and in peace.

When Abraham was thrown into the fire of Nimrod, various
heavenly beings came to offer their assistance to him. Abraham,
in his great faith and trust in God Almighty, kept repeating: "I am
not in need of your help. God's own knowledge of my condition is
sufficient for me." When his submission, acceptance of God's will
and trust manifested as true, God Almighty then said to the fire:

"O fire! Be cool and harm not Abraham."

God's help [عَزَّ وَجَلَّ] comes generously and without question to reward a servant who exercises true patience in this world. In the hereafter, God's blessings and plenitude come without reckoning. God Almighty has said: **"Verily those who exercise patience will be generously rewarded without reckoning**."

«اِنَّما يُوَفَّى الصّابِرُوْنَ اَجْرَهُمْ بِغَيْرِ حِسابْ»

Difficulties which one experiences for the sake of God are not hidden from Him. Be patient with Him for even one hour, and you will experience His forbearance, kindness and blessings for years to come. In fact, true courage is to exercise patience for one hour. **"Indeed Allah helps those who are patient**."

«اِنَّ اللّٰهَ مَعَ الصّابِرِيْنَ»

Be not unmindful of Him. He is the One Who helps and brings about victory. Do not be unmindful of Him. Let not your attention drift away from him, even for a moment. Wake up now from your heedlessness before the day comes when you are awakened without your will. On that day, your present stupor will become regret. That is a time when regret will be of no benefit to you. Correct your heart now. Once it becomes true, your existence and circumstances will change and advance smoothly in the right direction. That explains why the Prophet, upon whom be peace, said: **"In the son of Adam is a morsel of flesh. When it is healthy, his entire body will be fit, but once spoiled, his entire body will be diseased. That morsel of flesh is the heart**."

فِي اِبْنِ آدَمَ مُضْغَةٌ اِذَا صَلَحَتْ صَلَحَ لَهَا سَائِرُ جَسَدِهِ

وَاِنْ فَسَدَتْ فَسَدَ لَهَا سَائِرُ جَسَدِهِ ، اَلَا وَهِيَ الْقَلْبُ»

A pure, true heart is a state achieved through piety, trust in God Almighty, praise of His sole sovereignty and lordship, and devout sincerity within one's actions. Otherwise, your heart will prevent you from accomplishing what you intend. The heart is like a bird in a cage and its constitution is like a jewel in a box, a treasure in a safe. The emphasis should be given to the bird, not the cage. The jewel, not the box. The treasure, not the safe.

Our Lord, keep our hearts constantly obeying Thy commands. Fill our hearts with Thy Knowledge. Night or day, make us wholly engage in Thy service. Gather us in the company of the righteous, those who served Thee before us. Grant us sustenance like they received, and be unto us as Thou were unto them. Amen. O ye people! Be unto God Almighty such as the righteous and pious ones were unto Him, and receive the divine benevolence they received. If you want God [عَزَّ وَجَلَّ] to be on your side, then engage in fulfilling your obligations to His commands and exercise patience with each one of His decisions. Be always content with the way He treats you. Accept in full agreement what He destined for you and others. The pious ones first renounced the world. They then took their share from it with the hand of piety and fear of God Almighty. They sought the hereafter and performed the actions necessary to attain it. They disobeyed their mind and desire, carnal self (**nafs**) and obeyed their Lord and Cherisher [عَزَّ وَجَلَّ]. First, they advised themselves, then they went to share their advice with other others.

Child, teach yourself first, then advise others. Start by correcting your own faults. Do not transgress your own boundaries when you still have even the slightest corrections to make on yourself. How unfortunate you truly are. Do you really know how to save others? When you are blind, how can you guide others? A leader needs eyes. Only a good swimmer can be an able lifeguard. Thus, only one who knows God Almighty can bring people back to Him. How can someone who is ignorant lead people to Him? Say nothing about God's work until your heart is filled with love for Him and none else. Serve Him and no one else, fear Him and no one else.

This can be achieved only with the heart, not the mumbling of the tongue. This is done inwardly and privately, not by mere public display. Praising and proclaiming God's Oneness outside the door of the house while associating anything else with Him inside the house is pure hypocrisy. O poor and unfortunate one. Your tongue sounds pious, but your heart is exploding with filth. Your tongue speaks of gratitude, but your heart is full of objections. God Almighty has said: "**O son of Adam, My favors come to help you, but your evil is still directed towards Me.**"

«يَا ابْنَ آدَمَ خَيْرِي اِلَيْكَ نَازِلٌ وَشَرَّكَ اِليَّ صَاعِدٌ»

How unfortunate you are. You are a slave of God, but you obey the orders of someone else. If you were truly dedicated to

serving Him, you would defy any falsehood for His sake and pay
allegiance to His praises alone. A pious believer does not obey his
mind and desire (**nafs**), satan, passion or lust. A true believer does
not know satan in order to follow him. He has no interest in this
world, then how could he be humiliated by it? Instead, he brings
the world to its knees, bowing humbly before him. He strives
towards the hereafter. Once attained, he frees himself from its
attractions and connects with his Lord and Sustainer [عَزَّ وَجَلَّ]. At
all times, he remains sincerely dedicated in his devotion and
worship. He has learned and acknowledged the saying of God
Almighty: "**They were commanded to solely worship Allah,
dedicating their religion to Him, in truth and sincerity.**"

﴿وَمَا أُمِرُوا الاَّ لِيَعْبُدُوا اللّهَ مُخْلِصِينَ لَهُ الدِّينَ حُنَفَاءَ﴾

Thus, abandon associating the creation with God Almighty
and your dependence on the creations. Worship God Almighty as
the sole sovereign Lord [عَزَّ وَجَلَّ]. He is the Creator and ruler of
everything. Everything is in His Hands. You who seek your needs
from other than Him, you have no wisdom. Is there anything
which is not kept in God's hands? God Almighty says: "**The source
of everything is (inexhaustibly) in Our Hands.**"

﴿وَانْ مِنْ شَيءٍ اِلاَّ عِنْدَنَا خَزَائِنُهُ﴾

Child, in order for you to profit from this, sit still under the
font of God's decree and destined measures. Use patience for a
pillow. Adorn yourself with the acceptance of God's will [عَزَّ وَجَلَّ].
Be a true and obedient worshiper to Him, then await your
redemption. When you do that, He will shower His favors upon
you. He is the Supreme Authority Who controls all destinies. He
alone can bestow upon whomever He wills whatever abundance,
benevolence, favors, and grace He chooses. This is a wealth which
no one has the ability to conceive of, ask or even wish for. O people,
agree with the divine decree of God Almighty. Learn that from this
humble worshiper of His. Accept the words of this devotee and
student, Abdul-Qādir. Learn from him and practice his acceptance
of God's decree. In fact, it is my unconditional consent to that
divine decree that brings me closer to the powerful Lord [عَزَّ وَجَلَّ],
Who decrees all matters and rules everything.

O ye people! Let our assembly come together and humble
ourselves before God Almighty, accepting His decree, will and

doing. Let us bow our heads in form and in spirit before Him, accept His will, and join the caravan of our destiny. The divine decree is the emissary of our King and Ruler [عَزَّ وَجَلَّ]. Let us receive the messenger with grace, in honor of the One Who sent him. If we do so, he will keep us in his company and carry us before the Omnipotent Lord Himself, and: **"Thereat, the sovereignty belongs to God Almighty alone, the True Lord."**

«هُنَالِكَ الْوِلاَيَةُ لِلّه الْحَقّْ»

Indeed, thereat you will enjoy drinking from the ocean of His knowledge, and eating at the table of His benevolence and favors. You will find peace in His peace and immerse yourself in His all-encompassing mercy. Such a divine gift is bestowed upon rare ones, the very unique ones. Maybe one in a million from of all the tribes and nations receives such a gift.

Child, arm yourself with piety and the fear of wrongdoing. Abide by the divine laws of **shari'a**, persevere in opposing your mind and desire, your carnal self (**nafs**), passion, lust and satan, and do not mingle with like evil companions. A true believer is in a constant state of inner struggle against them all. He does not take the warrior helmet off his head, nor does he ever sheath his sword into the scabbard. The saddle is never taken off the horse's back. His only rest is the light sleep of the true servants of God Almighty. Little do they eat. Rarely do they speak, and they struggle to remain silent. It is the divine decree of their glorious Lord alone that makes them speak. God Almighty does their work for them. He makes their wisdom and common sense react in this world involuntarily, such as on the day of judgment when the limbs of the people speak and confess to the truth. He is the One Who gives the faculty of speech its sound. Like the inanimate objects which He causes to speak on the day of judgment, He makes them speak. He provides them with the faculty of reason to speak and thus, they speak.

Once the proof of the people's guilt was established, God intended to warn them as well as to give the believers His glad tidings. He then sent prophets and messengers who were commanded to carry His message to the people, and He caused them to speak. When He took the prophets and messengers back, He appointed in their places servants who were endowed with knowledge and who acted upon it as their representatives. Such are those whom He causes to speak wisdom and advise the people. These are the representatives of the prophets and messengers of God Almighty. The Prophet, upon whom be peace, said: "**People of knowledge *('ulama)* are the heirs of the prophets.**"

«الْعُلَمَاءُ وَرَثَةُ الأَنْبِيَاءِ »

O ye people. Be grateful to God Almighty for His countless favors upon you. and await them from Him only. The Almighty Lord [عَزَّ وَجَلَّ] said: "**No matter which blessing you enjoy, they all come from Allāh.**"

«وَمَا بِكُمْ مِنْ نِعْمَةٍ فَمِنَ آللهِ»

So, where is the due gratitude on your part? O you who are constantly immersed in His favors, you who see God's favors as coming from someone else. One time you consider them to be coming from other sources, another time you claim them to be insufficient or to be your own personal achievement. One time you desire to have what does not belong to you, and another time you use His favors as means of disobedience.

Child, in your privacy you need inner consciousness, piety and the fear of God [عَزَّ وَجَلَّ] to help you rid yourself of disobedience, sins and pitfalls. You need to have a contemplative awareness that reminds you that God Almighty is constantly looking at you. You are a beggar in dire need and under a strong obligation to have these qualities within yourself. You need them to fight your carnal self (**nafs**), passion, lust and satan. The majority of people experience destruction through the accumulation of their sins. The downfall of the ascetics (**zuhhād**) comes through failure to control their desires and craving. The defeat of the representatives of God Almighty (**abdāl**) comes when, in their privacy, their focus on God Almighty is mixed with intellectual tendencies and personal thoughts. As for the trustworthy faithful and righteous ones (**siddïqïn**), they lose their status if for even a split second they worry about keeping their hearts safe, even though they sleep at the King's door. Their main function is to guard their hearts, particularly since they have come this far to reach the gate that opens to God's own Presence [عَزَّ وَجَلَّ]. Their duty is to spread God's message and call the people to their Lord. They must have patience and perseverance in inviting people onto the path, calling out:

"O hearts of the people. O souls. O human beings. O jinns. O seekers of the kingdom, come in. Come to the door of the King [عَزَّ وَجَلَّ]. Hasten to Him, walk on the feet of your hearts. Climb up with the feet of your piety, the feet of your belief in His sole sovereignty and lordship. Strive towards Him with your knowledge, exalted piety, and fear of wrongdoing. Distance yourselves from any attachments to the world or the hereafter, and renounce anything other than the Lord."

This is the type of duty that the true people of God perform. They are wholly committed to fulfilling their duties. Their main concern is to help people recover their losses and correct their faults. Their utter determination (**himmah**) pervades the heavens and the earth, stretching from the feet of the Divine Throne down to the dust of this earth.

Child, free yourself from your carnal self (**nafs**), ego, passion and lust. Become like the ground under the feet of such true beings. Be like the dust their hands collect. God Almighty has said: "**He brings forth the living out of the dead and the dead out of the living.**"

«يُخْرِجُ الْحَيَّ مِنَ الْمَيِّتِ، وَيُخْرِجُ الْمَيِّتَ مِنَ الْحَيِّ»

He brought up Abraham, upon whom be peace, and gave him freedom from his parents who were dead through their disbelief. A believer is a living being, but a disbeliever is a dead one. One who proclaims lordship to be solely the dominion of God Almighty is alive, but one who associates anything with God's all-pervading sovereignty is dead. That is why God Almighty has said: "**Satan was the first of My creation to die. He disobeyed Me and that sin caused him his life.**"

This is the end of the world. The market of hypocrisy and falsehood has surfaced and is widespread everywhere. O ye people, do not mix with hypocrites, liars or impostors. O poor unfortunate man. Your mind, desire and ego are liars and disbelievers, arrogant ones and polytheists. How can you trust yourself to mix with such evil qualities? Oppose them, tie them up and let them not roam free. Imprison them and make them pay what they owe. Give them only the bare necessities, and repress them to keep them under control. As for your passion, grab firmly unto its reins and ride upon it. Never let it overtake you. As for your karmic habits (**taba'**), do not become their friend. Karma is like a little child, it has no judgment. Would you sit at the feet of a child and accept everything he says? As far as dealing with satan, remember that he is your avowed enemy and the enemy of your father Adam, upon whom be peace. How can you trust him or accept his advice when there is an ancient blood feud between you and him? Never trust him, for he is the murderer of your father and mother. If the opportunity were to come, he would surely make his best attempts at your own life as he did to theirs before. Thus, make piety your sword. Let your strength be made of continually celebrating God's Oneness. Contemplate His all pervading sovereignty, fear Him [عَزَّ وَجَلَّ] within you, be truthful and seek His help in every act. This is your weapon and these are your armed forces. They have the power to conquer satan, destroy him and crush his army. How will you not be victorious against him when God Almighty is on your side?

Child, think of this world and the hereafter as one entity, put them aside, and be alone with your Lord and Cherisher[عَزَّ وَجَلَّ]. Cleanse your heart from the slightest attachment to this world or the hereafter. Come not before your Lord unless you become absolutely free from anyone besides Him. Let not the world impair you from being with your Creator [عَزَّ وَجَلَّ]. Bar these causes from getting to you, and permanently root out these patrons. Once you achieve that, you may use the world to serve your basic needs, the hereafter to satisfy your heart, and your Lord as the sole Guardian of your treasured secret.

Child, follow not your mind and desire. Become free from passions, the world and the hereafter, and seek the companionship of none besides God Almighty. Only then can you reach the undiminishing wealth of both worlds. In that state your guidance will come directly from Him, and there can be no straying after that. Repent from your sins and escape to your Lord [عَزَّ وَجَلَّ]. Do so inwardly and outwardly, for repentance is the essence of changing one's condition. Take the garment of sins off your shoulders now by repenting with true sincerity, and by feeling truly ashamed of your actions before your Lord, not just as a figure of speech.

These are the actions of true hearts as they cleanse their bodies from sin by devoutly adhering to the rules of the divine laws of **shari'a**. The body has prescribed duties and the heart has different ones. The heart of a true believer, once it leaves the

wilderness of the world and attachment to its creation, abandons
its dependence on the cause and seeks the Causal Being Himself,
it sails the ocean of trust in God Almighty, the ocean of the inner
and outer knowledge. Once it reaches the deep of the ocean it will
cry out: "**He Who created me is surely my Guide.**"

"اَلَّذِى خَلَقَنِي فَهُوَ يَهْدِيْن"

Thus will the heart of a true believer be guided from one
shore to another, from one dwelling to another until he reaches the
straight path. Every time he remembers his Lord [عَزَّ وَجَلَّ], the road
will unfold and become more distinct before him. The bewilderment of the thick jungles he crosses will dissipate before his eyes.
The heart of the seeker is contemplative. It crosses vast distances
and leaves everything behind. Should he at any point on the road
become afraid of failure or destruction, his faith will immediately
manifest before him to encourage and comfort him. Thus, the fires
of fear and loneliness will be extinguished and replaced with the
effulgent light of peace, joy and nearness of God Almighty.

Child, when illness comes your way, receive it with the hand
of patience. Be tolerant until the medicine comes. When the
medicine arrives, welcome it with the hand of gratitude. If you
persevere in that state, you will experience in the present the
intended success of the hereafter. To a believer, even the mere
thought of hell-fire can cut through his stomach, shatter his liver
into pieces, turn his face yellow and throw his heart into the gloom
of sadness. When such a state seizes him, God Almighty will pour
the cooling spring water of His divine mercy and kindness over his
heart. He will unveil to his heart the sight of the gate of the
hereafter and he will see its haven. Once his fears are appeased
and he feels gratified in God's peace, He opens to him the door of
His divine majesty. The glory of that sight will shatter his heart and
innermost secret being. Thus his fears will become increasingly
reverent, and beyond his early ones. When he attains such a state,
God Almighty will open to him the gate of divine beauty. At that
point, he will regain the state of peace and comfort. His awareness
will increase as he rises on the ladder of the stations of grace, step
by step, from one station to another.

Child, do not worry about what you eat and drink, what you
wear, whom you marry, where you dwell, what type of home you
own or wealth you gather in this world. All of these are the worry

of the mind, desire and karmic habits. Where did you lose the concerns of your heart and innermost secret being? That is, the great striving towards God Almighty. Your worries are your burdens. Be concerned with your Lord [عَزَّ وَجَلَّ] and that which He has reserved for you. There is a replacement for this world, which is called the hereafter, and there is a replacement for your attachment to creation, which is your connection to the Creator of all things. Every time you discard one thing in this temporal world, He replaces it with something better for you in the permanent abode of the hereafter.

Think as though this were your last day in this world. Be forever ready for your return to the hereafter, and always await the coming of the angel of death. The world seasons the true servants of God Almighty, and the hereafter is created for them. Their true wealth is gathered therein. Once God's greater love is cast upon them, when that divine want (**ghïrah**, protective jealousy) comes, it will separate them from the hereafter. At that point, the most exalted stations of the hereafter will be replaced by an even higher rank of existence (**takwïn**) in which they will no longer need either the world or the hereafter.

O liar, you only love God Almighty when He endows you with His favors. Once difficulties befall you, you run away from Him, as though He were never your beloved. It is certainly true that the nature of a true servant is demonstrated when undergoing his test. When you remain steadfast and forbearing under the pressure of such trials, that will be the proof of your love for God Almighty; but if you waiver, your lies and pretenses will quickly surface, and your earlier claims of love will surely be refuted.

A man came to the Prophet, upon whom be peace, and exclaimed: "O Messenger of God, I truly love you." The Prophet replied: "**Be then ready to wear the cloak of poverty**."

«اسْتَعِدَّ لِلْفَقْرِ جِلْبَابًا»

Another man came to the Prophet and exclaimed: "Truly I love God Almighty." The Prophet replied: "**Then wear a cloak that can shelter you from trials**."

«اتَّخِذْ لِلْبَلاَءِ جِلْبَابًا»

Thus, the love of God Almighty and His Messenger, upon whom be peace, are associated with poverty and trials. As a righteous man once said: "Loyalty is associated with adversities so truth cannot be falsely claimed." If that were not true, anyone could profess that he loves God Almighty. Thus, patience and steadfastness are a good indication of the truth of one's love for God Almighty and His Messenger, upon whom be peace.

"Our Lord, grant us the benefits of a good deed in this world, the reward of a good deed in the hereafter, and protect us eternally from the sufferings of hell-fire."

❀ ❀ ❀ ❀ ❀

Chapter 2

On Poverty

Your delusions about your virtues in God's sight have separated you from Him and veiled Him from you. Cease your self-deceiving pride and arrogance before you are justly punished and humiliated. Wean yourself from such sickness before the snakes and scorpions of affliction overpower you. No doubt, you have not yet experienced the taste of afflictions, and that is why you persist in your practices. Do not relish your indulgences today, for soon they will vanish. God Almighty has said: "**Once they become intoxicated in the enjoyment of their gifts, We seize them back by surprise.**"

«حَتَّىٰ اذَا فَرِحُوا بِمَا أُوتُوا أَخَذْنَاهُمْ بَغْتَةً»

God's treasures can be attained only through patience. That is why God Almighty constantly emphasizes the extreme importance of exercising patience. Poverty and patience do not coexist except in the identity of a true believer. When true lovers experience difficulties, they exercise tolerance and are inspired to do good, while enduring what fate their Lord [عَزَّ وَجَلَّ] has destined for them.

In fact, had patience not been the cause, you would not have seen me sitting amongst you people. I was made like a hunting net which is spread to catch birds at night. At night, my eyes become open and my feet untied. During the day, my eyes remain closed and my feet are fastened to the net again. God Almighty ordained it thus for your own benefit, but you do not understand.

If it were not in compliance with God's commands, would anyone who has wisdom dwell in this town or mingle with its people? Do you not see that affectation, hypocrisy, injustice, suspicion and sins are widespread? Do you not see how ingratitude toward God's favors has surfaced everywhere? Today most people are corrupt and are desecrating God's favors upon them by using them for immoral acts. The outburst of dissolute life is a common practice everywhere. More and more, the aged, the weak and the defenseless are confined to their homes. The pious man retires to his shop and minds his own business. The atheist is struck with alcoholism, and the friend betrays the trust of his friend.

By God Almighty, if it were not the divine decree, I would be tempted to break through the screen of silence and reveal what you hide in your homes. However, I have a duty to accomplish, a foundation to lay, and a building to construct. I have children who need to be brought up in the proper way. Were I ever to unveil some of what I know, it would bring about our separation. Under such conditions, and in order for me to continue my work, I need the strength and determination of the prophets and messengers of God Almighty. I need the combined patience and tolerance that have existed since Adam up to this time, and I need the divine sustaining power to be on my side. Our Lord, show us Thy kindness and help us to do what pleases Thee. Amen.

Child, you were not created to dwell permanently in this world and indulge in its pleasures. Straighten up and avoid what displeases your Lord. You appear to be satisfied by merely saying: *"Lā ilāha il Allāh, Muhammadur Rasūl Allāh,"* (There is no god but God, Muhammad is the Messenger of God). This testimony does not benefit you unless you add to it. True faith is a combination of words and deeds, otherwise it will not be accepted from you or benefit you. If you persist in your indulgence in sinful and abominable actions and neglect your prescribed prayers, fasting, charity and doing good deeds, what benefit can you draw from merely proclaiming these two testimonies?

When you merely say: *"Lā ilāha il Allāh,"* (There is no god but God), that is not enough. That is just a proclamation. Someone may ask you: "Do you have proof of it? What is the proof?" In fact, to adhere to God's commands and abstain from what is forbidden, to exercise patience over calamities and submit to His decree are the proof of your claim. However, such deeds are not acceptable unless supported by devotion and sincerity towards the rights of God Almighty upon you. Thus, words without actions will not be accepted by God Almighty, nor will actions without sincerity and conformance to the leading example (**sunnah**) of the Prophet, upon whom be peace.

O ye people! Comfort the poor by sharing some of your

wealth with them. Send not a mendicant away unsatisfied when you can afford to give him something, whether a little or more. Adopt God's love of giving, and be grateful to Him for allowing you to be in that position. O poor unfortunate man. When someone in need comes to your door, and you have the means to assist him, he is a gift from God Almighty to you. Then how dare you reject the gift of your Lord [عَزَّ وَجَلَّ] and return it to its Sender? You come here, you listen to these words and cry, but when a needy person knocks at your door, your heart hardens. This proves that your crying and coming here was not solely for God's sake.

In order for you to hear what is being said here and benefit from it, first you need to listen with your innermost secret being (**sirr**), then with your heart, then with your senses, and then act accordingly. When you come here, leave behind your personal knowledge, deeds, speeches, titles, lineage and wealth; forget about your money and family. Come here only when your heart is empty of everything but God Almighty. Let His proximity, favor and bounty be the cloak that shelters your naked heart. If you do this when you come here, your needs will be satisfied like those of a bird who wakes up hungry in the morning and returns with a filled stomach to his nest in the evening.

The radiance of one's heart comes from the radiance of God's light. That is why the Prophet, upon whom be peace, said: "**Be aware of the clarity of perception of a true believer, for he sees with God's light**."

«اتَّقُوا فِرَاسَةَ الْمُؤْمِنِ فَإِنَّهُ يَنْظُرُ بِنُورِ اللهِ»

O insolent sinner, beware of such a true believer (**mu'min**). Do not appear before him while you are stained with the filth (**najas**) of your sins of disobedience. Remember that he sees with God's light all that is in you. He sees the perjury of your ascribing associates to God Almighty, and he sees your hypocrisy. He sees what is hidden under your garment, and what money you carry with you. He sees what shameful, dishonorable and scandalous actions you bring with you.

Listen. Unless you meet a successful person you cannot achieve success. You are a true fool and you mix with like people. (Someone in the audience asked: *"For how long will this blindness last?"* Our shaikh replied): Until you find a physician and use his doorsteps for a pillow, think good of him, trust his diagnosis, and restrain your heart from falsely accusing him. Take all your family and children and camp at his doorstep. Tolerate the bitter taste of his medicine. Only that can cure your blindness.

Humble yourself to God Almighty and bring all your needs to Him. Assume that you have not done one good deed. Stand before Him on the feet of bankruptcy. Close the door to the world of creation, and open that intimate door between you and your Creator [عَزَّ وَجَلَّ] Acknowledge your sins and apologize to Him for your failures. Finally, have perfect faith that none can harm or benefit you, none can give to you or deprive you but Him. When you understand that, the blindness of your heart will be cured, and God [عَزَّ وَجَلَّ] will reinstate your sight and clarity.

Child, wearing coarse garments and eating coarse food are not the point. It is the chastity and abstinence of your heart that counts. For a sincere and true believer, his coarse woolen garment is first worn inwardly, then outwardly. At first he clothes his innermost secret being (**sirr**), then his heart (**qalb**), then his mind and desire (**nafs**). Only after that does he cover his body with it. When he becomes wholly coarse-textured, then God's hand of kindness, compassion and favor will come to change his condition for the better. the garment of mourning will be stripped away, and he will be vested with the garment of joy and happiness. His adversities will be replaced with blessings, loathing with joy, fears with peace and tranquility, separation with proximity, and poverty with riches.

Child, take your share from this world with the hand of detachment, not the hand of desire and greed. One who eats with tears in his eyes is not like one who eats with joy. Take your share from this world, but keep your heart with God Almighty. That will protect you from any evil your portion may bring. It is safer to eat from the hand of your physician rather than to reach for something of doubtful content.

O ye people! How hard are your hearts. Trustworthiness has vanished amongst you. Mercy and compassion no longer link you together. The divine laws of **shari'a** are a trust which you have betrayed and no longer practice. O unfortunate one, if you do not commit to that trust (**amāna**), a cataract will impair your sight. Your hands and feet will be tied up in chains and the door of God's mercy will be closed to you. He will order the hearts of His creations to be harsh towards you, and restrain them from helping you. O ye people. Be on guard with your Lord [عَزَّ وَجَلَّ]. Save your heads, for His retribution is extremely painful. He can deprive you of your safety and health. He can curb your greed, insolence and vanity.

Fear God Almighty, for He is the Sovereign Lord of the heavens and the earth. Maintain the flow of His favors through gratitude. Hearken to His commands by hearing and obeying them. Face your hardships with patience (**sabr**) and welcome ease with gratitude (**shukr**). This is how the prophets, the messengers and the righteous ones were before you, grateful for His favors and forbearant during their adversities. Leave the table of the sinful food of disobedience, and eat only from the table of obedience to His commands. Observe His boundaries. Be grateful for His favors, and when in difficulty, ask forgiveness for your sins. Question yourselves when in difficulty and search for its real cause, for God is not unjust towards His creation.

Remember death and what comes after it. Constantly remember Your Lord and Cherisher, the day of judgment, and the fact that you are never away from His sight. Wake up! How long will you remain asleep? For how long will you remain in ignorance and doubt, falling prey to falsehood and satisfying the greed of your mind and desire, passion, lust and karmic habits? Why do you not adopt good conduct (**adab**) which can be attained through worshiping God Almighty and submitting to His divine laws of **shari'a**? Worship is absence from one's karmic habits. Why do you not learn and practice the exalted conduct which is taught in the Holy Qur'an and the teachings of the Prophet, upon whom be peace?

Child, do not intermingle with people when you are blind, ignorant, heedless and asleep. Mix with them when you have attained clarity, knowledge and vigilance. If you find in them what is praiseworthy, follow it, but if you discover in them what may harm you, avoid it and advise them for the better. O people. You seem to be totally unaware of the truth of God Almighty. Shake off your slumber. Your sole remedy is to faithfully and regularly attend the mosques and maintain constant invocations of blessings (**salawāt**) upon the Prophet, upon whom be peace. He said: "**Should fire fall from the skies over the world, only the regular worshipers in the mosques will be safe from it.**"

«لَوْ نَزَلَ مِنَ السَّمَاءِ نَارًا لَمَا نَجَا مِنْهَا الاَّ أَهْلُ المَسَاجِد»

If you neglect your regular prayers, your connection to God [عَزَّ وَجَلَّ] will be severed. That is why the Prophet, upon whom be peace, said: "**When in prostration, the worshiper becomes the closest possible to his Lord.**"

«أَقْرَبُ مَا يَكُوْنُ الْعَبْدُ مِنْ رَبِّهِ اَذا كَانَ سَاجِداً»

O unfortunate one! How many times, under the claim of authenticity, do you license yourself to commit perjury in religious interpretations? Such a presumptuous person is most deceitful. If only we would sail on the ship of certitude and determination, hold fast to the rope of united consent (**ijmā'**) to God's revealed words and be devoutly sincere in our actions. That will save us from God's wrath. Otherwise, what would happen should we license ourselves to brag or give personal opinions? Resoluteness is no longer in practice, and its determined people have gone.

This is a time of affectation, hypocrisy, and the unlawful seizing of people's money. Today, the number of those who regularly attend the mosques and perform their prescribed prayers, those who fast the month of **Ramadān**, join the pilgrimage to Mecca, give alms and do good deeds is on the rise. However, they do so for worldly gains, not for the sake of their Creator [عَزَّ وَجَلَّ]. The majority of this world seems as though it were a creation of creations without a Creator.

All of you are dead at heart and alive with carnal self (**nafs**), mind, desire and passions, seeking the world. One's heart comes to life only when it separates from the creations to abide by the Creator [عَزَّ وَجَلَّ] in essence. The heart comes to life only by adherence to God's commands, abstinence from His prohibitions, patience with His trials, acceptance of His judgment and consent to His divine decree.

Child, surrender to what God decrees, then follow that with abiding by His commands. Progress on the path requires a solid base followed by a sound structure. Then you must guard that state by night and day. O unfortunate one, reflect on your state. Reflecting is the duty of the heart. Thank God Almighty if you discover a good quality in yourself, but beg for His forgiveness should you realize that you have a bad one, and repent. In fact, repentance revives your faith (**deen**) and deadens your satan. This is why they say: *"To contemplate for one hour is greater than praying all night."*

O ye followers of Muhammad, upon whom be peace. Be grateful to your Lord, for He required very few deeds from you, in comparison to nations before you. You came last, but you shall be foremost on the day of judgment. On that day, you will be princes, and all nations will be your subjects.

You cannot reap such success if you remain prisoner in the house of your carnal self, mind, desire, lust and karmic habits. You cannot become true as long as you are busy stripping the people of what God Almighty gave them, through your affectation and hypocrisy. Whoever is true amongst you, there is no one like unto him. You cannot become a true human being as long as you have the slightest desire for this world. You cannot achieve that exalted station when your heart has the least trust in anything besides God Almighty.

O God, make us be true unto you. Amen.

«رَبَّنَا آتِنَا فِي الدُّنْيَا حَسَنَةً وَفِي الآخِرَةِ حَسَنَةً وَقِنَا عَذَابَ النَّارِ»

"Our Lord, grant us the benefits of a good deed in this world, the reward of a good deed in the hereafter, and protect us eternally from the sufferings of hell-fire."

❀ ❀ ❀ ❀ ❀

Chapter 3

Wish not for Wealth

O poor man. Wish not for wealth in this world. It may become the immediate cause of your downfall. O you who are afflicted with a disease, pray not for recovery. It may bring about your death. Be wise. Keep the fruits of your work, and your illness will be cured. Be content with what you have and ask for no more. Whatever God Almighty may grant you as a result of your prayers will become a burden and a distressing agony. I have experienced that myself. You will experience the same unless your heart is commanded to seek God's bounty and pray for change.

Once you are inspired to do this, the endowment will carry God's blessings and be free from improprieties. Should you have to ask, pray for forgiveness, for chastity and for the well-being of one's faith and one's life in this world and the hereafter. Be satisfied with this alone.

Be not selective with God Almighty, and surely not haughty, for He has the power to crush you. Be not arrogant with Him or with His creation. Show no pride in your youth, strength or wealth, for the impact of God's power is fatal. He can seize you in the way He obliterated such ones before you. Surely His retribution is most painful.

O impostor. Your tongue sounds Muslim, although your heart is not. Your words are those of a Muslim, but your actions are not. Publicly you profess to be a Muslim, but privately you are not. Are you not aware that even if you were to perform all the prescribed prayers, fast the month of **Ramadan** and do all the good deeds known to a Muslim, unless you do so for God's pleasure they will not be accepted, and you will be shown to be nothing but a hypocrite who is far removed from God's nearness? Repent now and rid yourself of your abominable actions, words and disgraceful endeavors.

True believers are not flattered by their deeds. They are the true winners, the servants of God's all-pervading sovereignty, the sincere worshipers who exercise patience and forbearance when adversities and trials befall them. They are the ones most grateful for His favors, bounty and magnanimity. They constantly remember Him inwardly and outwardly, with their tongues, in their hearts and within their innermost secret beings. When they suffer harm from the creations, they smile at them. They see the kings of this world as powerless. They understand that all the creations of this earth are transient, impotent, ailing and poor, having constant needs. Paradise, compared to what they have, appears as ruins, and hell-fire is deadened. To them, there is no earth and no heaven, and no one dwells therein. All directions turn into one.

First they are inhabitants of the world and companions to its people. Then, they become the inhabitants of the hereafter and its people. Next they join their Lord [عَزَّ وَجَلَّ] and the company of those who love Him. In their hearts they first walk along with Him until they attain His presence. Rightfully, they choose their Companion before the road. They open that ultimate door between themselves and God Almighty. He will extol them as long as they keep His remembrance, until their constant invocation (**zikr**) lifts their burdens.

When with others, they are extinct, and when with Him they exist. They hear and understand His words saying: "**Remember me, then I will remember you. Be grateful to Me and never deny Me.**"

«فَاذْكُرُونِي اَذْكُرْكُمْ وَاشْكُرُوا لِي وَلاَ تَكْفُرُونْ»

Thus, they keep His constant remembrance, eager that He remember them. They hear and cherish His saying: "**I am the Companion of the one who remembers Me.**"

«أَنَا جَلِيسُ مَنْ ذَكَرَنِي»

With that promise, they renounce social gatherings and find satisfaction in invoking His remembrance, in order to remain in His company.

O ye people! Let not your confusion be the cause of your hallucination. Without deeds, book knowledge will bring you no benefits. You have to work to cultivate your own farm. This is God's decree. You have to do your duty, day by day and year after year. Keep working at it until you reap its fruits.

Child, your knowledge is saying to you: "Unless you act upon me, I will become your indictment. Otherwise, I am your defense on the day of judgment." The Prophet, upon whom be peace, said: **"One's knowledge calls to be acted upon. If not satisfied, it will depart."**

«يَهْتُف الْعِلْمُ بِالْعَمَلِ فَانْ أَجَابَهُ وَالاَّ أَرْتَحَلَ»

The blessings of knowledge will depart but its trials will remain. Its interceding role (**shafā'a**) before your Lord [عَزَّ وَجَلَّ] will break off, and it will cease to be of help when you need it. Knowledge is of no avail when it becomes a husk, because actions are the kernel of knowledge.

You cannot be called a follower of the Messenger, upon whom be peace, unless you act upon what he taught. If you do, he will embrace your heart and innermost secret being and bring them before their Lord and Cherisher. Your knowledge is calling to you, but you have no heart with which to hear. Hearken with the ears of your heart and innermost secret being to that call. Follow what it says, and that will benefit you. To act with knowledge will draw you nearer to the Omniscient Lord [عَزَّ وَجَلَّ] Who revealed this knowledge.

If you follow this decree, which is the basic knowledge, then the fountain of inner knowledge will gush forth. You will have two overflowing springs that will permeate your heart with both inner and outer wisdom and knowledge. At that point, you will have to pay the due-alms (**zakāt**), Twhich is to confront your brothers and the seekers on the path. The alms of knowledge are to spread it and to call the people to their Lord.

Child, with patience, one can win. God Almighty has said: **"Truly those who exhibit patience will be generously rewarded."**

«انَّمَا يُوَفَّى الصَّابِرُونَ اَجْرَهُمْ بِغَيْرِ حِسَابْ»

Earn your livelihood with your own sweat, not with your religious knowledge. Work for a living. Eat from your own earnings and share with others. The earnings of the true believers are placed on the plates of the righteous ones. Notice that the business of the righteous ones cannot be successful unless the profits are shared with the poor and the indigent ones. The constant endeavor of the righteous ones is to be able to bring God's mercy to the creation, seeking God's pleasure and love. They heard and understood the saying of God's Messenger, upon whom be peace: "**God Almighty is the sustainer of all people. Amongst them, He loves best those of most benefit to others.**"

«النَّاسُ عِيَالُ آللهِ وَأَحَبُّ النَّاسِ

الى آللهِ عَزَّ وَجَلَّ اَنْفَعُهُمْ لِعِيَالِه»

God's deputies (**awliyā**) are deaf, dumb and blind in comparison with other people. Once their hearts reach God's proximity, they hear none beside their Lord [عَزَّ وَجَلَّ], and they see none besides Him. He allows them to be in His immediate presence. His divine majesty renders them oblivious, and their love benefits them most when in the company of their beloved. Standing surrounded by the divine majesty and beauty, they lean neither to the right nor to the left. They become one face in every direction, with no sides. Humans, jinns, angels and all types of creation serve them. Both the divine decree (**hukm**), and knowledge serve them. They are constantly nurtured by the divine bounty, and their thirst is quenched by the comfort of His nearness. Their food is the benevolence of His favors, and their drink is the satisfaction of His presence. Their preoccupation in Him prevents them from lending an ear to any worldly speeches.

They dwell in one valley and the creation in another. They command the people, by God's decree, to do what is lawful and to abstain from the unlawful. They are the deputies of the Prophet, upon whom be peace, and they are his real heirs in truth. Their duty is to direct the people back to their Lord, to establish the proof behind each judgment and to truly place things where they belong. They pay homage where it is due and do not wait to collect a reward, nor do they nurture the desires of their mind or karmic habits. They love in God Almighty and become angry for His sake. They are entirely His, and no one else has a share in them. Whoever attains that state of being will win the ultimate companionship, salvation and success. Human beings, jinns, angels, earth and the heavens will all love him.

As for you, O ye hypocrite, O worshiper of the creations and powers of this world. You who forgot about God Almighty. Do you truly expect this honor to come your way despite all your qualities? You certainly have no honor or integrity. Here is your way out: Surrender to God Almighty first, then repent, learn, and act upon what you learn with sincerity. Otherwise, you cannot find guidance to salvation.

O poor unfortunate one. You surely realize that there is no enmity between me and you, but I must speak the truth. There is no partiality in God's religion. I was brought up hearing direct and impartial words of true shaikhs. I also studied under adverse conditions and poverty away from home. If you can perceive some clarity in what I speak, then take it as coming directly from God Almighty, for He is the One Who causes me to utter it.

If you come before me, come stripped of your personal image, mind, desire and passions. If you had insight, you would see me stripped of my personality, too. However, your real sickness is your thick-headedness. If you want my company and its benefits then realize that my state of being has no connection to the creation, the world or the hereafter. If someone repents at my hands, remains in my company, thinks good of me and acts upon my words, he shall, God willing, become like me.

The prophets are reared by God Almighty through His revelations (**kalām**). However, He rears His deputies with His words by directly inspiring those words (**ilhām**) to their hearts. He does so because they are the guardians of the message of the prophets and their viceregents and servants.

God Almighty does speak. He spoke to Moses, upon whom be peace. He spoke to him directly without an intermediary. That was no creature who spoke to Moses. It was the All-Knowing Lord Who spoke to him with words which Moses could understand. God Almighty conveyed to his understanding what He intended to convey.

He also spoke like that to our Prophet, upon whom be peace, without an intermediary. The Qur'ān, this unbreakable rope of God Almighty, is your connection with your Lord and Sustainer. Gabriel, upon whom be peace, brought that revelation from the heavens by command from God Almighty. Gabriel delivered it to God's Messenger , upon whom be peace, precisely as revealed by God Almighty, and exactly as it is given in the Qur'ān itself. It is a great sin and a sacrilege to deny that. O Lord, guide everyone, turn unto everyone and have mercy upon us all.

It is related that the Caliph **Al-Mu'tasim**, God rest his soul, said on his death bed: *"God be my witness that I repent from all that I caused **Ahmad Ibn Hanbal**, although the reins of power were not in my hands, and the supreme rulership is in someone else's hand."*

O poor fellow, stop talking about things which are of no use to you. Abandon this zealous and fanatical stand about your school of religious thought (**mazhab**). Occupy yourself with something more advantageous for your life in this world and in the hereafter. Soon you will realize what has happened to you. Tomorrow you will hear your sentence and you will remember my words. As soon as you reach the battlefield you will realize how many wounds you will receive with no helmet over your head. Empty your heart of any worries in this world, for soon you shall be taken away from it. Pray not for a good life in it, for that is not something you decide. The Prophet, upon whom be peace, said: **"Real life is living in the hereafter."**

«الْعَيْشُ عَيْشُ الآخِرَة»

Curtail your ambitions and hopes, so that you may attain abstinence and become detached from this world. Abstinence (**zuhud**) is the fruit of self-restraint. Give up your association with evil companions. Eliminate all courtesy between you and them, and instead, direct your efforts towards strengthening your loving kindness with the righteous ones. Walk away from your own kin when he is an evil companion, and seek the friendship of those who are not your relatives when they provide you with good fellowship. Any person whom you take for a friend will become your relative. Thus, reflect well and choose before you create such kinship. (Someone in the audience asked: "What is kinship?'" Our **shaikh** replied): "Kinship comes from kindness."

Stop asking for your share and desiring what is not. To plead for what is already your allotted share is a waste of effort, while desiring what is not yours will earn you repugnance and humiliation. This is why the Prophet, upon whom be peace, said: **"It is a form of chastisement to be in the position of asking for what is not your share."**

«مِنْ جُمْلَةِ عُقُوبَاتِ آللهِ تَعَالَى لِعَبْدِهِ
طَلَبُ مَا لَمْ يُقْسَمُ لَهُ»

Child, be guided unto God Almighty through His signs.

Reflect on His work and you will find the Maker. A true believer who is both pious and a gnostic has two outer and two inner eyes. Through his outer eyes, he sees God's creations on earth, while with his inner eyes he sees God's creations in the heavens. Then, when God Almighty lifts the veils from his heart, he will see his Lord and Cherisher without imagining or interpretation. He will then be brought nigh, and become a beloved, and nothing is hidden from a beloved.

Such is God's bounty. He raises the curtains between Himself and a true worshiper who washes his heart clean of the creations, mind and desire (**nafs**), passion, lust and satan. A naked heart throws away the keys of earthly treasure, and treats as of equal value both pebbles and pearls. Be wise, and carefully examine what I have just said. The meaning is deep and represents the core of understanding. In it there is good advice for you. Take it and you shall be victorious.

Child, do not complain about your Creator to His creations. Rather, bring all your complaints before Him. He alone has the power to satisfy your needs, others do not. One of the treasures of true relationship (**birr**) is to keep one's secrets hidden, and, when possible, not to talk about one's adversities, illnesses and charities. Give charity with your right hand and strive not to let your left hand know about it.

Beware of the ocean of this world, for countless people have drowned in it. Only the rare few are saved from it. It is a deep ocean that can swallow everyone. However, it is God Almighty Who saves whomever He wills from its dangers. Similarly, He saves the true believers on the day of resurrection from hell-fire. On that day everyone will come upon it, and only those whom God Almighty wants to save will be saved. God Almighty has said: "**There is not one of you but shall come upon it. This is the decree of your Lord and it shall be fulfilled**."

«وَاِنْ مِنْكُمْ اِلاَّ وَارِدُهَا كَانَ عَلَى رَبِّكَ حَتْمًا مَقْضِيًا»

God Almighty then will say to the fire: "**Be cool and harm not**," so that My blessed servants—those who believe in Me, the sincere ones in their devotion whose main desire is to be with Me, who discarded everything for My sake—may cross safely. He speaks to the fire thus, as He spoke to the fire which Nimrod kindled to burn God's prophet Abraham, upon whom be peace.

Similarly, God Almighty will speak to the ocean of this world: "O ocean of this world, O water, do not drown this beloved servant whom I want." Thus, the servant will be saved. He will walk in God's secret and be safe, exactly as God Almighty saved Moses and his people from drowning in the Red Sea. "**Certainly, God bestows His favor upon whomever He wills**," and "**He grants His bounty to whomsoever He wants without reckoning**."

"وَيَرْزُقُ مَنْ يَشَاءُ بِغَيْرِ حِسَابٍ"

Everything belongs to God Almighty. The treasures of this world and those of the hereafter are in His hands. Giving and restraining are His responsibility. Wealth and poverty are His endowment. Exalting and humiliating are His province. He owes nothing to anyone. That is why a wise man will seek shelter at His doorstep alone.

O man! Are you proud of yourself? I find you eager to please people at the expense of displeasing your Creator. You build your life in this world at the expense of your life in the hereafter. Soon you will be taken away from this abode by Him Whose retribution is extremely painful and Whose punishments are most diverse. At first, He may seize you by dismissal from your office by illness, humiliation or poverty, by casting you into adversities, trials, stress and worries. He seizes you by subjecting you to people's tongues and allowing them a free hand in dealing with you. He may let all of His creations get at you. Wake up, O heedless one. Be aware of your state. Our Lord, wake us up in You and keep us just for You. Amen.

Child, when you want something from this world, be not like a woodcutter working at night. In his effort to gather firewood, he may not know what he grabs. I find you acting like a woodcutter working on a dark night where there is no moonlight to see by, who does not carry a lamp to help him see his way. He walks through heavy brush, and as he tries to find his way through, he is constantly surrounded by poisonous insects, some of which may be deadly.

You should do this type of work only in the daylight. The sunlight will prevent you from gathering what is harmful. Likewise in your actions, stand under the effulgent sunlight of God's sovereignty, abiding by the divine laws of **shari'a** and piety. Such sunlight will prevent you from falling into the trap of mind, desire, carnal self (**nafs**) passion, satan and associating people with God Almighty. Such light will prevent you from being hasty.

O man. Be not hasty. One who is in a hurry may trip into wrongdoing or come close to it. However, one who walks cautiously may reach his goal or approach it. Hastiness comes from satan, but carefulness is the way of the merciful Lord. What mostly leads you to be hasty is your greed to amass the maximum you can from this world. Be satisfied with little, for contentment is an inexhaustible wealth. How dare you desire something which is not allotted for you! You will never get it. Restrain yourself and be happy to be with God Almighty alone. Renounce everything but Him.

Be steadfast in your commitment until you know God Almighty. Only then will you be wealthy and without needs. Your heart will then have trust and your innermost being will be pure and sacred. Then will your Lord teach you. In your head, the world will become contemptible. In your heart, the hereafter will become small, and through the eyes of your innermost secret being everything other than your Lord will become inconsequential. Nothing besides God Almighty will be great in your eyes any more. Only then will you become great in the eyes of all the creations.

Child, if you wish that no door ever close before you, then fear God and be pious, for that is the master key to every door. God Almighty has said: "**As for those who fear God , He (ever) prepares a way out**"

$$\text{«وَمَنْ يَتَّقِ ٱللَّهَ يَجْعَلْ لَهُ مَخْرَجًا}$$

$$\text{وَيَرْزُقْهُ مِنْ حَيْثُ لَا يَحْتَسِبُ»}$$

Have no objection to whatever God Almighty does to you, your family, your wealth or the people of your time. Do you not feel ashamed, commanding Him to change things and rearrange them to your liking? Do you have more wisdom, more knowledge or more mercy than He?. Remember that all of you are His creation and His servants. It is He Who governs and provides for your needs, as well as theirs. If you truly want to be in His company in this world and in the hereafter, then be quiet. Quiescence and composure are the nature of God's deputies in His company. They are resigned to Him in everything. They do not make one gesture or move one step except by clear permission from Him to their hearts. They do not even eat from what is lawful, buy a garment, have marital relations or act in any way except with clear permission from Him to their hearts. They remain in His custody, consenting to His command. They are the recipients of the favors of the One Who has the power to change the intention of the hearts and shift the focus of the eyes. Such people find no peace until they meet their Lord with their hearts in this world, and then with their physical form in the hereafter.

Lord, grant us the gift of Thy bounty, to be with You in this world and to meet you in the hereafter. Give us the joy to be in Thy proximity and to look upon Thee. Let us be amongst those who find contentment in none but Thee.

"Our Lord, grant us the benefits of a good deed in this world, the reward of a good deed in the hereafter, and protect us eternally from the sufferings of hell-fire."

❈   ❈   ❈   ❈   ❈

Chapter 4

On Repentance

The Prophet, upon whom be peace, said: **"Take advantage of a good opportunity when the door opens, for you never know when it will close again.**"

«مَنْ فُتِحَ لَهُ بَابٌ مِنَ الْخَيْرِ فَلْيَنْتَهِزْهُ فَإِنَّهُ لاَ يَدْرِي مَتَى يُغْلَقُ عَنْهُ»

O ye people! Seize the true opportunity of living for as long as the door of this life is open. Soon it will be closed again. Cherish good deeds for as long as you are capable of doing them. Repent from your sins for as long as the door of repentance is open. Ask for divine favors for as long as the door of prayer is open. Compete along with your righteous brothers in striving to please God Almighty, for that door is still open to you.

O ye people! Rebuild what you have destroyed. Wash clean what you have soiled. Correct what you have spoiled. Dissipate the clouds of any damages you have created, and give back to the people what you took from them. Turn yourselves over to your Lord and give up your life of a slave who has run away from his Master.

Child, there is none who is omnipresent except our Creator. If you turn towards Him, you become His slave. But if you turn towards the creations, you become their slave. Say nothing until your heart experiences the crossings of the wilderness and empty deserts. Say nothing until your innermost being becomes detached from everything. Did you not learn that the seeker of God Almighty is a wayfarer who bade farewell to everything? With certitude he realized that whatever distracts him by on the road, becomes a veil between him and his Master [عَزَّ وَجَلَّ]. Child, do not idle on the path. A lazy person is always deprived of God's bounty, while regret and sorrow weigh heavily upon him like a rope around his neck. Improve yourself with good deeds and discover how God Almighty will shower you with His grace and benevolence in this world and in the hereafter. **Abu Muhammad Al-'Aajami**, God bless his soul, used to say: "*Lord, make us of good character and of outstanding excellence.*" He used the word '**jayyideen**' but he really meant to say: "Make us as good as horses (**ajyād**) are amongst the animals," though his tongue would not obey.

It is true that one who experiences the taste of something will recognize it again. Good conduct when socializing with people while consenting to the laws of **shari'a** is a blessed and praise-worthy behavior. But if socializing will lead to breaking any of its rules and displeasing God Almighty, then it is despicable and dishonorable. Consent is shown through obedience to God's commands, while refuting it manifests through signs that people of clarity and nearness to God Almighty can see.

Child, spread out your net of prayers now and gather God's blessings and acceptance. Do not pray with your tongue while your heart is still objecting. On the day of reckoning, man will remember what good and evil he did in this world. On that day, regret is to no avail and remembrance is of no use. The benefits come from remembering what to do today, before death comes. Remembering plowing and seeding at the time of harvesting is useless. The Prophet, upon whom be peace, said: "**The world is the farmland of the hereafter. Whoever plants good in it will harvest joy, and whoever plants evil in it will harvest regret**."

«الدُّنْيا مَزْرَعَةُ الآخِرة، فَمَنْ زَرَعَ خَيْرًا حَصَدَ غِبْطَةً

وَمَنْ زَرَعَ شَرًّا حَصَدَ نَدَامَةً»

When your death comes, you will wake up. If you do not realize your state today, waking only then will be of no benefit to you. Our Lord, let us not fall into the sleep of the heedless people, the ones ignorant of Who You are. Amen.

Child, your association with evil companions is leading you to have bad thoughts about the good people. Therefore, walk under the umbrella of God's Book, and follow the leading example (**sunnah**) of His Blessed Messenger, upon whom be peace. Only then will you succeed.

O ye people! Be truly ashamed of yourselves before God Almighty. Do not remain heedless. You are wasting the precious hours of your life. You busy yourselves accumulating food which you do not eat, hoping for what you cannot reach and building what you do not live in. All that will definitely become a veil between you and your Lord. Remembrance of God Almighty shades the hearts of the gnostics, mingles with them and makes them forget about everything else. Once that state is attained, then the paradise of bliss will be their abode. This is the oft-denied paradise, the promised garden of bliss. Paradise which is lost to you in this world, can be found again through consenting to God's decree, through bringing one's heart close to God Almighty and communicating with Him, and through raising the veil of separation between one's heart and its Lord. Such a heart will always be with its Lord, and that state will prevail without imagining or interpretation. **"There is nothing like unto Him. He is the All-Hearing and the All-Knowing Lord."**

"لَيْسَ كَمِثْلِهِ شَئٌ وَهُوَ السَّمِيْعُ الْعَلِيْمُ"

As for the promised garden of bliss, it is the heaven which God Almighty created as the dwelling place of the believers. In it they can look, without any separating veils or doubt, directly at His divine countenance.

No doubt, all that is good (**khair**) comes from God; evil (**sharr**) is the property of others. Good comes from seeking God Almighty, while evil is the product of turning away from Him. Any deed for which you seek a reward, your wages are your compensation. If you do a good deed and ask for compensation, your reward will be material. But, if you do something good to please God Almighty, your reward will be His nearness and the direct gaze on Him. Once you attain that, you will never ask for compensation again.

In reality, what is this world worth? What is the hereafter worth? What is anything worth besides God Almighty. Seek the bestower, not the bestowal. Find a good neighbor before you look for a house. God Almighty is the primal Lord Who exists from the beginningless beginning (**azal**). He is the Originator of all things, and He will always be, after everything else is gone.

Child, constantly remember death, exercise patience in adversities and trust in God Almighty under all circumstances. If you can develop these three qualities, you will have whatever you wish for in the kingdom of your Lord. By constantly remembering death, your renunciation (**zuhd**) will become true, through patience you will receive whatever you wish from your Lord, and through trust (**tawakkul**) you free your heart from all attachments and depend solely on your Lord. The world, the hereafter and everything besides your Lord will turn away from you. Peace and tranquility will encompass you from every direction. Not one of God's creations will then have access to you, and God Almighty will seal all doors of admittance to you. Then your food and protection will come from every direction. Your Lord will protect you from your six directions, and you will become one of those about whom God Almighty has said: "**You certainly have no power over My servants.**"

«اِنَّ عِبَادِي لَيْسَ لَكَ عَلَيْهِمْ سُلْطَانٌ»

In that state, how could satan have any authority or access to God's true worshipers, the sincere ones whose deeds are not affected?

Speaking is something done at the end, not at the beginning. Silence dominates the life of a true seeker. In the beginning, silence is his trade. At the end, he reverberates with golden words. The kingdom of the sincere devotee is in his heart, and his authority is in his innermost being, regardless of what is displayed outwardly. The rarest amongst these exalted beings has both the inner kingdom and outer wealth. Be ever concealed within your state of being, Strictly remain thus until you become a perfect human being, until such time when your heart reaches its Lord. Once you become a perfect human being, and have reached your destination, then have no concerns. How could you ever worry then, when you have attained your realized station and fulfilled the terms of your journey. Once you realize yourself, all your concerns will dissipate. You will be seated on your own throne of light, surrounded by your vigilant guards, and the people will be the same as horsemen and trees in your eyes. Their praises and blame will be equal in your sight. Whether people seek you or forsake you will have no effect on you anymore. At that point you become their chieftain, raising them up or lowering them. In that station, you will deal with them according to their Creator's intentions, and you will dispose of their affairs by His leave. He will assign that authority to the hand of your heart. He will place the mark of His approval into the hand of your innermost being. Be wise, say nothing until you achieve that state. Do not lose control of yourself while you are blind. Ask for someone to guide you. You are ignorant, search for someone to teach you. Should you find someone like that, hold firmly to his robe. Accept his words and opinions and steadfastly follow his lead until you reach the straight path. Once arrived on the straight path, dwell stationary there until your knowledge of it becomes your inherent reality. Then, every lost soul will turn to you for guidance, and you will become the plate from which the poor, the meek and the hungry eat.

Some of the characteristics of chivalry are to keep God's secret and to observe good conduct with His creations. O man. How far are you from a state of truly seeking God Almighty and being content to be with Him alone and no one else. Have you not heard His words: **"Amongst you are those who seek the world and others who seek the hereafter."**

«مِنْكُمْ مَنْ يُرِيدُ الدُّنْيَا وَمِنْكُمْ مَنْ يُرِيدُ الآخِرَةَ»

and He said: **"Seeking His Countenance."**

«يُرِيدُونَ وَجْهَهُ»

If your destiny is written as happy, the hand of divine protection (**ghïrah**) will be there to save you from any other hand and take you to the gate of God's proximity, and: **"Thereat, the sovereignty belongs to God, the true Lord."**

«هُنَالِكَ الْوِلَايَةُ لِلَّهِ الْحَقِّ»

If you receive that endowment, both the world and the hereafter will become subservient to you, without any more pain or efforts on your part. At that station, knock at the door of God Almighty, and remain, unwavering. If you do so with certitude and determination, then you will understand with absolute clarity the nature of all thoughts. You will recognize and differentiate among the thoughts of one's mind and desire, passion, the inclinations of the heart, and the suggestions of satan, whose hopes of salvation are dead (**iblïs**). Also, you will clearly perceive God's intentions. It will be said unto you: "This is a true intention and this is a false intention." Once you understand the nature of things, you will recognize each thought by its mark. Once you reach that station, then God's intention will come: to teach, strengthen, establish, appoint, animate you, immobilize you, and command you to do or not to do.

O ye people! Pray not for more or for less. Ask not to progress or digress. Surely the divine decree encompasses each and every one of you. Each of you has his own personal records and history. The Prophet, upon whom be peace, said: "**Your Lord has finished creating , allotting shares and life span. The pen of destiny has dried with what is written.**"

«فَرَغَ رَبُّكُمْ مِنَ ٱلْخَلْقِ وَالرِّزْقِ وَالْأَجَلِ جَفَّ الْقَلَمُ بِمَا هُوَ كَائِنٌ»

The decree which God Almighty predestined is conclusive. Then came His judgment proclaiming what is lawful, what is unlawful and what is incumbent. Thus, no one has the right to object to what was established in God's preexistent knowledge of things. Rather, one should say: "**He is not to be questioned about what He does, though they are subject to His questioning**."

«لَا يُسْأَلُ عَمَّا يَفْعَلُ وَهُمْ يُسْأَلُونَ»

O ye people! Act upon what was revealed outwardly. Follow these black and white instructions and they will lead you to perform the inner work. When you correctly abide by the outer revelations, that will lead you to understand the inner meanings. Your innermost being, (**sirr**) will understand them first. Your heart will then dictate the inner meanings to your 'self (**nafs**), which in turn will dictate them to your tongue, and finally your tongue will deliver them to the people. In this way, words will come to help the people and serve their interests.

Oh, what blessings you receive when you consent to God's decree and love Him. O stuporous ones. You merely claim to love God Almighty. Did you not know that there are stipulations to that? One of the conditions of loving God Almighty is to consent to His decree in regard to your destiny and that of others. Another condition is that you never seek comfort from anyone besides Him. Seek peace and tranquility in Him. Feel no bewilderment as long as you know that He is with you. Once God's love dwells in one's heart, it will satisfy him and make him be disgusted by any distractions. Thus, repent from your false claims. Such a state does not come through disdain, desire, lies, hypocrisy or pretense. Repent and maintain your repentance. But, your repentance alone is not sufficient, you need steadfastness. It is not enough to merely plant the seedlings; they must take root, branch out and bear fruits.

Remain consenting to God's will, whether you face adversities, hurt, poverty or riches; whether in difficulties, comfort, illness, or health; in good, bad, bounty or shortage; or in the giving or taking away. Be always content with Him. I find no cure for you except surrender (**Islām**) to God Almighty . Do not feel bewildered by His decree. Do not argue with His will. Do not complain to others about His doings with you; that will broaden your difficulties. Rather, be quiet, silent and passive. Be steadfast with Him and watch what He will do to you and through you. You will be happy when His changes come. If you care to be with Him in such a way, have no doubt that He will change your bewilderment into peace, and you will find joy in worshiping Him alone. O Lord, keep us on Your side and with You. Amen.

«رَبَّنَا آتِنَا فِي الدُّنْيَا حَسَنَةً وَفِي الآخِرَةِ حَسَنَةً وَقِنَا عَذَابَ النَّارِ»

"**Our Lord, grant us the benefits of a good deed in this world, the reward of a good deed in the hereafter, and protect us eternally from the sufferings of hell-fire.**"

✺ ✺ ✺ ✺ ✺

Chapter 5

The Reason Behind God's Love For His Servant

Child, where is the true worship of God Almighty you claim? Bring about a true state of worship, and receive a guaranteed satisfaction for all your needs. You are a slave who has run away from your Master. Humble yourself before Him. Turn yourself back to Him. Submit to His commands by compliance. Do what is lawful and abstain from the unlawful. Go back to your Master, be patient with and consent to His judgment. When you achieve that state, your worship of your Lord will be crowned with success. Your satisfaction comes from Him. He said: **"Isn't God sufficient to His servant?"**

«اَلَيْسَ آللّهُ بِكَافٍ عَبْدَهُ»

When you truly worship Him, God Almighty will love you and strengthen His love in your heart. He will comfort you with His company, bring you nigh unto His own presence and spare you any further roiling, once you ask for the company of no one besides Him. In every way, He will make you pleased with Him. Even if He restricts the entire earth and shuts all the doors with all its worth, you will never be dissatisfied with Him. You will near the door of no one else, you will eat no one else's food, and you will be joined in the company of Moses, upon whom be peace, about whom God Almighty has said: **"We foreordained that he sucks no milk from anyone besides his mother."**

«وَحَرَّمْنَا عَلَيْهِ الْمَرَاضِعَ مِنْ قَبْلُ»

Our Lord and Cherisher is witnessing everything. He sees everything, is present everywhere, is watchful over everything, and is near to everything. You cannot forego Him. How can you deny the truth, even though you know it? O fool. You know God Almighty. How dare you deny your own cognizance?. Turn not away from Him, for you will then be deprived of His immeasurable wealth. Be patient with Him and bear no patience with being away from Him. Do you not know that the patient ones will win? What kind of brain do you have? How do you explain your hastiness? God Almighty has said: "**O ye who believe, persevere in patience and constancy. Live in such determination, strengthen each other with unity, and fear God, so at the end, you may triumph.**"

« يَا اَيُّهَا الَّذِيْنَ آمَنُوا اصْبِرُوا وَصَابِرُوا وَاتَّقُوا اللهَ لَعَلَّكُمْ تُفْلِحُوْنَ »

There are many more verses in the Qur'ān on the subject of patience. They all point to the undiminishing wealth and blessings contained within the virtue of patience. They describe the exalted reward, bounty and comfort which are reserved for such believers in this world and in the hereafter. Have patience and you will experience its benefits in this world and in the hereafter. Visit the graveyards and learn the lessons. Visit the righteous people and learn from them. Do good deeds and your life will be properly aligned. Be not amongst those who ignore good advice and disdain to comply with what they hear.

There are four sections that make you lose your faith (**deen**): You do not practice what you know; you follow what you do not understand; you remain ignorant because you do not even attempt to learn what you need; and the fourth is that you hinder people's efforts to acquire the knowledge necessary for their own salvation.

O ye people! When you join spiritual study circles (**halaqātu zikr**) you mainly go there as spectators, not to cure your illnesses. You refrain from hearkening to the advice of the gnostic shaikh, You criticize his counsel and meticulously mark down any mistake or slip of the tongue he makes. You sarcastically make fun of him, laugh at him and just play around. Guard yourselves. You are endangering your heads with God Almighty. Repent from this attitude. Do not resemble the enemies of God Almighty, and try to reap the benefit of what you learn here.

Child, your progress has been curtailed by your karmic habits, though God Almighty is strict about the allotment of shares. Your current dependence on created resources and your forgetting to trust the causal being Who created everything are hindering your growth. Resume serving Him, and be sincere in your devotion.

God Almighty has said: "**I have created the jinns and the humans solely to worship Me.**"

«وَمَا خَلَقْتُ الْجِنَّ وْالانْسَ اِلاَّ لِيَعْبُدُوْنِ»

He did not create them so they could live their wild fancies, nor did He create them for fun, to play, eat, drink, sleep or have sex. So wake up, O heedless ones. Wake up from your slumber. Let your heart walk one step towards Him, and see how His love will foster many more steps towards you. His yearning is more ardent towards His beloved ones than theirs is to meet Him. "**He grants His bounty to whomsoever He wills without reckoning**."

«يَرْزُقُ مَن يَّشَاءُ بِغَيْرِ حِسَابْ»

When God Almighty intends something for His servant, He prepares him for it. This relates to the essence, not the form. Once the servant achieves what I have just explained, his renunciation of this world, the hereafter and anything besides his Lord will become true. Such state will come to him, and the kingdom, the sovereignty, and the power to command will also come to him. Every atom he carries will have the weight of a mountain. A drop from him will fill an ocean. His planet will radiate like a moon, and his moon will be brighter then the sun. The little he has will become abundance, his effacement becomes redemption, his annihilation becomes continuity, his movement becomes stillness. His tree towers up towards the Divine Throne, and its branches spread throughout the world and the hereafter. What are these branches? They are wisdom and knowledge. To him, this world will be like the hollow of a small ring. The world has no dominion over him, and the hereafter does not attract or distract him. No king compels him, and no slave obliges him. No veil separates him, no one can overtake him and nothing can disturb him.

Once these conditions are satisfied, then it will be appropriate for such a being to serve the people, assist them and save them from the ocean of this world. Thus, when God Almighty decides to grant His servant His blessings, He will appoint him as the guide of the people, as their physician, teacher and trainer. He will make him their interpreter and exegete. He will make him their opportunity. He will become God's gift to them, as their lamp and sun.

Either God Almighty will require this from him, and such it shall be, or He will keep him veiled in His presence, away from others. It is only the rare ones who reach that state whereby He sends them back to serve the people, armed with His total protection, guardianship and safety. God will grant them success in serving people's interests and guiding them back to Him. The trial of the ascetic who renounces the world is the hereafter, and the trial of the renunciate (**zāhid**) in both the world and the hereafter is the Lord and Sustainer of the world and the hereafter.

You became heedless as if you were immortal, as if you were not the subject matter of the great gathering on the day of reckoning, and as if you were unaware that you are going to walk over the bridge (**sirāt**) towards your destiny. These are your attributes, while you still claim to have surrendered (**Islām**) and to have faith (**imān**). This Qur'ān and knowledge you have are the incriminating evidence against you if you do not apply them in your daily life. If you go to those who have knowledge (**'ulamā'**) but do not accept their advice, this again will become your sin, and its consequence will fall on you later. It will be as if you had met God's Messenger, upon whom be peace, and did not accept his warnings or believe in the glad tidings he brought to this world.

On the day of resurrection, the entire creation will be seized by fear engendered by the glory, majesty, supremacy, and justice of God Almighty. On that day, all the kings of the world will vanish and His lordship alone will remain. On that day, everything returns back to Him. Also on that day the exalted stations, honor and undiminishing wealth God Almighty bestowed upon His chosen servants will manifest. Today, in this world, they are the testimony of God's providence to the people and the land. They are the pillars of the earth. They are the leaders of the people and their chancellors. They are God's deputies on earth. This is in essence, not in form. Today they are the expression of divine providence, and in the hereafter they will become its physical manifestation.

The courage of one who opposes disbelief is to face the disbeliever with steadfastness. The courage of the righteous ones (**sāliheen**) is to face their own mind and desire (**nafs**), passions, karmic habits, satan and evil companions who are the human satans. Finally, the courage of the chosen elite to God's proximity, is to renounce the world, the hereafter and anything beside God Almighty.

Child, wake from your slumber before death comes and forces you to rise. Become religious and mix with religious people, because these are the real people. The wisest of people is one who obeys his Lord, and the most ignorant is one who disobeys Him. The Prophet, upon whom be peace, used the term: '**tarubat yadāk**,' meaning "bless your hands." The root of the word, **tarubat,** comes from the word '**turāb**' in Arabic, meaning earth or dirt. (*Tarubat* is a kin to the word *Iftaqarat* from the root of the word *fiqr.*) The word: "**Fiqr**," means poverty and in that sense, the expression: '**tarubat yadāk**,' means to be without needs. Thus, if you associate with religious people and love them, your hands will become filled with the treasures of contentment and satisfaction because of the wealth which is inherent in their company, and your heart will be able to escape from hypocrisy and its people. A hypocrite and a deceiver have no actions.

Nothing will be accepted from you unless it is intended for God's sake. It is the intention behind your deed that makes it valuable, not its form. If you counteract your carnal self (**nafs**), vanity, malice, passion, satan and your love for the world in offering a deed, then God will accept it from you. Practice good deeds. Be sincere and do not look back at them boastfully. Only what is meant for God will be accepted, not what is meant for people's praise. How unfortunate you are. You solicit people's recognition for your deed but you expect God Almighty to accept it from you. This is mere craziness. Renounce your love for fame, your greed, your covert desires, and your pleasure in this world.

Instead, foster the feeling of sadness, for this world is the abode of sadness. This is a prison. Our Prophet, upon whom be peace, was most contemplative. He showed little joy and was mostly pensive. His laughter was little more than a smile to comfort the hearts of others. His heart was occupied with greater concerns. If it were not for the sake of his companions and duties in this world, he would have not left his house or sat with anyone.

Child, when your retreat to God Almighty is true, your innermost being will see wonders and your heart will become pure. Your gaze will become a meaningful admonition, your heart will become contemplative, and your essence and soul will reach their Lord. To be occupied in thinking about the world is a punishment and a veil. To reflect about the hereafter is true knowledge and life for one's heart. Whenever a servant is granted the gift of contemplation (**fikr**) he will also be given knowledge of life's hidden mysteries in both the world and the hereafter.

O unfortunate one. How can you waste your heart with concern about this world, when God Almighty has finished allotting its portions? Each one of your portions has a destiny and a time. Each day your sustenance will be given anew, whether you ask for it or not. Your anxiety to get hold of your share and more is defaming your character before God Almighty and the people. The weaker your faith, the more you pray for wealth. When your faith increases, you will refrain from asking and when your faith becomes perfect you will sleep on it.

Child, do not mix serious matters with play. This can bring you no success. When your heart is with the creation, how can you then bring the Creator into it? When you place your dependence on created things, how can you then reach the Causal Being Who created everything? How can you combine form and formlessness? Inner and outer? What you understand and what you do not understand? What the creation has at hand and what the Creator has? How ignorant is he who forgets about the Causal Being and turns to the elements. One who supports the next and forgets about the First is one who forgets about the Eternal and seeks the mortal.

Child, if you remain in the company of ignorant people, some of their ignorance will rub off on you. To be with an ignorant person is a companionship of losses. Seek the company of true believers, the pious, the gnostics who act on their knowledge. In every act they do, what a blessed state the believers live in. What a mighty power they have when battling and conquering their desires and passions. That is why the Prophet, upon whom be peace, said: "**A believer keeps his smile on his face and hides his sadness in his heart.**"

«بِشْرُ المُؤْمِنِ في وَجْهِهِ وَحُزْنُهُ في قَلْبِهِ»

It is a sign of one's strength to display cheerfulness to comfort people and to keep his sadness in his heart, between himself and his Lord. His stress is constant, his thoughts are flowing, he cries often and laughs little. That is why the Prophet,

upon whom be peace, said: **"There is no peace for a believer
other than in meeting his Lord."**

«لاَ رَاحَةُ لِمُؤْمِنٍ غَيْرَ لِقَاءِ وَجْهِ رَبِّهِ عَزَّ وَجَلَّ»

Thus, a believer veils his sadness with cheerfulness. Outwardly, he is involved in earning his livelihood, but inwardly he
remains with his Lord. Outwardly, he works for his family and
children, but inwardly he praises his Lord. He does not divulge his
secret even to his wife, children or neighbors, nor to any one of
God's creations. He has understood the saying of the Prophet,
upon whom be peace: **"Be discrete in the management of your
affairs."**

«اسْتَعِينُوا عَلَى أُمُورِكُمْ بِالْكِتْمَانِ»

In this way, he guards his secret. Should he be overcome by
a slip of the tongue, he retrieves his word and changes the
expression. He changes the subject, covers up his mistake and
apologizes for what he said.

Child, make me your mirror. Make me the mirror of your
heart and innermost secret being, the mirror of your actions.
Come near unto me, and see in yourself what you may not be able
to see when distant from me. If you need religious advice, find me,
for I will not pamper you at the expense of God's religion. I may be
forthright in speaking about God's religion. That is because I was
brought up at the forthright hand of my teacher, not a money-
making nor a deceiving hand. Leave your world at home and come
near unto me, for I am standing at the gates of the hereafter. Come
here and hearken to what I say and act according to it before your
death comes tomorrow.

The main point is to be Godfearing and reverent before His
glory and majesty. If that fear is not there, you will not find safe
refuge anywhere in this world or in the hereafter. Fear of God
Almighty is what knowledge is all about. That is why God Almighty
has said: **"Verily, those endowed with knowledge among God's
servants fear Him the most."**

, «إِنَّمَا يَخْشَى ٱللَّهَ مِنْ عِبَادِهِ الْعُلَمَاءُ»

Actually, those who fear and revere God Almighty are none
other than His servants who are endowed with knowledge and
actively practice it. They ask for no reward for their deeds other

than the pleasure of their Lord and His nearness. They ardently seek His love and seek to become free of the veils of separation from Him. They pray that the doors of God Almighty never be closed to them, whether in this world or in the hereafter. They have no desire for the world, the hereafter or anything besides Him.

This world belongs to one category of people. The hereafter belongs to another category, and God's nearness belongs to a people of a different state of being. Those are the faithful ones who have true certitude, knowledge, love, piety and reverence for God Almighty. They are the ones who are broken hearted and grief stricken for His sake. They are the ones who have fear and reverence for God's promise (**ghayb**), the unseen. He is unseen to their physical eyes only, but omnipresent to the eyes of their hearts. How could they not fear Him, when every day He brings a different manifestation of His Powers? He changes things and replaces them. He helps one and defeats another. He gives life to one and causes another to die. He accepts one and rejects another. He brings one nigh and distances Himself from another. Such is God, **"Who is not to be questioned about what He does, though they are subject to His questioning."**

«لَا يُسْأَلُ عَمَّا يَفْعَلُ وَهُمْ يُسْأَلُوْنَ»

O God, bring us near unto You and never distance us from You.

«رَبَّنَا آتِنَا فِي الدُّنْيَا حَسَنَةً وَفِي الآخِرَةِ حَسَنَةً وَقِنَا عَذَابَ النَّارِ»

"Our Lord, grant us the benefits of a good deed in this world, the reward of a good deed in the hereafter, and protect us eternally from the sufferings of hell-fire."

❈ ❈ ❈ ❈ ❈

Chapter 6

Importance of Brotherly Advice

The hearts of the true believers are pure, sacred and crystal clear. They forgot about the creation but kept the remembrance of the Creator. They think no more of the world but keep their focus on the hereafter. They ignore what you have and solicit what God Almighty has. In contrast, you have been kept in the dark, where they are veiled from you and you cannot recognize their true state. That is because you have been absorbed in your worldly affairs to the detriment of your life in the hereafter. You have abandoned your modesty and shyness before your Lord, and you are belligerent with Him. Accept your believing brother's advice and do not contradict him. He sees for you what you cannot see for yourself. That is why the Prophet, upon whom be peace, said: "**A believer is the mirror of another believer.**"

«المُؤْمِنُ مِرْآةُ المُؤْمِنِ»

A believer is sincere and truthful in advising his believing brother. He explains to him things which otherwise would be imperceptible. He makes him discern between good and evil, and clarifies for him his rights and obligations.

All praises be to God Who cast upon my heart the duty to admonish the people and made that my biggest concern. I am only offering sincere advice. I am not asking any reward for it. My Lord has already awarded me my final destiny. I am not a seeker of this world. I am not a slave to this world or the hereafter. I worship none besides my Lord. I worship only the Creator, the One and only God, the Absolute, the Eternal Lord Who existed before the beginningless beginning, and I celebrate His praises.

I rejoice when you are successful and become distressed when you fall. When I look at the face of a truthful seeker who has attained success at my hands, I rejoice and have no more hunger, thirst or needs. I smile, wondering, and say to myself: "How could

such an attained being have reached such success at my hands?"
Child, my goal is you, not me. If you change for the better, it will
be for you not me. I have already crossed into my destination. Now
it is your turn. I am here for your sake, so grab onto me so you may
cross the bridge faster.

O ye people! Refrain from your arrogance with your Lord and
haughtiness towards His creations. Acknowledge your worth and
humble yourselves within. You have all commenced from a filthy
dash of sperm ejected as discarded water, and you will end as a
discarded decaying cadaver. Be not like someone who is dragged
by his greed and hunted by his lust. His passion will carry him to
the doors of the rich to ask for something which is not written for
him, or to receive his share, but through humiliation and deg-
radation. The Prophet, upon whom be peace, said: **"God's
strongest chastisements to His servant in this world come
from his asking for what is not his share."**

«أَشَدُّ عُقُوبَاتِ اللّه عَزَّ وَجَلَّ لِعَبْدِه طَلَبُهُ مَالَمْ يُقْسَمُ لَهُ»

O fool, you are certainly ignorant of the divine decree or the
One Who preordained it. Do you think that the people of this world
can give you something which is not written for you? Your
thoughts are no more than satan's whisperings which have
already taken hold of your heart and brain. You are not God's
slave. You are the slave of your mind and desire (**nafs**), passions,
satan, karmic habits, pennies and dinars.

Thus, search for and associate yourself with a successful
person so you may achieve victory by his method (**tarïqa**).
Someone, God bless his soul, said: *"One may not recognize what
success is unless he meets a successful person."* However, when
you are lucky enough to meet such a person, you look at him with
the eyes of your head, not the eyes of your heart and innermost
being. Even the image you project about your faith is not yours,
but a copy of someone else's practices. That is why you do not
possess the vision with which to see someone other than yourself.
God Almighty has said: **"It is not the physical eyes that become
blind, but the hearts which lie in the breast that lose sight."**

«فَإِنَّهَا لَا تَعْمَى الْأَبْصَارُ وَلٰكِنْ تَعْمَى الْقُلُوبُ الَّتِي فِي الصُّدُورِ»

One whose greed impels him to extort the world from the
hands of the creation, has in fact sold his religion and faith in God

Almighty for a handful of dried figs. He sold what is eternal for the price of what is perishable. That is why, unfailingly, he will end by having neither one of them.

Child, as long as your faith is not thoroughly developed, strive to correct the way you earn your livelihood. Do it in such a way that you do not become dependent on people, or debilitate your faith by swindling people's money with it, putting a price tag on your religious obligations. However, once your faith becomes stronger and matures, then trust in God Almighty and become His dependent. Become free from your psychological dependency on the creations, sever your connection to your worldly patrons, and fly away with your heart to be forever free from them. Let your heart journey away from your home town, family, business, and connections. Entrust what you have to the hands of your immediate family, brothers and close friends. Become dead to the world, as though the angel of death had come and taken back your soul, as if he had come like lightning and robbed you of them, as if the earth cleaved and swallowed you, as if the waves of the divine decree and preordained destiny have swept you away and carried you and drowned you in the ocean of knowledge. For one who reaches such a state, there can be no created force (**asbāb**) that could ever harm him. Even should such created forces ever touch him, their effect would be outward not inward. These forces are for others, not for him.

O ye people! If you are incapable of practicing what I just told you, of becoming free from worldly entanglements, or renouncing them with your hearts from every angle, then do it from one angle. Try to take one step at a time. If you cannot do them all, then do no less than a few. Our Prophet, upon whom be peace, used to say: **"Free yourselves, as much as possible, from your worldly concerns."**

«تَفَرَّغُوا مِنْ هُمُومِ الدُّنْيَا مَا اسْتَطَعْتُمْ»

Child, if you have the strength and determination to free yourself from your worldly entanglements, then do it. Otherwise, hold on to your heart and run fast towards your Lord. Grab the tail of His divine mercy and implore Him incessantly until He casts any worldly worries out of your heart. He is the One Who has the power over everything. He is the All-Knowing Lord. Everything is under His command. Remain at His door, and pray to Him to purify your heart from everything besides Him. Implore Him to fill your heart with true faith, knowledge of Him, acknowledgement of His being, and satisfaction in Him alone. Ask Him to endow you with certitude and determination (**yaqïn**). Ask Him to comfort your heart with His own presence, to engage you in serving Him and obeying His command. Ask for everything you need from Him, and none else. Asking from the creation is humiliation. Humble yourself to God Almighty alone. Let all your dealings be with Him alone, for His sake and none else.

Child, a knowledgeable tongue will not advance you one step nearer to your Lord unless your words are correlated with the deeds of your heart. The walking is the walking of the heart. Nearness is the nearness of one's innermost being unto God Almighty. Deeds are what they imply in truth, while physically observing the rules of **sharï'a**, humbling oneself to God Almighty and to His creations.

One who values himself to be important is of no value. One who exhibits his deeds publicly for show has no deeds. Real deeds are those which are not disclosed to others. Only the necessary obligatory precepts (**farā'idh**) should be done in public. Previously you have neglected to properly lay the foundation of your building, thus constructing any structure on top of a shaky base would be of no benefit to you. When the foundation is strong, you can repair any damaged structure above it, or even replace the entire house, should the need be. Thus, the foundation of good deeds are belief in the Oneness (**tawhïd**) of God Almighty and sincerity (**ikhlās**) in one's actions. For one who has no such faith, his work is in vain.

Properly construct the foundation of your deeds with the pillars of belief in God's Oneness and true sincerity. Once that is accomplished, then proceed in building your actions with God's will (**hawul**) and power (**quwwa**), not yours. The hand of glorifying God's Oneness (**tawhïd**) is the builder, not the hand of hypocrisy and polytheism (**shirk**). Only the actions of such a true believer (**muwahhid**) will rise in value, not those of a hypocrite.

O Lord, make hypocrisy distant from us in all circumstances. Amen.

«رَبَّنَا آتِنَا فِي الدُّنْيَا حَسَنَةً وَفِي الآخِرَةِ حَسَنَةً وَقِنَا عَذَابَ النَّارِ»

"Our Lord, grant us the benefits of a good deed in this world, the reward of a good deed in the hereafter, and protect

us eternally from the sufferings of hell-fire."

Chapter 7

On Patience

اللَّهُمَّ صَلِّ عَلَى مُحَمَّدٍ وَعَلَى آلِ مُحَمَّدٍ

Lord, bestow Thy choicest blessings upon Muhammad and the followers of Muhammad. "**Endow us with patience and endurance, and make us gain a strong foothold and resoluteness in our struggle.**"

«وَأَفْرِغْ عَلَيْنَا صَبرًا وَثَبِّتْ اَقْدَامَنَا»

Lord, increase Thy bounty upon us, and grant us the gift of gratitude

O ye people! Be patient, for this world is only a prison of adversities and plagues. Rarely, is it different. Alongside every blessing there is an adversity. There is not one pleasure without grief, and no prosperity without restraint.

Spend your life in this world taking your share from it with the lawful hand of the divine law, **(shari'a).** This is the only medicine which cures anything taken from this world. Child, when you are a true seeker, you receive your destined share with the hand of **shari'a.** When you become a chosen friend, you take your share by command, and when you attain the state of true devotion, piety and proximity, you receive it from the hand of God Almighty. Your share will be hastened to you, the Sovereign Ruler will command your innate capabilities to do or not to do, and all actions will be His doing.

There are three categories of people: the common man, the chosen and the select. The common man is the pious Muslim. He holds fast to the divine laws and abides by them. He subscribes to God Almighty's directives: "**Follow what the Messenger brings you and refrain from what he forbids.**"

« مَا آتَاكُمُ الرَّسُوْلُ فَخُذُوْهُ وَمَا نَهَاكُمْ عَنْهُ فَانْتَهُوا»

Once that is attained and complied with inwardly and outwardly, he joins the blessed rank of the chosen ones (**khawās**). He becomes an illuminated heart with which he sees. When he takes something with the hand of the divine laws, his heart is satisfied, and seeks inspiration (**ilhām**) from God Almighty. In fact, God's direct inspiration encompasses each and every one of his actions. God Almighty has said: "**and He inspired each soul (nafs) with both its insolent and its pious nature.**"

«فَأَلْهَمَهَا فُجُورَهَا وَتَقْوَاهَا»

Being aware, his heart will fear wrongdoing and await God's inspiration. The immediate sign of God's inspiration is shown by the outer command. In other words, whatever is in the shop of this poor vendor is his property, and his responsibility to manage. Still, in the light of his own heart, he again examines and determines what belongs to him and what belongs to others. When he completes his obligations in full compliance with the **shari'a** and with the full power of his faith and affirmation of God's Oneness and sole sovereignty (**tawḥïd**), when his heart becomes free from the creation and the world (**dunyā**) by cutting his way through its wilderness and crossing its oceans, his daylight will dawn. The light of his true faith will gleam, the effulgent light of his nearness to his Lord will shine and the light of good deeds, the light of patience, the light of careful assessment, serenity and peacefulness will radiate in him. All of that is the fruit of complying with the **shari'a** and the blessings of submitting to it.

As for the representatives (**abdāl**) who are the elite amongst the chosen ones, they first deliberate every action in accordance with the laws of **shari'a.** Next, they await God's command, His doing, His propelling and His inspiration. For other than these three categories of people, there is nothing but destruction and death, sufferings within perdition, devastation of unlawfulness, a migraine for one's religion, a malignant growth in one's heart, and debilitation of one's body. O ye people! God Almighty created these conditions within you in order to see how you will perform. Will you assert your faith or run away? Will you believe or deny? One who does not agree with the divine decree cannot be trusted or consented to. One who does not agree with God's judgment is not blessed. One who does not give is not to be given to, and one who does not urge his horse does not travel far.

O ignorant one. You want to change things and move them around. Are you another god who wants God Almighty to agree with him, rather than the reverse? Reverse your direction direction and you will be on the right track. If it were not for God's antecedent decree (**qadar**), anyone could infringe upon the truth.

Testing reveals the real substance; oppose your carnal self's denial of God's decree. When you succeed at this, you can then advise others. The stronger your faith, the easier it will be for you to abolish objectionable actions, and the weaker your faith, the better it will be for you to sit at home and play dumb when you see wrong. The strong foothold of faith secures victory against the satans of the humans and the jinns. These are the feet that are unfailingly invincible against adversities. However, the feet of your faith are frail and shaky. Thus, do not claim to have faith. Start by disliking everyone and love the Creator of everyone. If it is His will to make you love what you earlier hated, He will then protect you from it, for He will be the One Who placed that love in your heart. That is why the Prophet, upon whom be peace, said:

"There are three things from your world which I was made to like, They are perfume, women, and placing the delight of my eyes on prayers."

"حُبِّبَ إِلَيَّ مِنْ دُنْيَاكُمْ ثَلَاثٌ :الطّيبُ، وَالنّسَاءُ،

وَجُعِلَتْ قُرَّةُ عَينِى فِى الصَّلَاةِ"

He was made to like them after he had disliked, renounced and abstained from them. Thus, empty your heart from anything besides God Almighty and let Him make you love His will.

❈ ❈ ❈ ❈ ❈

Chapter 8

Be Not Pretentious

A pretentious deceiver exhibits a clean appearance, but his heart is utterly defiled. Outwardly, he renounces the permissible, is lazy about earning his livelihood, and swindles others while wearing a religious garb. Privately, he does not have the slightest hesitation to accept what is clearly impermissible. He attempts to conceal his nature from the common people, although his presumption is not hidden from God's people. His asceticism and religious observances are entirely for show. His religious commitment seems outwardly sound, but inwardly it is conspicuously devastated.

O straying man. Obeisance to God Almighty is the work of the heart, not merely of the form. It should emanate from the heart, the innermost being and essence. Take off your false garb and let me procure for you a garment from your Lord that does not wear out, the value of which cannot be estimated. Remove the garb of your choosing and let Him fit you with the raiment of His choice. Take off the garment of contempt and neglect of honoring God's rights upon you. Throw off the robe of seeking after people and attributing to them a share (**shirk**) in God's power.

Throw off the garment of passions, frivolous action, vanity, hypocrisy, and love of fame, recognition or received favors in acknowledgment of your status. Throw off the robe of this world, and put on the robe of the hereafter. Eradicate your trust in your own capabilities or means, power and will, and lie motionless in the hands of your Lord. Be there without presumption. Stand without status, and associate no one with God Almighty.

If you heed this advice, you will discover His subtle kindness surrounding you, His Mercy encompassing you, His favors and bounty showering you and embracing you. Run towards Him! Give yourself up to Him, naked of the creation and of yourself. Walk over to Him in the state of being removed from yourself or others. Walk over to Him unprejudiced and without partiality. Let

Him restore you, grant you continuity, and strengthen you inwardly and outwardly. In that state, even if He were to banish you from all of universes and load you with their impediments, that would be of no harm to you. Rather it would be a protection for you. One who transcends the creations with the help of his faith in God's Oneness (**waḥdāniyya**), who transcends the world with the help of his ascetic detachment, and who transcends everything beside God Almighty with the help of his yearning for Him, will have achieved his success and victory in life. He will have won the wealth of this world and the hereafter. You must let your mind, desires, passions and satans die before your physical death comes, and die inwardly before you die outwardly.

O ye people! Hearken to my call, for I am God's caller to you. I call upon you to hasten to His door to obey Him. I am not calling you to come to me. A hypocrite calls the people to satisfy his selfish needs. He hopes for fortune, position and recognition.

O ignorant fool. You fail to take these words to heart, and prefer to be in your private cell in the company of your mind and desire (**nafs**) and passions. First of all, you need to seek the company of true shaikhs. You need to conquer your mind, desires, karmic habits, and everything besides God Almighty. You need to become a regular attendant at their doorsteps—I mean the true shaikhs. Learn at their hands. Only after that may you move to your hermitage and be alone with God Almighty. Once you satisfy these conditions, then you may become a cure for people's illnesses, a guided caller by God's leave. However, your tongue sounds pious, but your heart is rebellious. Your tongue sings God's praises, but your heart protests against His decree. Outwardly you are a Muslim, but inwardly you are a disbeliever. Outwardly you are a monotheist, but inwardly a polytheist. Outwardly you are an ascetic and religious, but inwardly you are like mildew on bathroom walls, a lock at the door of a garbage dump. If you become like that, satan will cast his shadow over your heart and dwell therein.

A true believer commences by building his inner life first, and then turns to finish the outside. Like a builder, he spends a fortune in structuring the inside of a house, while the door may remain a piece of board until the construction is finished. Once completed, he turns towards finishing the entrance and secures the house. Beginning on God's path and receiving His blessings are like that. First obtain His blessings, then you may turn towards the creation by His leave. It is like that on this path. You commence by attaining the hereafter, and then go back to collect your share in this world.

Chapter 9

The Trials of a Believer

The Prophet, upon whom be peace, said: "**God does not make His beloved suffer, but He may let him experience adversities**."

«إِنَّ ٱللَّهَ لَا يُعَذِّبُ حَبِيبَهُ وَلَكِنْ قَدْ يَبْتَلِيهِ»

A true believer is convinced that God Almighty will not put him through any adversity unless there are benefits to follow, either in this world or in the hereafter. With such faith, he consents to any trial, exercises patience, and has no hidden blame towards his Lord. A state of full absorption in his Lord keeps him pondering His glory and unconcerned about adversities.

O ye people who are engrossed in worldly concerns. Refrain from engaging in mere talk about these exalted stations. You speak with your tongues only, not from your hearts. You turn away from God Almighty and object to His words, oppose His prophets and their heirs (their true followers), their viceregents and their custodians. What you are disputing is the irrefutable authority of God Almighty and His irresistible power and will. You content yourselves with what the creations give you instead of seeking the bestowal and bounty of God Almighty. God Almighty and His righteous servants will not listen to your arguments or accept your pleas until you repent, are sincere in your repentance, and resolve in your penitence to agree with the divine decree and destiny regarding what you receive or what you owe, what exalts or what humiliates, riches or poverty, health or illness, and what you like or dislike.

O ye people! Comply, so you may be sought. Serve, so you may be served. Pursue the path of the righteous ones who preceded you and consent to the divine decree so that they may look after you and serve you. Humble yourselves before your destiny so it may be subservient to you. Have you not heard the saying: "**As you judge you shall be judged**," "**Your rulers reflect**

your rulings."

«كَمَا تَدِيْنُ تُدانُ، كَمَا تَكُونُوا يُوَلَّ عَلَيكُمْ»

Your deeds are your laborers. God Almighty is not unjust towards His servants. He rewards small deeds with bounty. He does not call what is correct rotten, and He does not call the truthful one a liar.

Child, serve and you shall be served. Whatever you devote yourself to will become your endowment. Serve God Almighty and be not distracted from serving Him by being preoccupied in serving worldly kings. They have no power to harm or benefit you. What can they give you? Can they give you what is not written for you? Can they allot you a share which God Almighty did not portion for you? They cannot initiate anything on their own. Should you ever say that what they allotted you is by their initiative, then you become a reprobate (**kāfir**). Do you not know that there is no bestower or depriver, no one who can harm or benefit, no one who initiates or delays except Allah, the Almighty Lord? If you say: "I know that ." I will reply: "How could you know that and still have the audacity to approach someone else for your needs?"

How could you harm your everlasting benefits in the hereafter for the sake of your worldly passions? Why would you harm your obedience to your Guardian Lord for the sake of serving your carnal self, mind and desire (**nafs**), your passions, your satan and the creations? Why would you encroach on your piety by complaining about your conditions to other than God Almighty? Do you not know that God Almighty protects and helps the pious ones, defends them, teaches them, points them towards Himself in order for them to know Him, and takes them by the hand to save them from adversities? It is He Who is the One Who looks at their hearts and grants them their sustenance from sources they do not anticipate.

God Almighty has said in one of His books: "**O son of Adam. Shy from Me the same way you shy from your righteous neighbor.**"

The Prophet, upon whom be peace, said: "**When a servant closes his doors, lowers his blinds, hides from the people and secretly indulges himself in sins, God Almighty will say to him: 'O son of Adam. You made Me despise you most amongst**

those who see you.'"

« إِذَا أَغْلَقَ الْعَبْدُ أَبْوَابَهُ، وَأَرْخَىٰ سَتَارَهُ، وَاخْتَفَىٰ مِنَ الْخَلْقِ، وَخَلَا بِمَعَاصِي اللهِ عَزَّ وَجَلَّ، يَقُوْلُ اللهُ عَزَّ وَجَلَّ:يَاابْنَ آدَمَ جَعَلْتَنِي أَهْوَنَ النَّاظِرِيْنَ إِلَيْكَ»

Chapter 10

Worship Without Constraint

The Prophet, upon whom be peace, said: "**I and the pious ones amongst my followers are free from unnatural mannerism.**"

«أَنَا وَالأَتْقِيَاءُ مِنْ أُمَّتِي بُرَاءٌ مِنَ التَّكَلُّفْ»

A pious person is free from presumption with regard to worshiping God Almighty. His devotion becomes inherent. He worships God Almighty outwardly and inwardly without constraint. As for a hypocrite, his entire mannerism is fake and pretentious, particularly with respect to his worship. He feigns devotion outwardly, though inwardly he neglects to practice it correctly. His nature fails to let him walk the avenues of the pious ones. Hence, each state has its prevalent characteristics, and each duty has its people. Indeed, God Almighty created a particular type of warrior for each struggle.

O ye hypocrites. Repent from your hypocrisy. Stop being slaves who have run away from their master. Why would you let satan laugh at you, trick you and quench the thirst of his jealousy with your failure? If you fast, you do so for social reasons, not for the sake of your Creator, likewise are your charities, community deeds and pilgrimage. Your state is as hopeless as "**Laboring in vain.**"

«عَامِلَةٌ نَاصِبَةٌ»

If you do not reshape your conduct, soon you will be cast into the blazing fire. Repent now and sincerely apologize to your Lord. Follow and do not invent. Carry on the fundamental precepts (**mazhab**) practiced earlier by the righteous people. Walk on the straight path as it is, without ascribing human characteristics to God Almighty (**tashbīh**) or denying the functions of His divine attributes (**ta'atīl**). Instead, clearly emulate the leading example (**sunnah**) of God's Messenger, upon whom be peace, without presumption, falsification, unnatural mannerism, fanaticism, vanity, or intellectualism. Sufficient for you are the good practices of your predecessors.

O man. You memorize the **Qur'ānic** text but you do not practice it. You learn the **sunnah** of God's Messenger, upon whom be peace, but do not act according to it. So what is your purpose? You admonish people but do not practice what you preach, and you forbid them from what you do not hesitate to do. God Almighty has said: **"It is grievously odious in God's sight that you say things which you do not practice."**

«كَبُرَ مَقْتًا عِنْدَ اللهِ أَنْ تَقُولُوا مَالاَ تَفْعَلُونْ»

Why do you act opposite to what you say? Are you not shy with God Almighty? Why do you profess to be believers when in fact you have no faith?

Faith is the antidote to all illnesses. True faith is the patience which bears our burdens. It is the real combatant and true fighter in our struggle. Faith is the true, generous donor that shares what it has in this world. Faith is generous for God's sake, but passion's generosity is solely for satan's sake and that of other selfish purposes which are generated from the carnal self, mind and desire (**nafs**). One who dwells at the doors of the creation has missed God's door. One who is strolling on the road of the creation has missed God's path. Yet for one whom God Almighty chooses to bless, He will make people shut their doors in his face and prevent their assisting him. Thus God makes him turn towards Himself. He pulls him out of the ocean of perfidy and deception onto the shore of safety. He brings him out of nothingness into reality, out of nowhere into somewhere.

O you fool. In winter's rainy season you seem happy to sit near the water hole. Wait and see, for soon the summer will arrive, the pond will dry and you will die on the spot. One who lives by the bank of the pond has water supplies aplenty in the winter, but when summer comes, the rainfall ceases and his reserve dries up.

Remain constantly with God Almighty and you will become wealthy and strong, a leader, a prince and a guide. Everyone needs one who suffices himself with God Almighty. However, this state cannot be attained by mere words or exaggerated hopes, rather through anchoring the truth in one's heart, the sign of which is compliance with one's knowledge.

Child, in the beginning strive for silence, wear the garment of apathy, and intentionally stay away from people. If you can, dig a hole and hide in it. Maintain such endeavor until your faith grows, until the foothold of your certitude becomes stronger, the wings of your truthfulness are plumaged and crowned, and until the inner eyes of your heart open. Only then will your station be raised high, and will you climb and soar in the realms of God's knowledge. You will encompass east and west, cross every land and sea, visit every valley and mountain, and go across the heavens and the two earths accompanied by the Guide, the Guardian Lord, the Compassionate Friend. Only then, may you untie your tongue and speak, remove the robe of apathy, and come out of your hole, unprejudiced, to serve the people as a cure for their illnesses. You will have no concerns whether they are few or many, whether they turn towards you or away from you, whether they praise or blame you. You will be confident that as long as you remain in the company your Lord, no matter what raging water you fall in, He will pull you out.

O ye people! Know your Creator and behave yourselves before Him. As long as your hearts remain distant from Him, your conduct will be ill-natured. However, once brought nigh, it will be well-behaved. Footboys may be raucous outside the door of their king, but when he rides out, they either shut up and behave themselves while near him or run and hide in different corners.

Like this parable, seeking others is the essence of turning away from one's Lord. Child, you will reap no success until you break away from your worldly patrons, eliminate your dependence on created causes (**asbāb**) and refute the notion that the creation can benefit or harm you. O ye people! You are healthy but sick, rich but poor, living but dead, existing but extinct. For how long are you going to remain ungrateful and heedless slaves who have run away from their Master and Lord? How far do you want to go in building your world at the expense of ruining your life in the hereafter? Certainly, none of you has more than one heart. Then how can it love both the world and the hereafter? How can the Creator and the creation coexist in one heart? How can this happen in one consciousness, in one heart? That is a sheer falsehood. The Prophet, upon whom be peace, said: "**Lies are alien to faith**."

«اَلْكَذِبُ مُجَانِبُ الاِيْمَانِ»

A clay pot sweats only from its own contents. Actions are proof of your belief, and your attitudes are the reflection of your thoughts. That is why someone said: *"What is manifest is the clue to what is hidden."* Thus, what you hide is known to God Almighty and to the chosen ones amongst His servants. If you meet one of them, then behave in their presence, and repent from your sins before you go to see them. Be submissive and small with them, humbling yourself to them. When you humble yourself before the righteous ones, you have humbled yourself to God Almighty. Be humble, for one who is humble will be raised high by his Lord.

Behave yourself (**adab**) when in the presence of your seniors. The Prophet, upon whom be peace, said: "**There are grace and blessings in your elderly ones (shaikhs).**"

«اَلْبَرَكَةُ فِي أَكَابِرِكُمْ»

Our Shaikh added: The Prophet, upon whom be peace, did not mean to mention the age bracket only (**shaikh**). Rather, this institution of blessings can only be realized with true piety, obeisance to the commands of God Almighty, abstinence from the forbidden, conformance to the Qur'an and following the leading example (**sunnah**) of the Prophet, upon whom be peace. For how many elderly people are not even worthy of respect, nor is it permissible to greet them with 'salām,' nor is there any blessing in seeing them. The true elders are: the pious, the righteous, the conscientious, those who apply knowledge ('**ilm**) to their actions, and those who are sincere in their duties. The true elders are the clear hearts which disdain everything but God Almighty. The true elders are the hearts of the gnostics who know God Almighty and are near unto Him.

The more knowledge the hearts acquire, the nearer to their Lord they become. Any heart which possesses the slightest love for the world will be veiled from God Almighty, and any heart that loves the hereafter will be veiled from the proximity of its Lord. The more you desire the world, the less you want the hereafter, and the more you desire the hereafter, the less you love God Almighty.

O ye people! Know your own worth and do not claim for yourselves (**nafs**) a position which God Almighty has not ordained for you. That is why someone said: *"One who does not recognize his true worth, one day his fate will teach him about it."* Do not sit in a chair from which you will be ordered to move. When you enter a house, do not sit until your host seats you, otherwise, you will be told to move from it without your will. Should you disdain to obey, you will be forced to do so, or you will be humiliated and expelled from the house.

Child, you have wasted your life in learning and memorizing books, the knowledge of which you do not practice. What benefits can that bring you? The Prophet, upon whom be peace, said: "**On the day of judgment, God Almighty will say to the prophets and the people of knowledge: 'You were the guardians of the creations, what did you do to your subjects?' And He will say to the kings and the wealthy ones: 'You were the safe keepers of my treasures. Did you help the poor ones, care for the orphans, and spend in My way the portions I prescribed to you?**"

«يَقُولُ ٱللَّهُ عَزَّ وَجَلَّ يَوْمَ الْقِيَامَةِ لِلْأَنْبِيَاءِ وَالْعُلَمَاءِ :أَنْتُمْ كُنْتُمْ

رُعَاةَ الْخَلْقِ فَمَا صَنَعْتُمْ فِي رَعَايَاكُمْ؟وَيَقُولُ لِلْمُلُوكِ وَالأَغْنِيَاءِ :

أَنْتُمْ كُنْتُمْ خُزَّانَ كُنُوزِي هَلْ وَاصَلْتُمُ الْفُقَرَاءَ وَرَبَّيْتُمُ الأَيْتَامَ

وَأَخْرَجْتُمْ مِنْهَا حَقِّي الَّذِي كَتَبْتُهُ عَلَيْكُمْ؟

O ye people! Heed the advice of God's Messenger, upon whom be peace, and accept his words. Truly, how hardened are your hearts. Glory be to God Who endowed me with the strength to endure people's heedlessness. Every time I intend to fly away, the scissors of divine decree come and cut off my wings. However, I do receive consolation and satisfaction from being where my Lord has placed me.

Woe to you, O hypocrite. You certainly wish that I would leave this town. Should you attempt one more move, things will change for you. Your limbs will start to disjoint, and the subject of our talk will be different then. But I fear God's punishment for any hastiness on my part. I am not rolling up my sleeves. Rather, I an straightening things and placing them the way the currents of divine decree indicate. I am in agreement with the divine decree, and submit as a Muslim to it. O God, I beseech Thee to grant us safety and peace.

O ignorant one. How dare you belittle me or make fun of me when I am standing at the gate of the true and mighty Lord, calling the creations to Him. Soon you will find your answer. For every yard I raise upward for the sincere ones to climb on, I also dig thousands of yards downwards for those who will fall. O hypocrites, soon you will discover God's chastisement and punishment that will be inflicted on you, both in this world and the hereafter. Time (**zamān**) is my rope. Soon you will find out how far it stretches.

I am an instrument in the hands of God Almighty. He turns me around as He pleases. One moment He makes me a mountain, another moment He turns me into an atom. At onetime He makes me an ocean, another time a drop of water. Once He makes me a sun, and later a sparkle and a ray. He turns me around in the way He rotates the night and the day. "**Each day, He manifests a different bounty**."

$$\text{«كُلُّ يَوْمٍ هُوَ فِي شَأْنٍ»}$$

He even manifests different bounties each moment. But the day is for people like you, and the moment is for others.

Child, if you wish to have forbearance and a good heart, do not listen to what people say, and pay no heed to their conversations. Aren you not aware that they are not even pleased with their own Lord? Then how could you expect them to be pleased with you? Do you not know that the majority of them have no wisdom, no insight and no faith? Instead they lie and do not accept the truth. Follow the people who understand nothing but their true Lord, God Almighty. They hearken to none but Him, and see no one besides Him.

In anticipation of winning God's pleasure, be tolerant with the sufferings people inflict on you in this world. Be patient with all kinds of adversities He may inflict upon you. This is God's way with His chosen ones and those who humbly submit to Him. He ostracizes them from everyone, puts them through all types of adversities, plagues and tests. He constricts them with the whole world, the hereafter and everything that exists beneath the divine throne down to the soil of this earth. In such a way, He annihilates their existence. Once extinct, He reinstates them solely for Himself, not for others. He keeps them with Himself, not with others, and He grants them a whole new existence, as God Almighty has said:

"**Then We developed out of him another form of creation, so blessed be God, the best to create**."

«ثُمَّ أَنْشَأْنَاهُ خَلْقًا آخَرَ فَتَبَارَكَ اللّهُ أَحْسَنُ الْخَالِقِينَ»

The first form is common to all creation, but this new one is unique to itself. God Almighty distinguishes him in superiority to his own brethren and his own kind amongst the children of Adam. He changes his primal essence and replaces it with a new one. He raises him in stations and brings down what was above him to be under him. He makes him a godly and spiritual person. He makes his heart constrict at the sight of the creation, and locks the door of his innermost being to the creation. He makes him perceive the world, the hereafter, paradise, hell, and all the creations as one thing. God Almighty then hands over all that knowledge to his innermost being in trust to keep as his secret. He takes it in, and nothing of it will manifest in him.

Through him, God Almighty will demonstrate the divine power (**qudrah**) as He manifested it in the staff of Moses, upon whom be peace. Glory be to God Who demonstrates His divine power and will at the hands of whomsoever He chooses. The staff of Moses swallowed numerous ropes, beside other things, though its shape did not change. God Almighty wanted to teach those people that these demonstrations were a manifestation of His divine power (**qudrah**), which is different from divine decree and wisdom (**hikmah**). On that day, the magicians used engineered wisdom, but what came from of the staff of Moses, upon whom be peace, was the divine power of God Almighty, which was beyond the norm of common things and a divine miracle. That is why the chief magician said to one of his companions: *"Look at Moses how his face changes."* The other replied: *"His color changed while the staff was doing its work."* The chief magician responded: *"This is truly God's work not his, for a magician has no fear of his own magic, and the maker is not afraid of his craft."* Following that, the chief magician publicly declared his faith in Moses and his Lord, and the rest of the magicians followed suit.

Child, when will you rise from the sphere of engineered wisdom to experience the manifestation of divine power? When will your labor in the abode of wisdom bring you to have a firsthand demonstration of the divine power of God Almighty? When will your sincerity of action carry you to the gate of nearness to your Lord? When will the effulgent sunlight of inner knowledge permit you to see the true nature of the hearts of the common people as well as to recognize those of the chosen ones?

Do not run away from God Almighty because of the adversities you encounter. He only lets you experience them to find out whether you remain at His door or return to trust in your worldly instruments (**asbāb**). Will you look inwardly or outwardly? Will you turn towards the fathomable or the unfathomable? Will you search for what can be seen or that which cannot be seen?

Lord, we implore You to spare us from these trials. Grant us Thy proximity without facing such adversities. Lord, show us Your way and bless us with Your kindness. Lord, grant us to be with You without separation, for we cannot bear to be distanced from You, and we have no strength to incur the suffering of adversities. Grant us the wealth of Thy nearness without the fire of plagues. If You choose that we go through them, then make us like the salamanders that lay their eggs in the fire to hatch, and the fire does not harm or burn them. Make the fire to us like it was to Abraham, Thy intimate friend, (**Cool and unharmful**). Sprout grass around us as You did around him. Be sufficient to us as Thou were to him, comfort us and be our friend as Thou were his, and guard us as Thou guarded him. Amen.

Abraham, upon whom be peace, sought the companion before he chose the road. He selected the good neighbor before the house. He found the Comforter before loneliness attacked. He followed the good diet before illness came. He developed patience before adversities came, and contentment before fate arrived. Learn from your father Abraham, upon whom be peace. Emulate his words and actions.

Glory be to God Who showed Abraham kindness when he drifted in the ocean of adversities, Who had assigned to him the plague of swimming in the ocean and helped him through it, Who commanded him to charge against the enemy and lead his horse, and ordered him to climb up to a high position and pushed him forward, placing His hand against his back. Then God Almighty instructed him to prepare food to serve the people and provided him with the necessary sustenance. This is the hidden and subtle kindness of God Almighty.

Child, be silent with God Almighty as His decree and doings befall you so you may witness and experience the countless wonders of His bounties. Haven't you heard the story of Galinos the wise, how he played dumb, deaf and stupid while serving his master until he acquired every bit of knowledge his master possessed? Like that, you cannot learn God's wisdom through raving, absentmindedness, challenge and through opposition to His will.

Our Lord, grant the wealth of consenting with Thee, and free us from every objection to Thy will.

«رَبَّنَا آتِنَا فِي الدُّنْيَا حَسَنَةً وَفِي الآخِرَةِ حَسَنَةً وَقِنَا عَذَابَ النَّارِ»

"Our Lord, grant us the benefits of a good deed in this world, the reward of a good deed in the hereafter, and protect us eternally from the sufferings of hell-fire."

✿ ✿ ✿ ✿ ✿

Chapter 11

To Know God

O ye people! Know God and be not ignorant of Him. Obey Him and do not disobey Him. Agree with His will and do not oppose it. Accept His decree, and do not challenge Him. Know God Almighty by His work, as He is the Creator and Sustainer, the First and the Last, the Manifest and the Hidden. He existed from the beginningless beginning and He is the Eternal, the Everlasting One Who does whatever He wills. "**He is not to be questioned about what He does, though they are subject to His questioning.**"

«لاَ يُسْأَلُ عَمَّا يَفْعَلُ وَهُمْ يُسْأَلُوْنَ»

He enriches and impoverishes. He is the Beneficent Lord Who gives life and causes death, Who reprimands and chastises, Who is to be feared and implored. Fear Him and none besides Him. Implore Him and none other than Him. Willingly submit yourselves to the demonstrations of His divine power and the manifestations of His divine decree. Remain thus until such time when power (**qudrah**) supersedes decree (**ḥikmah**). Properly follow the rules which you were instructed to adopt, until the veils of changes come. Then you will be protected against ever breaking the rules of the divine laws (**sharī'a**). Hence you will experience the uncommon versus the common.

What I am explaining can only be experienced inwardly, not outwardly. It is in essence, not form, and only few and rare ones, even amongst the righteous, can reach that state. However, we have no need to seek beyond the boundaries of **sharī'a.** Only one who walks that path can understand this experience, as it cannot be understood through mere description of its character. In all of your affairs act as if you were standing before God's Messenger, upon whom be peace, alert and in readiness under his command to follow him, comply with his instructions and to abstain from what he forbids. Stand with firm resoluteness in the ranks of his followers, until the time when the Almighty King calls for you to come before Him. Then having sought permission for leave from God's Messenger, upon whom be peace, may you then go before the King.

The deputy-representatives (**abdāl**) were named thus because they follow no will besides God's will, and they make no choices besides His choice. They judge by the outer rules, and conform to the prescribed laws. then they turn towards the duties and functions that were assigned to them. The higher they rise in station, the stricter the orders. They remain thus until they reside where there is no command (**amr**) or restraint (**nahi**). Instead, the divine laws (**sharī'a**) will interact with them, rule their lives, while they are oblivious to it. They remain wholly absorbed in their Lord though they engage in fulfilling their commands and restrictions. They are protected therein from breaking the rules of the divine laws (**sharī'a**), because to omit the prescribed duties of worship (**farā'idh**) is atheism, and to commit wrongdoing is sin. Under no circumstances the prescribed laws of worship are to be abrogated by anyone.

Child, be and act in agreement with God's decree, infinite wisdom and knowledge. Do not veer from the plan, forget not the original covenant, and battle your mind, desire (**nafs**) satan, karmic habits, and worldly attachments. Despair not from God's help, for it comes with your resoluteness. God Almighty has said: "**Indeed God is with those who exercise patience,**"

«إِنَّ ٱللَّهَ مَعَ ٱلصَّابِرِينَ»

and He has said: "**It is God's party that will be victorious,**"

«فَإِنَّ حِزْبَ ٱللَّهِ هُمُ ٱلْفَائِزُونَ»

and He has said: "**Those who struggle for Our cause, We shall surely guide them unto Our ways.**"

«وَٱلَّذِينَ جَاهَدُوا فِينَا لَنَهْدِيَنَّهُمْ سُبُلَنَا»

Child, control the tongue of your carnal self when it has the tendency to express grievances to people. Be God's appointed opponent against the tendencies of your own mind, desire and those of the creation, command them to obey Him and abstain from disobeying Him. Forbid them heedlessness, inventions, failing prey to their passions and consenting to their carnal selves. Command them to follow the precepts of God's Book (**Kitāb**) and to emulate the leading example (**sunnah**) of His Messenger, upon whom be peace.

O ye people! Revere God Almighty's Book and respect its tenets. The Holy Qur'ān is your link with your Lord. Do not regard it as another creation. God Almighty says: "**These are My words**," and you retort: "They are not." Whoever argues God's word or considers the Book to be a created entity is an apostate (**kāfir**), and this Qur'ān will disown him and declare itself innocent from him. This Qur'ān which can be read, recited, heard and seen, these recorded revelations are the divine speech of God Almighty. Imām Shāfi'i and Imām Ahmad, God be pleased with them both, used to say: "*The Pen is created, but what is written with it is not created, and the heart is created, but what is preserved in it by memorization is not created.*"

O ye people! Respond to the Qur'ān with compliance in deeds, not contentious arguments. The proclamation of faith needs only a few words, but compliance requires limitless deeds. O ye people, have faith in the Qur'ān, believe it with your whole heart and act according to it with your entire being. Concern yourselves that which benefits you and never give heed to ideas which come from spiteful and lowly half-brains.

O ye people! Transmitted knowledge cannot be intellectually assumed. Similarly, the written law cannot be deemed unnecessary through deductive reasoning. Do not abandon what is true and clear in order to support ideas which are merely claimed. People's properties cannot be seized without proof of ownership. The Prophet, upon whom be peace, said: "**If people were to be granted whatever they claimed, some would lay claims to the blood and properties of others. That is why the claimant has to provide proof, and one who deny's has to swear to God in his own defense.**"

«لَوْ أُخِذَ النَّاسُ بِدَعَاوِيْهِمْ لَادَّعَى قَوْمٌ دِمَاءَ قَوْمٍ وَأَمْوَالَهُمْ ، لكِنِ الْبَيِّنَةَ عَلَى الْمُدَّعِي وَالْيَمِينُ عَلَى مَنْ أَنْكَرَ»

Thus , a knowledgeable tongue is of no benefit to an ignorant heart. The Prophet, upon whom be peace, said: "**The worst that I fear for my followers is the rise of a hypocrite who speaks**

with learned expressions."

«أَخْوَفُ مَا أَخَافُ عَلَى أُمَّتِي مِنْ مُنَافِقٍ عَلِيْمِ اللِّسَانِ»

O ye people of knowledge. O ye people of ignorance. O ye who are present in this congregation. O ye who are absent. Be shy with God Almighty. Humbly look at Him with your hearts, and exercise patience when experiencing the pounding blows of His decree. Oblige yourselves to be grateful for His bounty. Day and night, maintain a state of obeisance to Him. Once you achieve that state, He will grant you His blessings and honor which will become your paradise in this world and the hereafter.

Child, strive hard not to love anything in this world. Once you reach that state, you will not be left alone for even one moment with your carnal self. Should you forget, you will be reminded. If slumber overtakes you, you will be awakened. In short, He will not let you look at anyone other than Him. Only one who tastes that state will recognize it. It is a very rare kind of person, one of the elite, who categorically refuses to accept comfort from any one of His creations.

O ye hypocrites. Diseases and calamities are crowning your hearts. Once people look with the eyes of their hearts at anyone besides God Almighty, they have endangered their own safety. In fact, their security can be maintained only by turning towards Him, submitting peacefully to His will, and acting blind towards His creations. The power of objecting to Him is removed from their tongues. The days and nights, months and years pass them by and they do not change with their Lord. They are the wisest ones amidst God's creations. If you saw them, you would say: *"These people are crazy."* and when they see you, they say: *"These people do not believe in the day of reckoning."* Their hearts are broken, sad, and constantly in awe, fear and reverence of God Almighty. Every time He removes the veils of His divine majesty and glory and reveals that to their hearts, their fear increases. Their hearts are nearly shattered and their bodies nearly torn apart. Seeing that, God Almighty opens wide the gates of His divine mercy (**raḥmah**), beauty and subtle kindness, and gives them hope. With such endowment they return back to peacefulness. I love to look at no one but those who are the seekers of the hereafter and the seekers of God Almighty. Otherwise, what can I do with the seekers of the world, the creations, mind, desire, passions?

Nevertheless, I do like to treat their illnesses and cure them, for the best one to bear patiently with a sick person is his physician.

O man, you try to hide your condition from me, but to no avail. You pretend you are a seeker of the hereafter, while in truth you are a lover of this world. This foolishness which is nestling in your heart is clearly inscribed on your forehead. Your secret is written all over you. The coin which you possess may look like gold, but in fact, it is only gold-plated. Inside there is only plain silver. Do not brag about it before me, for I have seen plenty like it. Bring it to me, let me hold your coin and recast it again. I will extract the gold from it and throw away the balance. To have a small quantity of a good substance is better than having plenty of a worthless one. Bring your dinar coin to me, for I mint these pieces and have a special tool for that. Repent from falsehood and hypocrisy. Do not shy away from confessing and testifying against your carnal self, for the majority of the righteous ones were once hypocrites. That is why someone, God bless his soul, said: *"An affected person knows best what sincerity is ."*

Only one who is the rarest of the rare lives with devout sincerity from the beginning to the end of his life. Children, for example, may tell lies, play with mud and impurities, get themselves in trouble, steal from their parents and indulge in gossip and hearsay. But as soon as their awareness grows, they abandon these childish acts, one after the other. They try to emulate the conduct and character of adulthood as they see these in their parents and teachers. When God Almighty intends the welfare of someone, He shows him the proper conduct to follow and how to abstain from his earlier practices. Yet, one whom God Almighty intends to leave to his own evil, such a one lives as he pleases, and his evil practices will culminate in his own destruction, both in this world and the hereafter.

However, God Almighty created both the illness and the cure. He created sin as the illness, and obeisance as the cure, injustice as the illness and justice as the cure, wrongdoing as the illness and correct actions as the cure, disobedience to the commands of God Almighty as the illness and repentance from the intoxications of one's sin as its cure.

You can acquire such a cure once you free your heart from the creations and connect it with your Lord. Once you offer your heart to be exclusively your Lord's property, your heart will dwell in the heavens while your soul and abode remain on earth. Your heart will be elected inwardly to singularly partake of God's knowledge, while outwardly you share the work with the people. Do your duty in accordance with God's plans (**hukum**) and do not contradict them in any disposition thereof, so they would have no argument against you. Be inwardly alone with your Lord, while with the creations outwardly. Never let your ego swell. Control it, or it will control you. Conquer it, or it will conquer you. Should your carnal self not submit to your intentions in matters of subscribing to God's commands, then chastise it with the scourges of hunger and thirst, humiliation and shunning, isolation and segregation. Continue until your carnal self becomes peaceful and obedient to God Almighty under all conditions. Even when it becomes trusting and content, do not hesitate to chastise it when necessary. Remind it: *"Have you not done this and that?"* Keep it constantly brokenhearted and under control. To do that, you need to constantly intend God's will and obey Him, and never disobey Him. Then you need to become one, inwardly and outwardly by embodying consent without objection, obeisance without disobedience, thankfulness without ingratitude, remembrance without forgetfulness and goodness without evil.

Your heart will never succeed as long as there is anyone besides God Almighty in it. Even if you were to prostrate to Him for one thousand years on a pile of burning coals, as long as your heart seeks someone other than Him, your devotion will be to no avail. Your heart will be of no consequence as long as it finds love in other than its Lord. You will not enjoy His love unless you drop everything else. What benefits can you gain from displaying ascetic detachment from worldly things when in fact your heart keeps desiring them? Are you not aware that God Almighty knows what is concealed in each one of the hearts of the entire creations? Are you not ashamed to utter the words: *"I trust in God,"* while your heart follows some other intent?

Child, let not your heedlessness deceive you just because God Almighty is showing forbearance today. Remember that the impact of His sudden retribution is very painful. Be not boastful or deceived by those worldly religious doctors, ignorant of who God Almighty is, for their so-called knowledge is proof of their guilt. It is to their detriment, not their advantage. They are jurists who know God's laws but do not know God Almighty Himself. They admonish people to do what they themselves do not practice, and forbid them from doing what they themselves do not hesitate to do. They call people to God Almighty, while they themselves are running away from Him. They contest God's commands by disobeying Him and indulging themselves in forbidden sinful actions. I have a list of their names, number and dates.

Our Lord, turn unto me and unto them, accept my repentance and guide them, too. Lord, make us all Your gift to Thy Prophet Muhammad, upon whom be peace, and to our father Abraham, upon whom be peace. Lord! Make us not enemies to one another. Let us benefit from each other, and let Thy mercy encompass us all. Amen.

Chapter 12

Ask only From God

Child, your yearning for God Almighty is not true, nor do you truly seek Him. One who professes to follow God's will while he is calling for someone else's help has refuted his own claim. Amongst the so-called seekers of God, the majority love the world, few love the hereafter, and even fewer consent to God's will and truly seek Him.

They are as rare as red sulfur. These are unique individuals who are the rarest of the rare. It is even very rare to meet one of them. They are the select few, the beacons of faith, the pride of the lands, the gems of the earth and the true kings on it. They are God's providence to the land and its people. They are the pillars of the earth and its protection. They are the leaders of the people and their chancellors. Because of them, the people are saved from calamities and because of them, God Almighty makes the skies rain and the plants thrive.

At the beginning of their spiritual quest, they ran from one mountain peak to a higher one, seeking seclusion and privacy. They fled from one country to another, from the outskirts of one ruin to another. Once they were discovered to dwell in one place, they moved to another. They left everything behind and surrendered the keys of this world into the hands of its people. They remained resolute until the castle walls of protection were built around them, and rivers flowed towards their hearts until such time that God Almighty assigned guards to protect them.

Each of the heavenly soldiers who surround them has a unique duty to guard. Thus, these elect servants of God Almighty will be honored, protected, and raised to the station of deputy over the people (**wilāyah**). All these blessings take place beyond their mental fathoming. In that state of being, their return to mingling with people and serving them becomes obligatory (**faridha**). They become like physicians, and the people become their patients.

O man, you claim to be one of them. Tell me then, how do you recognize their signs? What is the mark of proximity to and kindness of God Almighty? What is your position and station in God's kingdom? What is your name and title in the upper circle? Tell me, why does the door of your fate close every night? Do you think that whatever food and water you take is unconditionally permissible? Where do you sleep, with the world, the hereafter, or proximity to your Lord? Who comforts you in your loneliness? Who sits with you in your solitude?

O liar. What comforts you in your privacy are your mind and desire (**nafs**), satan, passions and contemplation of your world. In public you comfort yourself with the company of the human satans who are the evildoers and the fellowship of hearsay. The success illustrated earlier does not come through raving, craziness, or mere claims, nor would your speaking on the subject benefit you. Be in a state of dead calm and be languorous in the hands of your Lord and thus correct your behavior. Should you be unable to control your impulse to speak, then at least intend to receive the blessings contained within the recitation of His revealed words and the blessings of recalling the example of His true servants. Let it not be an outer pretense when in fact your heart is void of luminous substance. An outward expression which does not correlate with a natural inward substance is mere craziness.

Have you not heard the saying of the Prophet, upon whom be peace: "**One who keeps eating people's flesh by backbiting them has no reward for his fasting.**"

«مَا صَامَ مَنْ ظَلَّ يَأْكُلُ لُحُومَ النَّاسِ»

The Prophet, upon whom be peace, thus clarified that fasting is not the mere denial of food, water, and other conditions that break the fast, unless all of it is accompanied by abstention from evildoing and abominable actions. Beware of backbiting, for it devours good deeds just as fire consumes wood. A rightful seeker will never achieve success through backbiting. People will have little or no respect for a person who is known to be a gossiper.

Beware! Beware! Never look passionately at anything, for such lustful desire will plant the seed of sin in your heart, the results of which are not praiseworthy either in this world or the hereafter. Beware of the false oath, for it will leave your house hollow and gutted, devastate your crop and take away the blessings from your earnings and religious life. O man, you are losing your religion and squandering your earnings by committing perjury. If you only had a brain, you would realize that this is total loss. You say: "I swear by God, there is no merchandise equal to this in this land, and no other merchant sells it but me." You say:"I swear to God it is worth so much, I swear it cost me more." while in truth you are lying in every word you say. You then commit perjury and swear to God Almighty that you are telling the truth. Wait. Soon blindness and old age will overcome you.

O ye people! Behave yourselves before God Almighty, and may He have mercy upon you all. If one does not conduct himself in compliance with the divine laws of **shari'a**, soon the fire of hell will teach him on the day of reckoning. (Someone asked a question: *"One who has these five qualities, would you consider his fasting and ablution void?"* He replied): "His fasting and ablution are not nullified, though what was said earlier came out as a strong warning, admonition, and as a mean to teach self-constraint.

Child, think. It maybe that when tomorrow or the day after comes, you will no longer be found on the surface of this earth. O ye people! What is this obstinacy and heedlessness? How hardened are your hearts. Are you rocks? I tell you and others speak to you but you remain unchanged. The Qur'ān is recited unto you, the news of God's Messenger, and the stories of your predecessors are recited to you, but you pay no heed to them. You do not avoid being on the side of wrong, nor do your qualities and actions change.

Whoever enters a place where there is admonition and does not accept these warnings is the most evil of people. Child, your scorning and belittling of God's deputies (**awliyā'**) are a result of the little knowledge you have of God Almighty Himself. You belligerently accuse them: "Why do they not work like us to earn their livelihood? Why do they not mix with us?" You say it out of ignorance of who you are. In fact, when you have so little knowledge of yourself, your understanding of people's worth is less than that. To the limited extent you know about this world and its consequences, you know even less of the hereafter and its worth; and to the limited extent you know about the hereafter, even less do you know God Almighty. O you who are toiling in this world, soon you will discover your losses, and soon you will suffer the agony of regret. These are your manifest signs for both this world and the hereafter. Greater will be your remorse on the day of reckoning, the day of mutual loss and gain, the day of defamation and exposure, the day of disappointment and loss. Judge yourself today before the hereafter comes. Do not be misled by the events of the acting decree (**hukum**) of God Almighty and His generosity towards you. Right now, you are living in the worst conditions of abominable sins, pitfalls, and injustice towards people. Disobedience is the precursor of disbelief as much as high fever is the precursor of death. You must repent before death comes, before the coming of the angel in charge of reaping souls.

O youth, repent now. Do you not see how God Almighty puts you through adversities, pressuring you to repent, while you do not heed His warnings and persist in your disobedience? Rare are the ones whom God Almighty subjects to trials these days they may reflect and repent. Fallacy and lying are afflictions, not blessings. They are retribution for one's sins, not an elevation of one's station or an increase in blessings. When true believers face adversities, they rise in station and become more exalted in the sight of their Lord. They exercise patience in their plight for the sake of seeing the effulgent countenance of their Lord. Once they achieve that, they receive the imperishable divine wealth. Otherwise, they tend to think that they are doomed to destruction. O beloved Lord, cause us no destruction. We ask Thee to admit us in Thy proximity. Make us look at You in this world and in the hereafter, in this world with our hearts and in the hereafter with our physical eyes.

O ye people! Despair not of God's endowments and His giving you relief, for He is near unto you. Despair not, for the Maker is God. "**You never know, perhaps God will soon create a new circumstance**."

«لاَ تَدْرِي لَعَلَّ اللهَ يُحْدثُ بَعْدَ ذلكَ أَمْرًا»

Do not try to escape from adversities. Facing one's trials with patience is the basis of every benefit and the way to triumph. Adversities are the fountainhead of prophethood, the root of the message, the pillar of deputyship (**wilāya**), gnosis and love. If you do not exercise patience in the face of adversities you have no basis to stand on. No structure can stand upright without a good foundation. Have you ever seen a house standing erect on a trash pile? You are running away from trials and tribulations because you feel no need to receive the trust of deputyship, inner knowledge or to be near God Almighty. Exercise patience and persevere with good deeds in order to soar with your heart, inner being, and soul to the door of God's proximity. Those endowed with knowledge (**'ulamā'**), the gnostics, the representatives and trustees (**awliyā'**) and the deputies (**abdāl**) are the heirs of the prophets. The prophets are the brokers and their heirs are the pitchmen.

A true believer fears no one besides God Almighty, and has no hope in anyone other than Him. He is endowed with such strength from within his heart and innermost being. How could the hearts of the believers not be strengthened by God Almighty, when He brought them in a nocturnal journey unto His own presence? That is their abode. The hearts remain in His presence while the bodies dwell on earth. God Almighty has said: "**Indeed they stand in Our presence amongst the elect of the best chosen ones**."

«وَإِنَّهُمْ عِنْدَنَا لَمِنَ ٱلْمُصْطَفِينَ الأَخْيَارِ»

Such blessed beings are chosen as superior to their own kin and the people of their time. Such are their privileges: Their essence is distinguished, and their bodies are effulgent. It is for the sake of such blessings that they bid farewell to the whole of creation and renounce the common things of this world. As they walk forward, the green pasture grows to cover their trails. They neither revert nor regress. They find comfort and peace in solitude. They choose to live in abandoned ruins, by the seas, in prairies and wilderness, but not in cities. They eat from the plants of the desert and drink from its brooks and oases. They live in the wilderness and survive estranged, like its dwellers. It is in that state that God Almighty brings their hearts nigh unto Himself and comforts them with His own presence. They stand amongst the ranks of the messengers, the righteous ones and the martyrs. God Almighty will keep the core of their being constantly engaged in His service. Night and day they are submerged in the retreat and comfort of the long awaited meeting of beloveds, and find fragrant solace in God Almighty.

Child, in this world you cannot escape from experiencing both sweetness and bitterness, goodness and insolence, stress and clarity. If you seek a genuine unblemished purity, then let your heart bid farewell to the creations and reconnect it with your

Lord and Cherisher. Depart from this world. Bid farewell to your
own family and entrust them to your Lord. Free your heart and let
it be empty of them all, then go closer to the gate of the hereafter,
enter and look therein. Should you not be able to find God
Almighty there, then escape from it and run in search of your Lord.
Only when you find Him will you discover the core of clarity and
peace for everything exists in His presence. What would someone
who is in love with God Almighty do with anything else? Paradise
is the abode of those who aspire for the exalted stations of honor.
It is the abode of merchants. They buy it for the price of this world.
That is why God Almighty confirms their barter by saying:
**"Therein is all that the souls (nafs) desire and all that the eyes
could find delight in."**

«وَفِيهَا مَاتَشْتَهِيْهِ الأَنْفُسُ وَتَلَذُّ الأَعْيُنُ»

In this verse, God Almighty did not mention the heart. He did
not mention the innermost being (**sirr**) or the essence. Paradise is
created for the industrious worshiper who perseveres in his
devotions of fasting and praying, who practices abstinence and
ascetic detachment, and who renounces desires and worldly
pleasures. Such worshipers have sold one type of fasting in
exchange for another, one garden for another garden, one house
for another.

I want from you deeds without words. A true gnostic who
practices what he knows solely for God's pleasure can be likened
to the anvil of a blacksmith. You hammer on it, but it does not say
a word. He is like ground on which you walk, a farm which you
turn upside down and rotate its crop, yet it remains silent. Such
true believers see no one besides God Almighty. They hearken to
no one other than Him. They have souls but no tongues with which
to speak. They are concealed from themselves as well as from
others. They thrive in secret. Only if God wills does He unfold
them, like the pages of a book, and reveal them to others and make
their souls tongues that speak. As though they were intoxicated
or numbed, the King carries them unto His divine presence with
the hand of His mercy and compassion, reclaims them, restores
them, and recreates them for Himself and none else. He reshapes
them again to be His servants, just as He refashioned Moses, upon
whom be peace, when he said unto him: **"I made thee for Myself
(to serve.) There is nothing like unto Him, and He is the All-**

Hearing, the All-Seeing Lord."

«وَٱصْطَنَعْتُكَ لِنَفْسِي - لَيْسَ كَمِثْلِهِ شَئٌ وَهُوَ السَّمِيْعُ الْبَصِيْرُ»

He will be reborn into tranquility without effort, peace without hindrance, blessings without wrath, joy without hate, sweetness without bitterness, a king without destruction. "**And thereat, the sovereignty belongs to God Almighty alone, the Rightful Lord.**"

«هُنَالِكَ الوِلَايَةُ لله الحَقِّ»

To one who reaches that state comfort will hasten towards him.

However, in your current condition you cannot experience such tranquility because this world is the abode of distress and plagues. Therefore, it is imperative that you walk away from it and let your heart be free from it. Should your hand not be able to let go of it, then keep holding it, but get it out of your heart. Once you become stronger, then release it from your hand and give it to the poor, the needy, and the indigent one. Make it a gift to all the dependents of God Almighty. Despite that, your share will still come to you. It has to come by divine decree, whether you be rich or poor, renunciate or desirous. What matters is the correct attitude of your heart and innermost being and their clarity. They become pure and clear as you become more knowledgeable, practice what you learn, become sincere in what you do, and become a truthful seeker of God Almighty.

Child, have you not heard the saying: "**Learn first then retreat.**"

«تَفَقَّهْ ثُمَّ اعْتَزِلْ»

First learn the outer jurisprudence, then retire to contemplate the inner meaning. Practice the prescribed laws so that your deeds may bring you to comprehend a knowledge of which you were unaware and have not practiced. This outer knowledge is the light of that which is manifest, and inner knowledge is the effulgent light of the innermost reality. It is a light linking you and your Lord and Cherisher. The more you put your knowledge into practice, the shorter your path to your Lord, and the gate becomes more open between you and Him. Your personal door will become wide open and the bar will be removed for you.

«رَبَّنَا آتِنَا فِي الدُّنْيَا حَسَنَةً وَفِي الآخِرَةِ حَسَنَةً وَقِنَا عَذَابَ النَّارِ»

"Our Lord, grant us the benefits of a good deed in this world, the reward of a good deed in the hereafter, and protect us eternally from the sufferings of hell-fire."

Chapter 13

Giving Preference to One's Life in the Hereafter Over the Life in this World

Child, give life in the hereafter priority over that of this world and you will win them both. If you attach more importance to your life in this world than to that of the hereafter, as punishment you will lose them both. You will be asked: "Why did you devote yourself to what you were not commanded to do?" If you do not occupy your life in serving of this world, God Almighty will lend you His support and help you to overcome it, then He will grant you success (**tawfiq**) when you take your share from it. At that time, whatever you take from it will be blessed.

A believer serves for his life in this world and that of the hereafter. He works in this world solely for his basic needs. He is content with as little as a traveler carries with him on the road, and does not care to take much from it. The ignorant person (**jāhil**) makes the world his entire concern, while the gnostic focuses his gaze first upon the hereafter and then his Guardian Lord.

Child, if you receive a loaf of bread from this world, but your mind and desire (**nafs**) question its fate and demand greater pleasures, then look for someone else with whom to break bread. Go against your carnal self by giving it less. You will reap no success until you can abhore your mind and desire and fight against them, with regard to God's rights.

The righteous ones know and recognize each other. Each one of them can smell the fragrance of divine acceptance and the perfume of truthfulness emanating from the other. O man who exhibits dissent and dares to reply to God Almighty and His righteous servants (**siddiqïn**) while seeking people to fulfil your needs. How long will you remain seeking them rather than God Almighty? What benefits can they bring you? They have no power to harm or benefit you, nor can they give or withhold from you. There is no difference between them and any inanimate object in these regards. The King is One. Only God can disadvantage, only He can bring benefits, only He can enable things to be animate or inanimate. The Ruler is One. The Subjugator is One. The Giver is One. The Bestower is One. the Depriver is One. The Creator is One, and the Sustainer is One, and that is God Almighty. He is the Primal One, the Eternal and Everlasting. He existed from the beginningless beginning before creation came into existence. That was before your fathers and mothers, your rich and wealthy ones were ever created. He is the Originator of the heavens and the earth, of what they encompass and what is in between, **"There is nothing like unto Him, and He is the All-Hearing and All-Knowing Lord."**

«لَيْسَ كَمِثْلِهِ شَيْ‏ٌ وَهُوَ السَّمِيْعُ العَلِيْمُ»

O ye people among God's creations. How sorry am I for you. You certainly do not know the true worth of your Creator. Should God Almighty grant me the fulfillment of a prayer on the day of reckoning, I will ask to carry all your burdens. I will say: "O Reader of the Records, pronounce their sentences to me alone and to no other creations of the heavens or the earth." Anyone who cares for his own duties, there will be a door through which he can bring his heart forth before God Almighty. As for you who claims to be a man of religious knowledge (**'ālim**), you busy yourself with hearsay, gossip and collecting money for religious functions. That is why nothing falls into your hands but material gains without real substance. If God Almighty decrees the welfare of one of His servants, He will endow him with knowledge. He will then inspire him to act upon it with sincerity. From there, He will bring him nigh unto Himself, exalt his knowledge, and teach him both the knowledge of the heart and of the innermost being. Such will be his exclusive endowment, and God Almighty will elect him as He chose Moses, upon whom be peace, and said unto him: "**I have made (and chosen) thee for Myself (to serve).**"

«إِصْطَنَعْتُكَ لِنَفْسِيْ»

Not for anyone else. Not to indulge in passions and pleasures, or to trifle in darkness. Not for the earth or the heavens, nor for paradise or hell. Not to reign as a king or be destroyed. I created you, so no image can obstruct you from being with Me, no creation can veil you from being with Me, and no desire can distract you from Me.

Child, despair not of God's mercy because of a sin you have committed. Instead, wash any impurities which are soiling the garment of your religion with the water of repentance, steadfastness and sincerity. Perfume and scent it with the fragrance of true knowledge (**ma'rifa**). Beware of the abode in which you dwell, for in whichever direction you turn, lions are surrounding you and trouble is aiming at you. Avoid it, and go back wholeheartedly to your True Lord, God Almighty. Do not eat with your karmic habit, desire and passion. Do not touch the food of this world without the testimony of the two lawful and just witnesses, the Book (**kitāb**) of God Almighty and the leading practices (**sunnah**) of the Prophet, upon whom be peace. Furthermore, call upon two more witnesses, which are the consent of your heart and God's own doing. Once the Book, the **sunnah**, and your heart permit you to eat, then await the fourth witness, which is God's own doing. Be not like the wood cutter who works at night. He goes to gather firewood but does not know what his hands grab. However, under the abovementioned four conditions, the act of the Creator and the created being becomes one. This state of being does not occur through adornment, exaggerated hopes, affectation or pretense. Rather, it is enshrined with subtle conviction in one's heart, and its sign is truthful deeds—deeds which are offered for God's sake and His pleasure.

Child, be healthy by not crying for good health. Be wealthy by not desiring wealth, and obtain the real cure by not asking for medicine. The true cure is contained in surrendering and trusting one's entire needs to God Almighty, cutting off one's dependence on created means, and expelling from one's heart the presence of any deities or lords. The true medicine is to glorify God's Oneness in one's heart, not only by the tongue. In fact, both glorification of God's Oneness (**tawẖïd**) and true ascetic detachment (**zuhud**) are not shown by the body or the tongue. **Tawẖïd** is in the heart, **zuhud** is in the heart, piety is in the heart, gnosis is in the heart, knowledge of God Almighty is in the heart, the love of God Almighty is in the heart, and to be near unto Him is in the heart.

So think. Do not hallucinate, be not pretentious, and be free from unnatural mannerisms. You are a mixture of actions which are filled with craziness, lies, presumption, affectation, falsehood, and hypocrisy. All that you are concerned with is attracting people to you. Do you not know that with every step you take towards the people in your heart, you will be distancing yourself from God Almighty? You profess to be a seeker of God Almighty, but in truth you are seeking the creation. Your parable is that of someone who says: "I want to go to Mecca." However, once he starts his journey, he walks in the opposite direction towards the city of *Kharasan (in Persia)*. Thus he distances himself from his original stated destination, Mecca. You claim that your heart has become free from attachment to the people, when in truth you still fear them and you place your hope in them. Outwardly you appear to have renounced the world, but inwardly you are infested with lustful desires. Outwardly you appear godly, though inwardly you are filled with the world.

Such an exalted state of purity does not come about through lip service. This station does not embrace people, the world, the hereafter, or anything besides God Almighty. God is One and does not accept other than oneness. He is One and does not accept any associate. It is He that manages your entire life. Accept what is being said unto you. In reality, the people are powerless. They cannot harm or benefit you, but He is the One Who manages your destiny at their hands. It is His doing that settles your fate and theirs as well. The ink of the pen of destiny (**qalam**) has dried out after having written God's decree and preexistant knowledge of what is entrusted to you and what you owe.

The righteous servants who glorify God's Oneness (**muwaḥḥidün**) are His testifying witnesses for the remainder of the creations. Some of them renounce this world both inwardly and outwardly, while others renounce it just inwardly in such a way that God Almighty will not find the slightest trace of it in their hearts. The latter ones have the purest of hearts. The people themselves will offer the rule of their kingdom to whoever achieves that state. Such ones are the true heroes and champions. A true hero is one who courageously cleanses his heart from anything other than God Almighty, stands at His gate carrying the sword of glorifying God's Oneness (**tawḥïd**), and holds true with steadfastness to the perfect resoluteness and purity of the divine law (**sharï'a**). Thus, he allows nothing of God's creation to enter his heart, and unites his heart with the divine controller of hearts. The law of **sharī'a** teaches proper conduct to the physical form (**zhāhir**) while glorification of God's Oneness and gnosis teach proper conduct to the inner being (**bātin**).

O man, wandering between hearsay and gossip will bring you no benefits. You say: "This is not permissible," but you do not hesitate to practice it. You also say: "This is lawful," but you do not use it or benefit from it. Truly, you are utterly confused and perplexed. The Prophet, upon whom be peace, said: "**An ignorant person is met with one calamity for his sin, but for one who knowingly commits wrongdoing, the calamities are seven fold.**"

«وَيْلٌ لِلْجَاهِلِ مَرَّةً ً وَلِلْعَالِمِ سَبْعُ مَرَّاتٍ»

An ignorant person will be chastised once for his sin, but the punishment of a learned person will multiply seven fold because he did not comply with what he was taught. The blessings contained within knowledge will be stripped away from him. What remains is his indictment.

Child, first learn, then let your deeds reflect what you have learned. Then be alone, away from the creations in your retreat, where you can in develop the love of God Almighty in your heart. Once your detachment and love become true and peerless, He will bring you nigh unto Himself, establish you in His proximity, and hold you without impediment, wholly absorbed in Him (**fanā'**). Then, should it be His Will, He will exalt your name, raise you to become known to the people, and then commission you to return to the world and collect the portions earlier destined in your name. He will then command the winds of His preexistent knowledge to demolish the walls of your privacy and expose you to the people. Thus you will be in their midst again, but by Him, not you. You will receive your destined share without the ominous darkness of your **nafs**, karmic habits, or passions. He will return you to collect your portions so that the law of His preexistent knowledge of you does not become void. You will redeem your share while your heart remains with God Almighty.

Hear me and act upon it, O people who are ignorant of Who God Almighty is and who His deputies (**awliyā'**) are. O ye who are discrediting God Almighty and defaming His representatives. Truth is God Almighty Himself, and falsehood is you, O ye people! Truth resides in the hearts, in the innermost secret being and essence, while falsehood dwells in the mind and desire (**nafs**), passions, karmic habits, the world, and anything other than God Almighty. This human heart will not achieve success unless it is joined together with the station of proximity to God Almighty, the Primal, the Eternal, the Everlasting and Infinite Lord.

O hypocrite. Do not compete on these grounds, for you have no knowledge of this. You are a slave to earning your bread, food, sweets, clothing, horses, power and riches. A heart which is truthful in its love for God Almighty flies away from the creations towards the Creator. During its journey, it pays respect to whatever it sees on the road, and merely passes by.

The learned religious doctors (**'ulamā'**) who practice the precepts of their knowledge are the representatives of their righteous predecessors (**tābi'īn**). They are the heirs (**wārithīn**) of the prophets and a branch of the remainder of their blessed progeny. They stand before them in the front row and hear their instructions. They stand like a foreman who stands before his boss to receive the plans to build the city of divine law and who forbids them from causing its destruction. They all gather on the day of reckoning, together with the prophets, upon all of whom be peace, who in turn will collect for them their reward from their Lord. As to the learned person who does not practice what he knows, God Almighty gives a parable likening him to a donkey. **"Like a donkey who is burdened with loads."**

«كَمَثَلِ الحِمَارِ يَحْمِلُ أَسْفَارًا»

Loads, (Sing. **safar**, pl. **asfār**), are the books of knowledge that are carried on the backs of animals and transported between towns. Can a donkey draw any benefit from carrying books? Nay, he gets nothing but exhaustion and fatigue. Therefore, one who receives extended knowledge, fear of God Almighty and obedience to Him should increase as well.

O you who claim to have knowledge. Where are the tears of your fear of God Almighty? Where are your vigilance and awareness? Where is the confession of your sins? Where is your repentance? Where is your assiduous engagement, night and day, in your devotions to Him? Where are the confrontations and training of your **nafs** to stand with resoluteness on God's side? Why do you not oppose its demands? All that you are concerned with is your religious garb, your turban, food, sex, properties, businesses, mixing with the creation and finding comfort in their company. Restrain your endeavors from all these things. If you are destined to have a share, it will come in due course. Your heart will then be at peace and free from the anxiety of waiting and the burden of envy. In that state, you will be on God's side. So, why should you trouble yourself or toil in a matter which is already decreed?

Child, your private thoughts are rotten, corrupt and stained with impurities. Your retreat is untrue. What can I do to correct you? True glorification of God's Oneness and sole sovereignty and true sincerity are, at present, alien to your heart. O heedless people in slumber, whose actions are not hidden. O objectors, who are not out of God's reach. O forgetful ones, whose actions are not forgotten. O disdainful ones, who are not left to roam free. O ye ignorant ones of Who God Almighty is, who His Messenger is, who are those who preceded you, or those coming thereafter. You are as useless as a rotten and discarded piece of wood.

«رَبَّنَا آتِنَا فِي الدُّنْيَا حَسَنَةً وَفِي الآخِرَةِ حَسَنَةً وَقِنَا عَذَابَ النَّارِ»

"Our Lord, grant us the benefits of a good deed in this world, the reward of a good deed in the hereafter, and protect us eternally from the sufferings of hell-fire."

❊ ❊ ❊ ❊ ❊

Chapter 14

Dispelling Hypocrisy

O hypocrite. May God Almighty cleanse the surface of the earth of people like you. Is the punishment of being a hypocrite not enough for you and your like brethren, that you continue to backbite, slander and eat the flesh of the learned ones (**'ulamā**), the guardians of God's trust (**awliyā'**) and the sincere ones in their love for God Almighty (**sālihïn**)? Soon will the worms of the earth eat your tongues, cut up your flesh and chop you into pieces. Soon will your graves hug you, crush you and turn you upside down.

There is no salvation for one who does not think well of God Almighty and His righteous servants or who disdains to humble himself before them. Why should you not humble yourself before them, when they are the true leaders and commanders in this world? Who are you compared to them? God Almighty has entrusted them with the decision-making. They are His deputies, in charge of the rainfall and the sprouting of vegetation in the fields. The entire creations are their subjects. Each one of them stands tall with the might of a mountain which high winds and turbulences of plagues and adversities cannot displace. They cannot be shaken from their stations of devotion to God's Oneness and sole sovereignty or from their great satisfaction in their Lord. They pray for their benefit as well as for others.

O hypocrites. Repent and return to God Almighty. Show regret and confess your sins. Plead with Him. Implore Him. If you only knew what is awaiting you, you would be different. Conduct yourselves in the presence of your Lord as others did before you. In comparison to their resoluteness and faith, you act deceptively and effeminately. Your courage and vehemence surface only when your mind and desire (**nafs**), passions and karmic habits command you to fulfill their demands. True religious courage is to fulfill your obligations towards your Lord [عَزَّ وَجَلَّ].

Do not take lightly or undervalue the words of wise men and

learned ones, for their speech is medicine for your illnesses and their words are fruitful. Their words are direct revelations (**waḥī**) from God Almighty. Today, there is no prophet dwelling amidst you in the physical form. Thus, to emulate the followers (**tābi'īn**) of the Prophet, upon whom be peace, the true realized ones who have established his leading example in their lives, is like following him personally, and if you see them, it is just like seeing him. Strive to remain in the company of the pious learned ones, for such company will bring blessings to your lives. Do not stay in the company of learned people who do not practice what they know, for that will be ominous for your lives. If you choose the fellowship of an old and mature person who is stronger than you in piety and knowledge, his company will be a blessing for you, but if you dwell in the company of an elderly person who has no piety or knowledge, that will be ominous for you.

Do your deeds solely for God's pleasure and none else. Work for Him and for no one else. Renounce everything for His sake and for no one else. To serve anyone besides God Almighty is disbelief, and to renounce anything for other than His sake is falsehood. One who does not recognize this truth and acts otherwise is entirely sick. Soon death will come and cut him off from his insanity.

O man, reach out with your heart to link yourself with your Lord, and cut off the connection to anyone else. The Prophet, upon whom be peace, said: "**Reach out to establish the link between you and your Lord in order to attain true happiness.**"

«صِلُوا الَّذِي بَيْنَكُمْ وَبَيْنَ رَبِّكُمْ تَسْعَدُوا»

Child, you can reap no success as long as your heart finds differences between the rich and the poor when you meet them. Honor the poor and the meek who patiently endure their adversities, and seek the blessings contained in seeing them and being in their company. The Prophet, upon whom be peace, said: "**Poor people who exercise due patience are amongst the select ones who sit with the Merciful Lord on the day of reckoning.**"

«الفُقَرَاءُ الصُّبَّرُ جُلَسَاءُ الرَّحْمَنِ يَوْمَ القِيَامَةِ»

Today, they sit with Him in their hearts, and tomorrow in their physical form. These are the ones whose hearts have renounced the world and rejected its glitters. They chose poverty

over worldly riches and exercise great patience towards its difficulties. Once they attained the station of true patience, the
hereafter came and asked for their hand in marriage. They
connected with it, but as it became attainable to them, they
discovered it to be other than their Lord and Cherisher. They broke
their engagement to it, turned their hearts away from it, and ran
away from its pleasures in modesty, shying away from their Lord
[عَزَّ وَجَلَّ]. They reproached themselves saying: "How dare we stand
with other than Him, or find solace and peace in a created being?"
How could they afford to entertain a moment of tranquility with a
created being like themselves? Thus, they relinquished to the
hereafter their good deeds and records of obedience to God's
commands, then flew further on with the wings of their truthfulness,
seeking the company of their Master and Creator.

In the hereafter, they discarded their cages. Once they
became free from the cages of their own existence, they flew to
meet their Maker. Seeking the Upper Companion (**Ar-Rafīq Al-A'alā**)
they called upon the First, the Last, the Manifest and the Hidden,
and reached the tower of His proximity. Thus, they emerged as
those whom God Almighty has said of their attainment: "**Indeed
they are, in Our presence, from amongst the chosen honorable ones.**"

«وَإِنَّهُمْ عِنْدَنَا لَمِنَ الْمُصْطَفَيْنَ الْأَخْيَارِ»

In both this world and in the hereafter, their hearts, wills,
and substance dwell in Our presence. Indeed their prime essence
dwells in Our presence. Once they attain such a station, neither
their share in this world nor that in the hereafter will be abrogated.
Meanwhile, the heavens, the earth and whatever is between them
will be folded closed like a book, together with their hearts and
innermost beings . He will make such attained ones die away from
anything but Himself and make their being subsist by Him alone.
Should their destiny have further share in the provisions of this
world, He will render them back to their human nature and
mankind to redeem their portions, so that the divine wisdom,
preexistant knowledge and decree are not altered. Thus, they will
behave according to God's knowledge, fate and decree for them
and they will take their shares with the hand of detachment and
abstinence, not the hand of desire, passion or personal will.
Meanwhile, under all circumstances, they will observe the pre-

cepts of the divine law (**shari'a**). They do not withhold anything from anyone, rather if they could they would bring everyone nigh unto their Lord. The entire creations and manifestations do not possess the weight of even an atom in their hearts.

Child, as long as you are attached to this world, you will have no connection to the hereafter; as long as you hold the hereafter dear to your heart, you will have no connection to your Guardian Lord. Be actively committed to your religion and play not the fool. Truly you are one of those whom God Almighty has left astray, knowing him as such. One of the aspects of being in touch with God Almighty is to offer the poor some of your wealth. Do you not know that charity is truly dealing with God Almighty, Who is the Self-Subsisting, Rich and Generous Lord [عَزَّ وَجَلَّ]? Therefore, would someone who trades with the Self-Subsisting, Rich and Generous Lord lose anything? If you spend an atom's worth on God's path, He will reward you with a mountain's worth. If you spend a drop, He will replace it with an ocean. In both this world and the hereafter, He will repay you for your efforts with further reward.

O ye people! If you trade with God Almighty, your tilth will grow and prosper, your rivers will flow in abundance, and your trees will branch out and become lush and fruitful. Command good deeds and forbid abominable actions. Support God's religion, even if it means going against your own friend. For one who is loyal to his Lord [عَزَّ وَجَلَّ] and sincere in his deeds, the friendship with his Lord [عَزَّ وَجَلَّ] will surely endure both privately and publicly, in comfort and adversity, during hardships and prosperity. Ask for all your needs from Him, not His creations. If it becomes inevitably necessary that you ask for something from them, then bring your heart before Him first, for He will inspire you from which direction to ask. Then whether you are denied or granted your needs, it will be His decision and none of theirs.

True believers have freed their hearts from any worries concerning their livelihood. They have understood that their sustenance was apportioned beforehand and was destined to be distributed at a preset time. Thus, with such awareness they stopped looking for it and resided at the gate of their King. They received their satisfaction from God's favors upon them, His proximity and His preexistent knowledge of their needs. With that attainment, they became the pillars of the creations and their deliverers, calling out their names before their King. They hold onto the hands of the seekers' hearts, labor for their sake in His service, and implore Him to bestow upon them the garment of His acceptance and blessings.

Someone, God bless his soul, once said: *"Those whose devotion became true ask for neither world nor hereafter, but seek God for Himself and none else."* O God! I implore Thee to guide the entire creation to Thy door. This is my ultimate prayer, and Thou art the One Who makes the decision. This is an open prayer for which I will certainly be rewarded, although God Almighty does whatever He intends with His creations. Once the believer's heart becomes true, it will be filled with mercy and compassion towards all of the creations.

Someone else, God bless his soul, once said: *"No one is more proficient in their good deeds and examines their mistakes better than the sincere ones in their love for God Almighty (**siddiqūn**)"* In fact, such a sincere one abstains from wrongdoing, whether major or minor, then carefully examines his own piety and reserve through abstinence from what is desirable, and denial of the common lawful pleasures, and seeks only what is infinitely permissible. Such a one who is sincere in his love for God Almighty (**siddīq**) dearly cherishes worshiping God Almighty, night and day. His devotion goes beyond common practices, which is why uncommon grace becomes unveiled to him. His needs are provided for from sources he does not anticipate. Whatever he is given, he is commanded to take. Everything he receives is pure and unblemished.

How often was he deprived from his needs? How many times did he need something but was vexed in his heart having his efforts rejected? He often prayed, but returned empty-handed; asked, but his needs were unanswered; complained, but his torment became harder to bear. He called for relief, but could not achieve it; exercised piety, but remained suffering; glorified God's sole sovereignty and showed true sincerity in his deeds, but could not find nearness to his Maker. Thus he was treated as though he were not a believer or a **muwahhid.** However, despite all that, he exercised patience and tolerance, realizing that his patience was the real medicine for the illnesses of his heart and the immediate cause for its purification in order to help him rise to the station of proximity. He understood that the true benefits would surely come after the test was passed.

Such trials were created to demonstrate the difference between: the believer and the hypocrite, the monotheist and the polytheist, the sincere and the affected, the courageous and the coward, the strong and one who wavers, truth and falsehood, the truthful and the liar, the loving and the hateful, and the true follower and the inventor. So listen carefully to the words of a wise man, God bless his soul, who said: *"Be in this world like a wounded person who carefully nurses his wounds and patiently takes the bitter medicine, in the hope that soon his adversity will pass away."*

The true reason behind all of your adversities and illnesses is your polytheism, attributing to the people a share in God's will, decision-making and sovereignty, and finding in them a source of harm or benefit, giving or withholding. On the other hand, the secret of the real medicine is in removing them completely from your thoughts. One needs determination to exercise extreme patience with God's judgment and decrees in relation to his destiny and fate, and he must never, ever be haughty or seek leadership over the people or to rise above them. One's heart needs to be detached, his innermost secret being needs to be pure and devoutly sincere towards God Almighty, and his resoluteness must intensify.

The more that state is availed to you, your heart will rise in station and hasten to take its place amidst the rows of the prophets, the messengers, the martyrs, the righteous ones, and the most exalted heavenly beings. The longer this state lasts, the greater, the loftier, the more exalted, the more advanced and the better friend you become, and the more extensive trust (**wilāyah**) you will receive. You will be entitled with leadership. You will be given back what you earlier declined. Entrusted with what you entrusted God Almighty, you will be given what you gave away. In truth, a truly deprived person is one who is denied hearing these words, believing in them, respecting such attained beings amongst God's servants or respecting their people.

O ye who are scrambling for your livelihood, come here to gain the wealth of living, come here and collect the true profits, come here to receive the provisions of the hereafter. At one time I beat the drum and announce the message. At another time, I become the pitchman and the broker and, like that, sometimes I am the owner. I render to things their true worth. Should I receive a special favor from the blessings of the hereafter, I do not eat it alone, for a truly generous person does not eat his meals alone, but instead shares them with others. Anyone who has tasted God's generosity will never be stingy. One who comes to know God Almighty will attach importance to nothing else. Avarice comes from the ego self, but the **nafs** of a gnostic is already dead in relation to the nature of the souls of the creations. His self has reached the perfect state of peacefulness and quiescence with its Lord, trusts the assurance of His promise of the reward of excellence, and fears His pledge to chastise the unworthy ones.

O God, grant us the sustenance of such blessed beings, "**and grant us the benefits of a good deed in this world, the reward of a good deed in the hereafter, and protect us eternally from the sufferings of hell-fire.**"

«وَآتِنَا فِي الدُّنْيَا حَسَنَةً وَفِي الآخِرَةِ حَسَنَةً وَقِنَا عَذَابَ النَّارِ»

❈   ❈   ❈   ❈   ❈

Chapter 15

Giving Priority to Others' Needs

The believer carries with him the rations of a traveler, while the disbeliever feeds on indulgence. The believer carries the minimum provisions because he knows he is traveling. He contents himself with a token of his money and spends the balance for his own benefit in the hereafter. He travels light as a traveler on the road. All of his wealth is in the hereafter. His heart and will are there as well. From that perspective, his heart is totally detached from the world. He focuses his devotion on the hereafter, not on the world or its people. When he has good food, he prefers the poor and needy to have it instead of himself. He knows well that his nourishment in the hereafter will be better.

The ultimate goal of the believer, the gnostic and the man of knowledge is to reach the gate of proximity to his Lord. His highest purpose is to have his heart connected with his Lord while in this world and before he reaches the hereafter. Proximity to God Almighty is the highest aim of the heart and the path the innermost being travels.

Child, I see you occupied in prayers, standing, sitting, bowing, prostrating, toiling hard in sleepless nights, while your heart remains unchanged and does not move out of the abode of its self-centered existence. Nor is it willing to reverse the course of its old habits. Be sincerely truthful in seeking your Lord and your truthfulness will save you from immense difficulties. Use the beak of your truthfulness and peck from within to crack open the egg of your self-centered existence. Use the pickax of your sincerity and glorification of God's Oneness to knock down the walls of your stubborn fetters and binding attachment to the people. Use the hand of your ascetic detachment from the world to break open the cage of desiring it. Rise up with your heart and fly away until you reach the shore of the ocean of proximity to your Lord. Be there waiting until the ship of divine providence arrives. Be there when the captain of preexistent knowledge comes to take you across that ocean to bring you before your Lord. This world is an ocean, and your faith is its ship. That is why **Luqman Al-Hakim**, God bless his soul, said: *"Son, this world is an ocean, your faith is its ship, the captain is your deeds of obeisance, and the hereafter is the shore."*

O ye who arrogantly persist in your sin, soon you will be seized with blindness, deafness, adversities of time and poverty. Soon the cruelty of people's hearts will reduce your possessions through loss, confiscation and theft. Be wise, repent to your Lord. Do not associate your wealth with God Almighty, do not depend on it or give it any power. That is polytheism itself. Be detached and let your heart be free from your wealth. Place your money in your homes and pockets and entrust it to the hands of your servants and employees to barter with. Sit back and await your own death. Curtail your possessiveness and do not exaggerate your hopes. **Abu Yazid Al-Bistami,** God bless his soul, once said: *"A believer who has true knowledge does not ask his Lord for the benefits of this world or those of the hereafter. Instead, he himself is sought by his Lord."*

Child, open your heart once again to your Lord. A penitent is one who returns to his Lord, and that is why God Almighty has said: **"And turn back to your Lord."**

«وَأَنِيْبُوا إِلَى رَبِّكُمْ»

That means literally to return to your Lord and submit everything to Him. Place your entire trust in Him. Surrender your carnal self **(nafs)** to Him. Lay it down before the equitable hands of His divine judgment, decree, commands, restrictions and effective changes. Lay down your hearts before Him. Let them remain there without tongues, hands, feet or eyes, and without "How?" or "Why?" Be there without argument or opposition. Instead, place your hearts before Him with absolute consent and belief. Say: "God's command is true, God's divine decree is true, and God's preexistent knowledge is true."

When you become like that, your hearts will be atoning and oft-returning to Him. They see Him. They solicit satisfaction from none but Him and feel bewildered about anything beneath the Throne down to the soil of this earth. They run away from all the creations, and remain thus, uprooted and withdrawn from all the created events. Only someone who has served and had a glimpse of some of God's favors upon the true shaikhs and their mystical connection with Him knows how to properly behave before them.

To such select few amongst God's favored ones, praises and blame are like summer and winter, or night and day, all of which are God's work. He alone can bring about their manifestations. Once they realized that, they did not find confidence or reassuring strength in people's praises, nor would they fight the defaming injuries of blame, all of which could no longer affect them. Their hearts became free from either love or hatred towards the people. They know no more the expressions of such love or hatred, and replace them with mercy and compassion.

O man, what benefits can you gain from knowledge without truthfulness? Indeed you are one of those whom God Almighty has, knowing him as such, left astray. You strive for knowledge, pray, and fast to please others. You search for their acknowledgment. You want them to offer you their money and you go to any length to get them to praise you in their homes and social gatherings. God Almighty knew what you will get from them, but once your death, and the sufferings, exasperation, horror and dismay of the grave overtake you, all that you sought will become inaccessible to you, and they can save you from nothing. Whatever money swindled from them will go to someone else, while the reckoning and punishment will befall you. O clever man of the world. O truly deprived one. Indeed you are one of those who strive in vain. In this world you toil hard, but in the hereafter you stand great losses in the hell-fire.

True worship of God Almighty is a craft. Its professionals are the trustees (**awliyā**), deputies (**abdāl**), the sincere ones in their love for Him (**mukhlisïn**), and the ones brought nigh unto God Almighty (**muqarrabïn**). The gnostics are God's true viceregents on earth. They are His deputies and emissaries. They inherited the prophets and the messengers, not you. O hallucinators, O agents of hearsay and gossip who outwardly appear to possess knowledge of the religious doctrine, but inwardly are a bag full of ignorance.

Child, what you are pursuing is nothing. Islām is not made for people like you. Islām is the foundation upon which everything is based. The testimony of faith, (**shahādah**) is not made for people like you. You say: "**Lā ilāha il-Allāh**" (There is no god but Allāh), but you lie. In your heart there is a host of deities. Your fear of your king and governor is a deity. Your trust and dependence on your wealth, earnings and status, your will, power, hearing, sight and inequities towards others are deities. To think that harm or benefits, giving or depriving are the hands of the creations is a deity. Many people depend on these things with their hearts, though outwardly they pretend to be dependent on God Almighty. Their remembrance of God Almighty became a habit spoken with their tongues, not their hearts. When they are questioned about it, they become annoyed and angry and retort: "How dare you question us, aren't we Muslims?" However, tomorrow the scandals will surface and the secrets will be divulged.

O unfortunate one. You are fully supported when you say: There is no sovereign god (**Lā Ilāha**), other than God (**il-Allāh**) as you universally disclaim sovereignty to any creation and proclaim and confirm God's authority, lordship and state of none other than Him. Thus, whenever your heart finds solace in depending on anything other than the ultimate truth (**haqq**) of God's sovereignty, then you are lying in your testimony, and whatever you depend on becomes your god. The outer appearance is of no consequence. The heart is the believer, the one who calls upon God's Oneness, whose love is sincere, who is pious, who is God fearing, who has ascetic detachment and is filled with certitude. The heart is the gnostic, the laborer and the commanding prince. All besides the heart are soldiers and followers.

Therefore, when you say: "There is no one worthy of worship other than Allāh," say it first with your heart and then with your tongue. Trust in the intuitions of your heart, and depend on them and nothing else. Engage yourself outwardly with fulfilling the divine command, but keep your heart focused on God Almighty Himself. Let the manifestations of good and evil be outward, but occupy yourself inwardly with the Creator of good and evil. One who comes to truly know Him will abase himself before Him, tie up his tongue, and humble himself to Him and to His righteous servants. For such a one, his grief, stress and crying will multiply, while his fears and reverence will increase. His shyness and shame will grow and his regret for his delinquencies and past squanderings will increase. He becomes more vigilant and fearful of the possibility of losing what he has gained of inner knowledge, outer knowledge and nearness to God Almighty (**qurb**). He knows of God Almighty that: **"He does whatever He wills. He is not to be questioned about what He does, though they are subject to His questioning."**

«فَعَّالٌ لَا يُرِيْدُ لَايُسْأَلُ عَمَّا يَفْعَلُ وَهُمْ يُسْأَلُونَ»

He vacillates back and forth between two states. The first is that of his past squandering, impudence, arrogance, ignorance and ecstatic enjoyments. Recognizing them for what they are, he practically melts out of shame, and constantly fears the questioning. Meanwhile, he contemplates with great anxiety the future of his state of being. Will he be accepted or rejected? Will he be stripped of what he has already been given, or will he be left with what he has earned? On the day of reckoning, will he be in the company of the believers or the disbelievers? That is why the Prophet, upon whom be peace, said: **"Amongst you, I know God the best, and I fear Him the most."**

«أَنَا أَعْرَفُكُمْ بِاللهِ وَأَشَدُّكُمْ لَهُ خَوْفاً»

One of the rare mystical particulars of a gnostic is that he receives nothing unless he already has knowledge of it. He knows what is destined for him and its refuge. His innermost being reads his allotted shares in the Preserved Tablet (**Al-Lowhul-Mahfūz**). Further on, it reveals them to his heart and commands it to conceal it from mind and desire (**nafs**). Such a state of attainment begins with surrender to God (**Islām**), submitting to what is commanded, abstaining from what is forbidden, while exercising patience in adversity, and culminates with ascetic detachment from everything except God Almighty. To the gnostic, gold or dust are of equal value. Praises or blame, giving or depriving, heaven or hell, blessings or wrath, richness or poverty, existence of the universes or their annihilation, all of them are equal in his eyes. When that state is achieved, God Almighty will be the real force behind it all, and further on will appoint him to his rank of leadership over the people as God's representative (**wali**). Whoever sees such a person will benefit from him, because of God's reverence and light which have dawned in such a one.

«رَبَّنَا آتِنَا فِي الدُّنْيَا حَسَنَةً وَفِي الآخِرَةِ حَسَنَةً وَقِنَا عَذَابَ النَّارِ»

"Our Lord! Grant us the benefits of a good deed in this world, the reward of a good deed in the hereafter and protect us from ever suffering in hell-fire."

Chapter 16

Become a True Human Being

Al-Hassan Al-Basri, God bless his soul, once said: *"Despise the world. By God, it does not taste good unless first rejected and humiliated."* Child! Your acting in accordance with the Qur'ān will make you realize its worth, and emulating the leading example (**sunnah**) of the Messenger, our Prophet Muhammad, upon whom be peace, will lead you to understand his station. His blessed heart and exalted endeavors (**himmah**) never cease to encompass the hearts of the true believers. He is the comforter of their hearts, the one who suffuses the hearts with aromatic perfumes and enhances the sweet fragrance of its incense, who purifies their innermost beings and beautifies them. He leads their way and draws them nigh unto the gate of proximity. He serves them and he is the ambassador between their hearts and their innermost being on one hand, and their Lord on the other. Every step you take towards him increases his joy.

It becomes incumbent upon whoever is endowed with such a state of attainment to be ever grateful and to increase his devotion and obedience. Otherwise, to be ecstatic about anything other than that state is mere hallucination. An ignorant person rejoices in the world, but one who has true knowledge experiences the reverse. An ignorant person disputes and considers himself a challenger of God's decree, while one who is acquainted with knowledge concedes and contents himself with what it brings.

O miserable one. Do not dispute your fate or attempt to rival God's decree. It can destroy you. Rather, your purpose should be to be content with the doings of God Almighty, to remove the creations from your heart, and to meet your Lord and Cherisher with it, free from everything other than Him. Meet Him with your heart, your innermost being and your essence. If you can perse-

vere on God's path, the path of His messengers and righteous
servants, if you can serve the righteous ones, do so, for that will
greatly benefit you in both this world and the hereafter. Otherwise,
even if you were to possess the treasures of the entire world and
yet your heart was not like theirs, your wealth would not be worth
even a penny.

Whosoever corrects his own heart towards God Almighty
and keeps it in His trust for this world and the hereafter will be
endowed with the privilege to judge amongst the common people,
as well as the select ones by God's decree.

O man, know your true worth. Who do you think you are
compared to them? Your striving is so mundane as it is merely
centered around your food, drink, clothing, sexual pleasures, and
the accumulation and control of worldly wealth. You are one of
those failing to serve the concerns of the hereafter. You are
nurturing the fat of your body to ultimately feed its flesh to the
worms and insects of the grave. The Prophet, upon whom be
peace, said: "**God Almighty has an angel who, morning and
evening, sounds a special call saying: 'O children of Adam!
Prepare for death, build towards the day of ruins, and rally for
your struggle against your enemies.'**"

"إِنَّ لِلهِ عَزَّ وَجَلَّ مَلَكًا يُنَادِى كُلَّ غُدْوَةٍ وَعَشِيَّةٍ:

يَابَنِى آدَمَ لِدُوا لِلْمَوت   وَابْنُوا لِلْخَرَاب وَاجْمَعُوا لِلأَعْدَاءِ"

A true believer (**mu'min**) always has good intentions and
sincerity in his deeds. He does not work for the benefits of this
world, but rather for those of the hereafter. He labors for the
benefit of his Muslim brethren by building mosques, bridges,
schools and roads. He also works to take care of his own
dependents, as well as widows, and the needy or to carry out other
fundamental obligations. He fulfills his duties, aspiring to attain
that which is built for him in the hereafter. His commitments do
not satisfy the impulses of his karma, passion or carnal self (**nafs**).

Like this, once the son of Adam becomes a true human
being, he remains with God Almighty in his entirety. In God he is
annihilated, and by Him he subsists. In this world, his heart joins
the company of the prophets and messengers. He accepts and
subscribes in word and deed to what they brought, and consents

to their directives with unwavering faith and certitude. That is why he will, no doubt, join their company in this world as well as in the hereafter.

One who constantly remembers God Almighty (**thākir**) is ever alive. He crosses from one life into another. His experience of death is merely for a moment. Once the remembrance of God Almighty permeates the heart, it becomes ongoing even when the tongue is not uttering the praises. The more he engages in that state of remembrance, the more clarity he gains and the more natural becomes his consent to and contentment with God's doings.

If you disagree with God Almighty about the coming of summer, summer will still come and prove you a liar, and the same goes for winter. The cold will make us feel its effects. Accepting the fact of their occurrence will, through preparedness, eliminate their harm and minimize their effects. Such will be the result of encountering adversities and plagues with acceptance of God's decree. It will eliminate any grief, stress, anguish, irritation, alarm or disturbance.

What a wonder is the character of the intimate servants of God Almighty, and what a beautiful state they encompass. Whatever comes to them from God Almighty is good. He gave them the drink of knowing Him and they floated in its ecstasy. He brought them nigh to rest in the cradle of His subtle kindness, and comforted them with His own presence. That is why being situated in His presence, while concealed from everything but Him, brings about their utmost satisfaction. They remain thus, dead to themselves and inanimate in His presence, being seized by the divine reverence. If He wills, He will expand their existence, raise them back to life again, restore them and awaken them. They become the 'Companions of the Cave,' concerning whom God Almighty said: "**And We turn them to the right side and that of the left**."

$$\text{«وَنُقَلِّبُهُمْ ذَاتَ الْيَمِينِ وَذَاتَ الشِّمَالِ»}$$

These are the wisest of people. All that they deeply aspire to is God's forgiveness and His granting their salvation. This is all they labor for.

O man. You behave like the companions of hell and still aspire for the heavenly paradise. Your greed is truly misplaced. Do

not be deceived by this worthless world or think it is yours. Soon
it will be taken away from you. God Almighty has loaned you this
life to teach you how to obey Him in it. Instead, you thought it
belonged to you and went on indulging in whatever pleased you.
Also, your health is a naked trust, riches are a naked trust, as well
as your safety, titles and each and every one of God's favors. Do
not abuse these trusts, for you shall be questioned about them
and everything that is generated from them. All the blessings you
have are God's favors. Use them wisely to help you better serve and
obey Him. Meanwhile, all that you desire is in the safe reach of the
righteous ones, though their main preoccupation is to remain on
God's side protected (**salāmah**) in this world and in the hereafter.

Someone, may God be pleased with him, once said: *"Agree with
God Almighty about the people, but do not agree with the people in
their opinions about God."* Whosoever his destiny has condemned
is condemned and whosoever his destiny has restored is restored.
Learn how to agree with God Almighty from His righteous servants,
who with absolute clarity and unwavering faith agree with Him.

«رَبَّنَا آتِنَا فِي الدُّنْيَا حَسَنَةً وَفِي الآخِرَةِ حَسَنَةً وَقِنَا عَذَابَ النَّارِ»

**"Our Lord, grant us the benefits of a good deed in this
world, the reward of a good deed in the hereafter, and protect
us eternally from the sufferings of hell-fire."**

Chapter 17

Do Not Worry
About Your Provisions

Do not worry about your provisions. They labor to reach you more avidly than you seek them. If you have received your food for today, then be not concerned about what may come tomorrow. As yesterday went with your not knowing whether tomorrow will come, then concentrate only on the needs of your livelihood today. If you truly knew God Almighty you would be concentrating more on Him rather than on your food. The reverence and awe of His presence would make you refrain from asking about anything, for one who truly knows God Almighty will stop wagging his tongue. A gnostic remains silent and still in God's presence until He returns him to serve people's interests. Once God Almighty reinstates him in that duty, He will remove the stuttering and stammering from his tongue. When Moses, upon whom be peace, was a shepherd, he used to stammer, rush, stutter, and hesitate. However, once God Almighty intended to send him back to Egypt to serve the people, He inspired him to pray: "**And untie my tongue so that they may understand what I say**."

«وَاحْلُلْ عُقْدَةً مِنْ لِسَانِى يَفْقَهُوا قَوْلِى»

It is as if he were saying: "When I was in the wilderness herding the sheep, I did not need to speak. Now that my duty is to be with the people and to admonish them, help me to do so by removing the stuttering and idling of my tongue." Consequently, when God Almighty lifted the obstacles from his tongue, Moses' speech became fluent, and he spoke ninety words of perfect diction and clarity in the time it took anyone else to speak only a few words. During his infancy, when brought before the pharaoh and his wife Asiya, Moses intended to tell pharaoh the truth, but as it was the wrong time, God Almighty made him touch a burning coal, the shock of which made him develop his stammering and stuttering.

Child, I see that you have very little knowledge of God Almighty and His blessed Messenger, upon whom be peace. I find that you have even less knowledge of God's representatives, prophets, deputies and viceregents amongst His creations. Truly, you have no sense. You are like a cage without a bird, like a vacant house in ruins, like a dead tree, withered with no leaves left on its branches. Building the heart of God's servant can only be done through **Islām** and by further on ascertaining its reality, which is **istislām**, the unconditional surrendering to and immersing oneself in His infinite truth. Submit even your carnal self (**nafs**) wholly to God Almighty. He will return it to you purified and entrust you with other people to serve. Extract your carnal self as well as the creation from your heart and stand before Him stripped of it all. In that state, if it be God's will, He will cover you, clothe you with brocades and bring you back to the people. You will fulfill His decree with regard to your fate or theirs, carry His orders with His blessings and those of God's Messenger, upon whom be peace, and you will always be waiting in readiness to carry out His commands and to accept His judgment towards you or the people. Whosoever can free himself from everything besides God Almighty, and stand before Him on the feet of his heart and innermost being in a complete state of resoluteness will have spoken with the tongue of his state of being (**lisanul-hāal**) as did Moses, upon whom be peace, who prayed: "**I hastened back to Thee, O my Lord, to please Thee.**"

«وَعَجِلْتُ إِلَيْكَ رَبِّي لِتَرْضَى»

I removed my attachments to the world, to the hereafter and to all of the creation. I cut off my dependence on any personal means (**asbāb**), tore down all the hindrances and personal deities (**arbāb**) and rushed back to meet Thee, hoping that Thou may be pleased with me and forgive me for having waited so long amidst them. O ignorant man. What chance of comparison do you have to that state? You are merely a slave to your mind and desire, passions and the world. You are a slave to creation by associating them with God Almighty, because you think they have the power to harm or benefit you. When you envision paradise, you still have hope of entering it, and when you see hell-fire, you fear having to enter it. O people! How distant are your current conditions from Him Who has the power of transforming the hearts and sights into a whole new existence —He is the One Who says to the thing: "**Be**" and "**It is**".

«كُنْ فَيَكُون»

Child, be not proud of your devotions or marvel at them. Instead, implore God Almighty to accept them. Be cautious and fear that He may choose to reverse your condition or remove you to another state. What assurance do you have that He will not choose to say to your obedience: "Be disobedient!" or to your clarity: "Become obscurity!" One who truly knows God Almighty fosters nothing, marvels at nothing, and trusts nothing until he departs from this world, having safeguarded his religion and sustained a sacred relationship between himself and God Almighty.

O ye people! Choose the work of the heart and act with sincerity. Perfect sincerity and loyalty are incumbent upon the creations, but knowledge of God Almighty are their foundation. I find the majority of you to be nothing but liars both in words and actions, privately and publicly. You seem to have no resistance to being such. You lack steadfastness. You have words but no deeds, you act without sincerity, and you have no faith in God's oneness. Even if my testing stone were worn away and mistakenly accepted you, what benefit could that bring ? You need God Almighty to accept you. Soon your metal coin, which you claim to be as valuable as gold, will be exposed in the forge when the heat separates the elements. It will be said to you: This is white, this is black, and this is suspicious. Like that on the day of judgment, every impurity will skitter to the side. This is what will be said to each and every act of hypocrisy you committed. Any deed which is not offered solely for God's sake is a sham. Therefore, strive, love, be with and ask only of Whom it is said: "**There is nothing like unto Him, and He is the All-Hearing, the All-Seeing Lord.**"

«لَيْسَ كَمِثْله شَئٌ وَهُوَ السَّمِيْعُ البَصِيْرُ»

Deny what is false and attest to what is right. Refute any attribute which is not befitting God Almighty, and credit Him with what is appropriately His. These are the attributes which God

Almighty has acknowledged for Himself and which His blessed Messenger, upon whom be peace, has praised as God's manifest powers. If you do so, you will eliminate from your heart any ascribing of human characteristics to God Almighty (**tashbïh**) or denying God Almighty His divine attributes (**ta'aṭïl**). Remain in the company of God Almighty, His Messenger, and the righteous ones of His servants. Be with them with reverence, exaltation, and respect.

O ye people! If you truly want success, then let none of you come before me unless intending to behave properly. Otherwise, do not come here. You are mostly curious about things. Drop intellectual curiosity from this hour. Perhaps there is someone in this audience who is worthy of respect and whose presence commands proper behavior, which point will go beyond your immediate perception and understanding. The cook knows what he is cooking. The baker knows what he is baking. The craftsman knows his craft, and the host knows whom he invited and those who are present. Your attachment to your world has blinded your hearts to the point where you cannot see anything. Beware of this world! In the beginning it entices you to enjoy it again and again, then gradually draws you into its trap to capture and butcher you. At first, it lets you drink from its intoxicants. Then, while under their influence, it hastens to cut off your hands and feet and pluck out your eyes. Once the effects of the anesthesia are gone and it is time for you to wake up, you will discover what harm has been done to you. These are the consequences of loving the world, running after its pleasures, holding it dear to one's carnal self (**nafs**) and being captivated by it. That is the nature of its work, so beware of it!

Child, as long as you love this world, you will reap no success. As to you who claim to love God Almighty, as long as you love the hereafter or anything else, you can reap no success and there is no truth to your claim. A true God-loving gnostic craves neither this or that, and desires nothing besides being with God Almighty. Once his love is ascertained and identified as true love, his allotted portion in this world will come to him, wholesome and gratifying. Similarly, when he reaches the abode of the hereafter, any portion which he earlier renounced to please God Almighty (**liwajhillāh**) will be waiting for him at God's door. God gives His representatives (**awliyā**) their shares, while they are oblivious to the giving or the receiving of them.

The treasures of the heart are hidden, and the pleasures of the carnal self (**nafs**) are tangible. Thus, the treasures of the heart do not manifest unless the pleasures of the carnal self (**nafs**) are curtailed. Once the mind and desire are restricted, the gate to the fortune of the heart will become wide open. Once the heart finds its satisfaction in God's treasures alone, mercy will dawn upon the mind and desire and encompass them. Such a devout servant will be told: Do not kill your 'self.' Then, one's adornments will come without hindrance, and the **nafs** will take its share with peace and serenity (**mutma'inna**).

Discard the company of one who stimulates your desire for the world, and seek the company of those who can help you find it repugnant, so that you, too, can become detached from it. Each quality relates to its own kind. People of the same type orbit around each other. A lover walks through the highways of lovers until he finds his beloved. Those who love God Almighty love one another in Him. No doubt, that's why He loves them, supports and cherishes them, and strengthens them with one another. Together, they share the duty of calling the people to God's path. They invite them to have faith, to glorify God's Oneness, and to be sincere in their devotions and deeds. They take them by the hand and bring them forth to walk on the straight path of God Almighty. One who serves others shall be served, one who shows kindness shall be treated with kindness, and one who is generous shall be rewarded with generosity. If you indulge in the work of the companions of hell today, then hell shall be yours tomorrow. "**As you judge, you shall be judged...Your rulers shall reflect your rulings .**"

«كَمَا تَدِينُ تُدَانْ . كَمَا تَكُونُوا يُوَلَّ عَلَيْكُمْ»

Your actions are your workers. However, you indulge in the conduct of the companions of hell-fire, and look to God Almighty to grant you heavens. How dare you aspire to paradise without practicing the qualities of its dwellers! The true masters of the hearts in this world are those who sustain each and every one of their actions with their hearts, not their limbs alone. An act that does not have the clarity and consent of the heart, how far can it go? An pretentious person acts with his limbs only, but a sincere believer acts with his body and heart. In fact, his heart acts first, then his body follows. A believer is alive, but a hypocrite is dead. A believer works for God Almighty, but a hypocrite works for people, seeking their praises and asking for compensation for his efforts. A believer's deeds are inherent and most natural, inwardly and outwardly, privately and publicly, during hardship or prosperity, while a hypocrite only acts in public, only in prosperity. Once hardship comes, he becomes selfish and his acts vanish. He does not remain in God's company. He shows no faith in God Almighty, His Messengers or revealed books. He no longer remembers the day of gathering, the resurrection or reckoning. His **Islām** is a tool to save his neck and money in this world, and not for his own salvation and protection from the hell-fire in the hereafter, which is God's punishment for such beings. He fasts, prays and studies knowledge in the company of people, but once alone, he reverts to his own nature, work and disbelief (**kufr**).

O God! We seek refuge in You from ever falling into such a state. We ask of You to endow us with sincerity in this world and in the hereafter. Amen.

Child, be sincere in your actions. Stop looking at your work or asking to be compensated for it from the people or from the Creator. Work for God's pleasure, not for the sake of His favors. Be amongst those who only seek His countenance. Keep asking until He grants it to you. Once He grants you your prayer, you will have reached paradise in both this world as well as the hereafter. You will have won His proximity in this world, and you will be able to physically look at Him in the hereafter. The reward He has promised is an assured pledge to His devotees. Child, entrust yourself and your wealth to the equitable hand of God's decree, judgment and will. Trust the merchandise to the Buyer, and tomorrow He will pay you.

O God's servants, completely surrender yourselves to God Almighty. Give back to Him both the price and the merchandise. Say to Him: "Our souls, wealth and paradise are yours. Everything beside You belongs to You. We want nothing but You." Search for the good neighbor before you look for a house. Look for the companion on the road before you embark on your journey. O you who are asking for paradise, the buying and building of it is done today, not tomorrow. Increase your rivers and let their waters flow today not tomorrow.

Child, on the day of reckoning, hearts will become despon-

dent, eyesight will falter and feet will slip and trip over themselves.
Only one in a million will be able to stand on the feet of his faith
and piety. To gain a foothold on that day will depend on the
strength of your faith today. On that day: "**The wrongdoer will
bite his hands (in regret).**"

«يَعَضُّ الظَّالِمُ عَلَى يَدَيْهِ»,

He will ask himself: "How did I do that? How did I oppress
others?" The wicked will bite his own hand in regret and ask
himself: "How did I cause corruption rather than doing good? How
did I become a runaway slave from my own Lord and Master?"

Child, have no pride about your deeds. The value of actions
is shown at the completion of one's work. You should pray and beg
God Almighty to make the conclusion of your life a good one. Pray
that when you die, your last action be the one He loves most.
Never, ever breach or violate your repentance. Never revert to sin
once you have repented because of any idle talk, irrespective of
whatever is said to you. Do not disobey your Lord and Master for
the sake of accepting the suggestions of your mind and desire,
passions, or karma. This by itself is a sin. Any action done today
should be weighed against its consequences tomorrow. If you sin
against God Almighty, He will forsake you and humiliate you both,
in this world and the hereafter, and deprive you of His help. O God!
Help us to be obedient unto You, and do not abase us by
disobeying You.

"**Our Lord, grant us the benefits of a good deed in this
world, the reward of a good deed in the hereafter, and protect
us eternally from the sufferings of hell-fire.**"

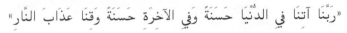

«رَبَّنَا آتِنَا فِي الدُّنْيَا حَسَنَةً وَفِي الآخِرَةِ حَسَنَةً وَقِنَا عَذَابَ النَّارِ»

❀ ❀ ❀ ❀ ❀

Chapter 18

Jihadu-nafs:
The Inner Struggle

God Almighty has informed you about two types of struggle, outer and inner. The inner struggle is directed towards the mind and desire (**nafs**) passions, karmic nature, and satan. It is to repent from sinful actions and errors, resolutely maintain that course of conduct and abstain from forbidden desires. As to the outer struggle, that one is against the disbelievers who are stubbornly waging war against Him and His blessed Messenger, upon whom be peace, and to rigorously endure their swords, spears and arrows. They kill and they are killed.

Thus, the inner struggle is more difficult than the outer one, because it is connected to one's carnal self which is tenaciously recurring. How could it not be harder to wage the inner struggle than the outer struggle, when it requires severing the common evil habits of the carnal self (**nafs**) and overcoming its indulgence in forbidden actions (**ḥarām**), subscribing to the jurisdiction of God's law (**sharī'a**), and doing what is lawful while abstaining from the unlawful? Thus, whoever, in submitting to God's will, engages in both struggles will receive his reward in this world as well as in the hereafter. Wounds to the body of a martyr are like a small vein in one's hand—they cause no pain. While death is regarded by a penitent and a warrior against his own carnal self (**nafs**) as a cold, fresh drink of water that quenches the thirst of a long journeying traveler.

O ye people! We ask you to give up nothing without offering you something better in return. Each moment, from within his heart, a servant who is sought by God Almighty (**murād**) receives instructions and guidance, commands and restrictions. That is contrary to the rest of creation, and particularly in contrast to the hypocrites and the enemies of God Almighty and His Messenger, upon whom be peace. Those nonbelievers enter the hell-fire through the gates of their ignorance of God Almighty and their animosity towards Him. Why should they not be thrust into hell-fire, when, in this world, they oppose God Almighty and consented to the commands of their carnal self (**nafs**), passions, desires, karmic nature, evil habits and satans? They favor the pleasures of this world to the detriment of their own salvation in the hereafter. Why should they not enter hell-fire, when, in this world, they heard the revelations of the Qur'ān but did not believe in it, nor did they act upon it, nor abstain from what it forbids.

O ye people! Believe in the Qur'ān, follow its precepts and be sincere in your actions. Be not affected or hypocritical in your actions. Seek not people's praises nor expect any compensation from them for your deeds. Only a few, singled out and rare people amongst God's creations do believe in the Qur'ān and act according to it solely for the pleasure of God's Countenance.That is why the sincere ones are few, the hypocrites many. O ye people! How lazy and slow you are to obey God's commands and how fervent and strong you are in obeying His enemy and yours, the accursed satan.

True believers wish never to be free from duties assigned by their Lord. They understand that in exercising patience towards His will and decree and by performing their assigned duties, they receive immeasurable wealth and blessings in this world and in the hereafter. They heed His measures and find solace in His vicissitudes. Whatever changing conditions He puts them through, they embrace them, one time with patience and another time with gratitude. In proximity or distance, in toiling or comfort, in wealth or poverty, in health or sickness, they constantly remain obedient to Him. All they aspire to is for their hearts to remain pure and true unto Him. They cherish this most. This is their safety (**salāma**), and the safety of the creation with their Creator. Thus, they keep praying to and imploring God Almighty on behalf of the people for their salvation.

Child, be true unto God Almighty and your speach will have clarity. Be true unto Him in the abode of destiny (**hukm**), then you will be precise and lucid. Be a true being inwardly and you will be articulate outwardly. The essence of safety is obeisance to God Almighty. That is, to be obedient to everything He commands, abstain from what He forbids, and accept His judgment and carry out His will with great patience. Whosoever answers God's call, God Almighty will answer his prayers, and whosoever obeys Him, God Almighty will subject His creation to be at his command.

O ye people! Accept my words without prejudice, for I am only advising you. I have no attachment to myself, to you, or to all the influences my being is experiencing. I am a remote spectator, observing His doings in me and in you. Do not brand me with your accusations, for I only want for you what I want for myself. The Prophet, upon whom be peace, said: "**The faith of a believer does not become complete until he loves for his brother what he loves for himself.**"

«لاَ يُكْمِلُ المُؤْمِنُ إِيمَانَهُ حَتَّى يُرِيدَ لأَخِيهِ المُسْلِمِ مَايُرِيدُهُ لِنَفْسِهِ»

These are the words of our prince and commander, our chieftain and magistrate, our leader and guide, our ambassador and intercessor, who is the leader, the predecessor and seal of all the prophets, messengers and the righteous ones since the time of Adam, upon whom be peace, and will remain thus until the day of judgment. He has refuted any claims of perfection of one's faith unless he loves for his Muslim brother what he loves for himself. If you wish to have the best food, the best garment, the best homes, the most beautiful wife and abundance of wealth, while wishing the opposite of that for your Muslim brother, you will have lied in your claim of having perfect and true faith. O man of little planning. You have a poor neighbor in need, you have relatives in need, and you have extra money on which alms tax (**zakāt**) is due. Each day you keep accumulating profits upon profits from your business, and though you have more than you need, to deprive them from their rightful share in your material comfort is plain acceptance, with either callousness or satisfaction, of their state of poverty. However, should your **nafs,** desires and satans provoke you, your certitude changes then, and you spare nothing to satisfy them. That is why it is not easy for you to do any good. You are a mixture of selfish greed, exaggerated hopes, lack of piety, love for the world, and of meager faith. You are a polytheist. You worship and boast about yourself, your money, and your worldly connections, but you do not realize this. Whoever is captivated by the desire for this world and holds niggardly to it, has forgotten about death and his final destination to stand before his Lord

[عَزَّ وَجَلَّ] , Whoever does not care to discriminate between what is permissible (**halāl**) and what is forbidden (**harām**) is imitating the disbelievers who boastfully say: "**Our life is only what we have in this world, in it we live and die, and only old age and time could ever destroy us.**"

«مَاهِيَ إلَّا حَيَاتُنَا الدُّنْيَا نَمُوتُ وَنَحْيَى وَمَا يُهْلِكُنَا إلَّا الدَّهْرُ»

You sound like one of such people. The only difference between you is that you wear the garment of **Islām** and you have spared your blood with the two testimonies, saying: "**Ash-hadu an lā ilāha il-Allāh, wa ash-hadu anna Muhammadur-Rasül Allāh**."*(i.e., I bear witness that there is no god other than Allāh, and I bear witness that Muhammad is the Messenger of Allāh)*. You adopt the practices of **Muslims**, that is, prayers and fasting as a matter of social norms, not as acts of worship. You display piety to people while your heart is filled with immorality and insolence. All of that will not benefit you. O ye people! What could you gain from hunger and thirst during the day, if you then break fast with what is unlawful at night? O filth mongers. You deny yourselves water by day, then you break fast by drinking the blood of **Muslims** at night. Some of you fast during the day, then commit abominable actions at night.

The Prophet, upon whom be peace, said: "**My followers shall not be forsaken or humiliated as long as they reverently honor the month of Ramadan**."

«لَا تُخْذَلُ أُمَّتِي مَا عَظَّمُوا شَهْرَ رَمَضَانَ»

The true way of exalting the month of **Ramadān** is to glorify it with piety, to fast during it solely to please God Almighty, while observing the law of **sharī'a**. Child, subscribe to the obligatory precept of fasting the month of **Ramadān.** When you break the fast, comfort the needy by sharing some of your food with them. Do not eat alone , for one who eats alone or disdains from sharing his food may have to experience poverty and have to beg for himself.

O ye people! How can you claim to be believers, when you satisfy your appetite though aware that your neighbor is hungry? Your faith is not true. Some enjoy abundance of food beyond the needs of his hunger or that of his family, yet a beggar who stands for a long time at his door, is still sent away with his needs unsatisfied. Soon you will discover what end is awaiting you, and soon you will become like him and will be driven from people's doors without success. You will be frustrated in the same manner that you have acted towards another when you blocked his way to your door, although you had the means to help him.

Alas! Why don't you get up, take what you have at hand and happily give it to him? By doing that, you will have combined the quality of humility in standing up to serve together with the quality of giving a share from your wealth. Our Prophet Muhammad, upon whom be peace, would give to the mendicant with his own hand, feed his camel, milk his goat and even mend his shirt for him. Then how can you pretend to be his follower when you oppose him in words and actions? Your case has no basis in truth. There is a proverb that says: *"Either be a true Jew or do not get passionately excited about the Torah."* And I say the same: Either you follow the precepts of **Islām** or do not say: *"I am a Muslim."* O ye people! Hold fast to the precepts of **Islām**. Hold fast to the truth of **Islām**, that is, surrender yourselves wholly to God Almighty (**istislām**). Comfort the people today and God Almighty will comfort you with His mercy tomorrow. Have compassion towards those living on earth, and He Who is in the heavens will have compassion on you.

Child, as long as you follow your mind, carnal self and desire (**nafs**) you cannot reach that station. As long as you keep satisfying its lust for pleasures in this world, you will be entangled in its rope. Instead, give only its basic rights to it and deprive it of its lust for pleasures. In fact, by providing it with its rightful earnings (**haqq**) you insure its safety and continuity, and by satisfying its lust for good luck(**hazz**) you cause its destruction. The carnal self's basic rights are the essential provisions of food, clothing, water and shelter, while its luck is its lust for pleasures, desires, intoxicants, and sexual delights. Ask for its rights and take them from the equitable hand of God's law (**sharï'a**). Entrust its good luck (**hazz**) to the hand of the divine decree and God's preexistent knowledge (**sābiqa**). Feed your carnal self (**nafs**) what is permissible, not forbidden. Take a seat at the door of the divine law and enlist your **nafs** to serve and do duty there. Only then will you have a successful life. Have you not heard the words of God Almighty: **"Practice what the Messenger brought you and abstain from what he forbade you."**

«مَا أَتَاكُمُ الرَّسُولُ فَخُذُوهُ وَمَا نَهَاكُمْ عَنْهُ فَانْتَهُوا»

Be content with little, and condition yourself to be satisfied with it. Under those circumstances, should the hand of destiny and preexistent knowledge bring you more, then enjoy it. That will be its good luck. Once you are content with only a little of this world, your carnal self (**nafs**) will not be destroyed nor be deprived of any predestined share.

Al-Hassan Al-Basri, God bless his soul, used to say: *"The hunger of a believer can be satisfied with the same amount of food that suffices a kid goat—a handful of dried dates and a sip of water."* A believer carries the rations of a traveler, but a hypocrite feeds on indulgence. The believer carries as little as his needs require on the road until he reaches home. He knows well that all his needs are stored there, while a hypocrite has neither home, path, nor purpose.

O ye people! How long do you want to continue wasting your days and months? You waste your life without deriving any benefit from it. I see you are careful not to hinder your love for the world, even at the cost of squandering your religious covenant with God Almighty. Turn around and you will be on the right track.

Eternal life in this world was not the lot of anyone before you, so do not expect this life to last. O ye people! Do you have a signed contract from God Almighty granting you eternal life in this world? What little planning you have done. Whoever builds another's world at the cost of ruining his own life in the hereafter and gathers the world for someone else while breaking his own religious covenant earns God's wrath, just to please a creature like himself. If only he knew with certainty that soon he will die and be brought for judgment before God Almighty, he would constrain himself from many of his wrongdoings.

Luqmān Al-Hakïm, God bless his soul, once told his son: *"My child, just as when you get sick and do not know how the virus entered your blood stream, similarly, you die and do not know how it happened."* I keep warning you and advising you, but you do not heed my warnings or advice. O ye who are bereft of true goodness, indulging yourselves in worldly gains. Soon the forces of the world will clutch at you and strangle you. On that day, nothing of what you gathered from its hands will benefit you, nor any of its enjoyments. Instead, all of that will bring you evil consequences.

Child, you must have patience and forbearance. You must shun all evil. You must understand that words have sisters that come to support their arguments. If someone makes a remark to you and you retort with a like word, the sisters will come and evil will break out between you and the other person. Only few and rare ones amongst God's servants will be trained and prepared to admonish the creations and call them to God's door. These rare beings are the living proof should the people refute the truth. They are a blessing to believers and a punishment for hypocrites, the enemies of God's religion.

O God, please wash us with the perfume of praising Your sole sovereignty and Oneness, purify us with the incense of annihilation from creation and anything but You, O Lord.

O monotheists. O polytheists. No created being has the power to do anything. All of them are powerless. The kings, the lords, the governors, the rich or the poor people, they are all prisoners of what God Almighty destined for them. He holds their hearts in His hands and transforms them as He wills. **"There is nothing like unto Him, and He is the All-Hearing, the All-Seeing Lord."**

«لَيْسَ كَمِثْله شَيْءٌ وَهُوَ السَّمِيْعُ البَصِيرُ»

Do not fatten your carnal self (**nafs**), for it will end by eating you. Its parable is that of one who raises a wild dog, stays alone with him and keeps fattening him. In his case, there is always the possibility that the wild dog might eat him. Do not let go of the reins on your carnal self (**nafs**) or ever let it run free, and do not sharpen its cutting edge. Otherwise, it will deceive you and throw you into the valley of destruction. Cut off its elements at the root and never let its passions run free.

O God please, we implore You to help us overcome our mind and desires (**nafs**). **"Our Lord, grant us the benefits of a good deed in this world, the reward of a good deed in the hereafter, and protect us eternally from the sufferings of hell-fire."**

«رَبَّنَا آتِنَا فِي الدُّنْيَا حَسَنَةً وَفِي الآخِرَة حَسَنَةً وَقِنَا عَذَابَ النَّارِ»

Chapter 19

Love God Almighty

God Almighty is most worthy of being feared and implored even if He had not created heaven or hell. Obey Him for the sake of His Countenance. Neither His endowments nor chastisements should swerve your focus. Make obedience to His commands your chief objective. Carry out His orders. Abstain from what He forbids and exercise patience with His decree. Repent unto Him. Cry to Him to accept you. Humbly bow before Him and shed the tears of your eyes and those of your heart for His sake. In fact, to cry before God Almighty is an act of worship, and it is an exalted form of humility.

If you die penitent, having good intentions and praiseworthy actions, God Almighty will show you the benefits of it. He will repay your debts and satisfy those whom you have caused injustice, for there is no one who can show mercy, love and compassion towards His obedient servants other than Him. Love God Almighty in this world and in the hereafter. Make His love the most important reality of your life, for that love will benefit you most. Everyone in this world wants you to serve his own purpose, but God Almighty wants you just for your sake.

O ye people! Your carnal selves (**nafs**) are claiming divinity, though you are unaware of it! They are intransigent and arrogant towards God Almighty. They desire to have other than what He chose for them. They love His enemy, the accursed satan, and have no love for God Almighty Himself. They do not consent or have patience with their fate, instead they object to His decree and show dissent. People in such a state have no idea what surrender (**istislām**) is all about. They only bear the name **Islām**, but the title alone is of no benefit to them and its benefits cannot, therefore, flow their way.

Child, maintain that state of reverence and fear of God Almighty and have no hopes until you meet your Lord [عز وجل]

and stand before Him with your body and soul. Only when He places the seal of safety in your hands will you then be safe. In fact, when God Almighty grants you His protection, you will discover and experience His undiminishing wealth and bounty. Once He chooses to safeguard you, then rest in peace, for once He bestows something, He does not take it back.

When God Almighty chooses to bless a servant, He brings him nigh unto Himself and cherishes him. Whenever the awe of reverence overcomes His servant, God Almighty bestows another light upon him that will dissipate his fears, comfort his heart, and his innermost being. Such a gift remains confidential between God Almighty and His servant.

O you ignorant man! You are walking away from your Lord [عَزَّ وَجَلَّ]. Turn your heart back to Him and engage in serving and comforting His creation. The true servants of God Almighty strive hard in serving Him, and make that their sole occupation. As a result, God Almighty draws forth their hearts and places them near unto Him. He makes Himself known to these precious hearts, and they immediately recognize Him as their Lord and Cherisher. When one of them grows to know his Lord; when he wins his inner struggle against his carnal self, passions, karmic habits and satan; when he liberates himself from them and from his own worldly attachments; and when finally God Almighty opens to him the door of His proximity and finds him asking for services to perform, such an intimate servant will be told: "Go back, serve the creation and lead them back to us. Go and serve the students and seekers on the path."

O ye people! You are truly heedless and unaware of what such beings have attained. You labor day and night toiling to serve the demands of your mind and desire (**nafs**). These are your enemies.

Many people give priority to pleasing their wives and children, instead of seeking to please their Lord [عَزَّ وَجَلَّ]. I find that your moves and gestures, intentions and concerns are all directed towards satisfying your own desires and pleasing your wife and children. You surely have not even the slightest idea of who God Almighty really is.

O fool! You cannot even be considered a man. A man whose chivalry and integrity are perfectly matured would labor for no one other than his Lord [عَزَّ وَجَلَّ]. Your heart is blind, the clarity of your innermost being is clouded and you have been veiled from your Lord, though you have no idea of it. This explains why some blessed souls, may God's peace be upon them, said: "*Woe unto the discarded people who are not even aware of being veiled from their Lord* [عَزَّ وَجَلَّ]."

O man, in your bowl of soup there are some chips of broken glass, but because of your gluttony, craving, passionate desires and stinginess, you are gulping everything down without even looking at it. Wait and see! In an hour's time the glass chips will cut through your intestines, and you will begin bleeding to death. All your problems are caused by your separation from your Lord [عَزَّ وَجَلَّ] and your choosing to obey someone else. If you only examine and experience people's qualities, you will be repelled by them. Instead, direct your love towards their Creator [عَزَّ وَجَلَّ]. The Prophet, upon whom be peace, once said: "**Experience the world and you will surely seek sanctuary from it**."

«أُخْبُرْ تَقْلُه»

He meant you will detest it. However, in your case, you still go about loving and hating without discrimination or clarity. It is the brain that discerns, but you do not have one. In reality, it is the heart that experiences and discerns, but still you have no heart. A true heart reflects, contemplates, heeds, obeys and worships God Almighty. God Almighty has said: "**Indeed, in this message there is a reminder for someone who has a heart and listens earnestly as he witnesses**."

«إِنَّ فِى ذلكَ لَذكْرى لِمَنْ كَانَ لَهُ قَلْبٌ
أَوْ أَلْقَى السَّمْعَ وَهُوَ شَهِيدٌ»

Witness here how the power of understanding (**aql**) becomes the heart. The heart (**qalb**) here is transformed into the state of the innermost being (**sirr**), then the latter ceases to exist as an entity and becomes a non-being (**fanā'**). Finally, his annihilation embodies a renewed existence. Adam, upon whom be peace, and the other prophets also had natural innate desires and wishes, but they opposed the intrinsic impulses of their mind, desires and carnal self (**nafs**). Instead, they sought to win the pleasure and blessings of their Lord [عَزَّ وَجَلَّ]. In truth, Adam, upon whom be peace, once had a single desire. He committed a single error, then repented once and for all. He never, ever disobeyed his Lord [عَزَّ وَجَلَّ] again. His new desire then was praiseworthy. His wish was never to part from the proximity of his Lord. The prophets, upon all of them be peace, also kept on opposing their mind and desires (**nafs**), karmic habits and passions until they attained the ranks of the angels from the point of realizing the ultimate truth (**ḥaqiqah**). They succeeded as a result of their endurance, determination and unwavering struggle against their enemies. In such an exemplary way, the prophets, the messengers and their heirs, the **awliyā'**, carried the torch of patience and perseverance. Shouldn't you also follow their example and emulate their patience?

Child, exercise patience when you receive a blow from your enemy. Soon in the hereafter you will exact retribution and return his blow, destroy him and repossess your rightful property again. Then you be knighted by the King and receive His endowment and robe of honor.

Child, strive never to hurt anyone and always endeavor to have good intentions towards everyone, except those whom the Law of **sharī'a** commands you to strike against. In that case, to attack their evil purpose is a rewarding act of worship. However, for the wise ones, the noble and true ones unto God Almighty and His righteous servants, the trumpet of resurrection has already been sounded. They called for the day of judgment (**qiyāmah**) against their own carnal selves (**nafs**). They shunned the doors of the world with their certitude and determination, and then crossed the ultimate bridge (**sirāt**) holding to the staff of their true faith and trust in God's words.

They walked steadily with their hearts until they stood at the gate of paradise. They stopped before entering and said: "We do not eat or drink alone." That is because a gracious person does not eat alone. Thus, they returned to the world, feeling the obligation to serve the people and to admonish them, to call upon them to obey their Lord [عَزَّ وَجَلَّ], and to explain to them about what is awaiting them at the end of their road. These tidings will comfort the believers and lighten their burdens.

When one's faith becomes strong, when one has mastery over his certitude and determination, he will see with his heart everything that God Almighty foretold of the day of reckoning. He will see paradise and hell-fire and what is gathered therein. He will see the trumpet and the angel in charge of sounding it. He will see things as they are. He will see the world and its end. He will see the reversal of the status of its dwellers. He will see the people as wandering coffins and walking graves. Even when he walks by these cemeteries, he will feel what blessings or sufferings each grave is experiencing. He will see the grand gathering and how everything there stands in perfect agreement with God Almighty. He will see the display of God's mercy for the believers and the punishment reserved for the dwellers of hell-fire. He will see the myriads of angels standing erect, and the prophets, the messengers, their deputies and representatives, each standing in his reserved station. He will see the family of believers in paradise visiting one another, and he will see the companions of hell-fire fighting one another. Once one's insight opens thus, he will look with his physical eyes at the world, while the eyes of his heart will see God's doing, moving the creations around or causing them to be motionless.

This is the nature of the blessed insight of God's trustee (*walï*). When he looks at someone, his physical eyes see the outer form, the eyes of his heart see what is hidden, while his innermost being (**sirr**) maintains its focus upon his Lord. One who serves shall be served. He will consent to what the divine decree brings, whether it carries him to the shore or the ocean, to the valley or the mountain, and whether it feeds him sweet or bitter food. He will accept his fate, whether it brings dignity or humiliation, riches or poverty, health or sickness. He willingly and submissively walks through whatever his destiny brings. In that state, should his fate find him tired, it will humbly lower its back to him and let him ride upon it. Thus, his fate becomes his vehicle and serves him when it discovers the station of proximity and honor God Almighty bestowed upon him. All of that honor is the result of one's opposition to the demands of his mind, desire, passions, karmic nature, ill habits, satan and evil companions.

O God, we beseech You to grant us the state of total consent to Thy divine decree and to make us consent to our fate under all circumstances.

"Our Lord, grant us the benefits of a good deed in this world, the reward of a good deed in the hereafter, and protect us eternally from the sufferings of hell-fire."

«رَبَّنَا آتِنَا فِي الدُّنْيَا حَسَنَةً وَفِي الآخِرَةِ حَسَنَةً وَقِنَا عَذَابَ النَّارِ»

❀ ❀ ❀ ❀ ❀

Chapter 20

Words Without Actions

O people of this town. Hypocrisy has spread widely amongst you and sincerity has diminished. There is much talk here but no actions. Words without actions are worthless. They become an indictment on the day of judgment, not an alibi. Words without actions are like a house without a door, rooms or amenities. They are like a solid bar of gold bullion that cannot be spent as petty cash, a claim without proof, a body without a soul, a wooden statue without arms, feet or ability to make an impact. Like this, the majority of your deeds are bodies without souls.

The soul (**rüh**) is sincerity and praising God's Onenness. It is the constancy of practicing the precepts of God's Book and following the leading example of His Messenger, upon whom be peace. Be not heedless, reverse the course of your actions, and you will be on the right track. Follow what you are commanded to do, abstain from what you are forbidden from doing, and consent to God's divine decree. The anesthesia of divine comfort and peace, the joy of being in God's presence, the sight of His beauty and being in His proximity are the true intoxicating drink which is given only to few, rare and select ones amongst God's creations. Such blessed beings do not feel the pain or blows of destiny. The days of adversities pass by while they are not even conscious of them, and their gratitude increases considerably. They thank Him for letting them be captivated by the awe of His proximity and for their nonexistence when difficulties befall them so that they could not object to God's will. Calamities befall such true beings as they befall you. Some exercise patience, while others will be made unaware of them or of having exercised patience therein.

The state of a true being grows step by step. Harm may touch him when his faith is weak and he is still a child. Patience is his recourse when he becomes a youth, consent to God's will when he becomes an adult, and contentment when he reaches God's proximity and looks through his knowledge at his Lord. Consequently when his heart blossoms into a new existence, he has reached the state of annihilation and concealment of one's self. Then his secret has been retained in God's knowledge. This is the stage of visual witnessing (**mushāhada**) and conversing with God Almighty. Inwardly and outwardly he will be annihilated and nonexistent alongside the remainder of the creations, though in God's presence he has a renewed existence. Thereat, he becomes nothing and dissolves (like melting snow). Should it be God's will, He will then renew his existence, and bring him to life again. Should He will it so, He will reassemble his shattered and dismembered being, in the same way He will raise the decomposed bodies of the dead on the day of resurrection. He causes the entirety of His creations to regain their individual bones reassembled, and their own flesh and hair reconstituted, and then commands the Archangel Isrāfeel to reanimate them by blowing their souls back into their respective bodies. This is what happens to the common creations, but as for the true beings, God Almighty reanimates them without an intermediary. One single glance of their Beloved annihilates them and another glance resurrects them.

True love is conditioned by the absence of personal will with one's beloved. It is never to busy oneself away from Him with either world, hereafter, or creations. To love God Almighty is not an easy thing that anyone can claim. How many people pretend to love God Almighty but are distant from truth? And how many have no such pretenses, but in truth do love Him?

O ye people! Never despise any Muslim, for the seeds of God's secrets are planted in such people. Humble yourselves and be not arrogant towards any one of God's creations. Wake up from your slumber. Truly you are oblivious of your state of heedlessness. You act joyfully as though you have received your account from God Almighty, crossed the bridge (**sirāt**) and seen your stations in paradise. What kind of arrogance and self deception is this? Each one amongst you has his share of major sins committed towards God Almighty, and still fails to reflect about them, nor does he repent from them, assuming that they have been forgotten. These abominable sins of yours are inscribed in your individual book of records. They are all dated and timed with perfect accuracy. God Almighty will reckon with whomever He wills, and He punishes whichever minor or major sins He wills.

Wake up, O heedless ones, O ye under the sedation of slumber. Wake up to awareness again and focus your attention on receiving God's mercy. Expose yourselves to His divine compassion. If one's sins and transgressions reach their zenith while he persists in behaving so without shame, repentance or regret, and should he not recognize his faults and further correct himself, he would be asking to be identified as an infidel, a reprobate and a disbeliever, unless he were to hasten to repair the damage done. O people who are a world without a hereafter, a creature who acts as though he has no Creator, who fear nothing but poverty, and hope for nothing but riches.

O man, God Almighty has already divided the sustenance of each one of His creations. Therefore, your share is not going to increase or decrease. It will not reach you sooner nor ever be late. You seem to have doubt about God's guarantee of delivering it, and you insist on going after what is not written in your name. Your covetousness has even deprived you from joining the religious study circles or from receiving any benefits or grace found therein. Your engrossment in business is thus causing you to fear losing some profits or missing a customer if you close your shop to go there and join them.

O fool, who do you think fed you when you were a fetus in the womb of your mother? Instead of trusting Him for all your needs, you continue depending on and trusting your carnal self, your dinārs and pennies, your buying and selling power. You go on placing your trust in other creations and you count on your connection with the governor of your town for personal benefits. Anything you depend on is your god. Anyone you fear and plead with is your god. If you do not realize that God Almighty is the One Who is running the show at the hands of His creations, anyone you place in the position of having the power to bring you benefits or harm is your god.

Soon you will find more about your final destination. Soon God Almighty will deprive you of your hearing and sight. Soon He will abolish your usurpation, seize your properties, deprive you of anything you depend on, disrupt your dealings with the creations, make their hearts hard towards you, make them reproach you and refuse to deal with you. He will censure you, curtail any success you may otherwise attain, and cause your business to bankrupt.

He will occupy you in going door to door without success. He will not give you a bite to eat or an ounce of satisfaction. Even if you were to pray and call upon Him, He will not answer your prayers. All of that is the consequence of associating partners with Him, depending on and trusting in other than Him, asking for His favors from other than Him, and using all of that to disobey Him. I have witnessed these happenings taking effect with the majority of this type of people, and especially the disobedient sinners. Some escape partially by hastening to correct themselves and repent their sins, whereby God Almighty will accept their repentance, look at them with mercy and compassion, and treat them with generosity and subtle kindness.

O creations of Allāh, repent! O learned ones, O theologians, O ascetics and mystics, O slaves of God Almighty, there is no one amongst you who does not need to repent from some type of sin. I have some knowledge about you and about your life and consequences after death. Even if something seems unclear about your beginning, it will certainly be identifiable at the end, when death comes. If some obscurity veiled the source and origin of someone's money, I wait and see after his death. If the inheritance goes to his children, family, the poor people amongst God's creation and serves the interest of the creation at large, I will know that his money came from a lawful source (**halāl**). If the distribution goes to benefit the endowments of the sincere ones in their love for God Almighty (**siddïqïn**) who are His true chosen ones (**khawās**), I will immediately understand that the origin of his money came from his absolute trust in God Almighty (**tawakkul**) and is invariably lawful. I am not with you in your shops and markets, but God Almighty made me understand the way you earn your livelihood through this type of observation, as well as through other vehicles.

Child, beware! Never let God Almighty find in your heart anyone other than Himself. Otherwise He will expose you. Beware! Never let Him see in it fear of anyone but Him, hope in anyone but Him, or love for anyone but Him. O ye people! Purify your hearts in God Almighty and cleanse them from anyone else. Do not think that harm or benefits can originate from other than Him. You are only guests in His house.

Child, the love which you have towards anything considered likable in the eyes of this world is an incomplete love and you shall be chastised for it. The only true love which never changes is the love of God Almighty. That is the love which you can see with the eyes of your heart. That is the love of the sincere ones, the spiritual ones (**ruhaniyyün**), whose love is not the result of their faith only, but a legacy of their eyewitness, certitude and determination. When the veils were lifted to open the sight of their hearts, they saw what is commonly unseen and witnessed a truth they have no power to explain. O God, grant us Your love along with Your pardon and a life of good health.

O ye people! Your shares are placed in trust in this world. They will come to you at such times known to God Almighty. No one can decline from surrendering them to you when the permission to release them comes from the True Owner. These shares laugh at people's faces, pull their legs, make fools of them, and mock anyone who asks for what is not his, or anyone who asks to receive his own share prior to God's decree and permission.

O ye people! If you step away from the door of the world and turn towards God's door, your shares will leave their treasure chest to come out and follow you. Ask God Almighty to grant you the wisdom to understand that. When worldly comforts present themselves before God's representatives (**awliyä'**), God's true friends will say: "You may pass by. Go and deceive someone else, for we know your true worth. We know what you labor for, so fake no glamour before us."

O man, your dinār coin is exaggeratedly adorned, and your ornaments are hung on a hollow wooden statue which has no soul. Truly you are an attraction without significance. The true attraction and significance belong to the hereafter.

Thus, once God's true friends realize the deficiencies of the world, they escape from it. When they discover the disgraceful actions of the people, they distance themselves from them and seek refuge from them. Estranged by such inadequacies, they seek peace and solace in the vastness of the desert and prairies, in the quiet of ruins and caves, and in the company of passing jinns and angels on this earth. Both the angels and the jinns pass by in appearances other than their real forms. Sometimes they manifest in the form of a mystic, a bearded monk, or even a beast. They appear in whatever form they wish. In fact, angels and jinns possess the ability to manifest in any physical form they wish, exactly like the wardrobe in one's home, where he may change his raiment or his shirt as he pleases.

In the beginning of his path, a seeker (**mureed**) who is truthful in his endeavors becomes impatient and nervous about meeting people or listening to even one word from them. He becomes quickly annoyed if he sees even an atom from this world, and he has no heart to see any one amongst God's creation. His heart becomes lost, his mind absent, and his sight glazes as though his eyes were fixed like marbles. He wanders about in such a state until the hand of divine mercy touches the tip of his heart, and only then does quiescence pervade it. He remains intoxicated in such delight until he inhales the fragrance of the proximity of his Lord. Only then does he wake up. Once his understanding of God's Oneness is strong, once his sincerity, acquaintance with his Lord, knowledge and love for God Almighty become whole, he will be endowed with resoluteness and nobility of character. His strength will come from God Almighty, and he will then carry people's burdens without any effort on his part. He will be brought back to their circles, seek their company and serve their interests. Not for even a twinkling of an eye will he be absent from his devotion to his Lord [عَزَّ وَجَلَّ].

A new student on the path of ascetic detachment (**zuhud**) from this world will run away from people, while a perfect mystic who becomes a gnostic has no such concerns. Instead, he calls for them, and never runs away from them. One who knows God Almighty runs away from no one and fears no one but Him. The beginner distances himself from the insolent people and the sinners, while the attained being calls for them. Why would he not call for them when he carries their medicine? That is why someone, God bless his soul, once said: *"Only a true wise man will smile in the face of an insolent sinner."* One whose knowledge of God Almighty is matured to perfection will become a guide who leads the seekers towards their Lord [اعز وجل]. He becomes a fishing net that catches the people and pulls them out of the ocean of this world. Such a person will be granted an awesome strength to conquer the accursed satan and his armies, and to pull the people away from him.

O you who in ignorance have renounced the world, come forth and listen to what I am saying. O ascetics of this earth, come here, demolish your hermitages and come near me. You have retreated to your cells, but without preparation, and you will gain nothing in that way. Come forth and pluck the fruits of wisdom, so that God's mercy encompasses you, too. I do not ask you to come here for my sake, but for your own.

Child, you need to labor hard before you can learn this trade. You need to build its structures then dismantle them one thousand times, over and over, before you can build what is impregnable. Should you die during the process of building, demolishing and rebuilding, then God Almighty will build for you a structure which is imperishable.

O ye people! When will you become wise? When will you understand towards what I am aiming? Look for God's seekers, be industrious in searching for their company. Should you find them, then serve them with your wealth and being. The true seekers have a musky fragrance. They have radiant lights on their faces which are easily recognizable. However, the sickness is in you, in your shortsightedness and poor understanding. You do not know how to discern between the true friend and the atheist, the lawful and the unlawful, the poisonous and the nonpoisonous, the polytheist and the monotheist, the sinner and the devotee, God's seeker and the seeker of the creations. This is your illness. Go and serve the hard laboring gnostic **shaikhs** who practice what they know, so that they may show you things the way they are.

Strive to know God Almighty, for once you get to know Him, you will know about everything besides Him. Know God Almighty, then love Him. If you cannot see Him with your physical eyes, then look at Him with the eyes of your heart. Once you realize that all favors come from Him, you will definitely love Him. The Prophet, upon whom be peace, said: **"You should love Allāh for His favors upon you, and you should love me for the sake of His love for me."**

«أَحِبُّوا اللهَ لِمَا يُغَذِّيكُمْ مِنْ نِعَمِه ، وَأَحِبُّونِي بِحُبِّ اللهِ عَزَّ وَجَلَّ لِي»

O ye people! He is the One Who fed you when you were still a fetus in the womb of your mothers, and He is the One Who nurtured you after you were delivered from it, and from Him comes your health, strength and will. Further on, He favored you to be obedient unto Him, and guided you to submit in **Islām** and be amongst the followers of His Prophet, upon whom be peace. Thus, obeying the Messenger is in part obeying God Almighty Himself, and to thank him and love him is an integral part of one's gratitude and love for God Almighty Himself. Once you realize that all favors come from Him, then no attachment or love for the creation will remain in your heart.

One who truly knows God Almighty, the gnostic who loves Him, who looks at Him with the eyes of his heart and recognizes that good and bad are under God's command will no longer consider them as coming from the people. If they show goodness, he realizes that God Almighty has subjugated them to do so, and if they cause him harm, he understands that the infliction is done by God's decree. In fact, he changes the way he looks at things, and shifts his sight away from the creation to focus on the Creator [عَزَّ وَجَلَّ]. Despite that, he remains loyal to observing the divine laws of **shari'a** and never abrogates their rulings. The heart of a gnostic keeps on rising from one state into another until he becomes irrevocably detached from the creation. His tolerance grows as he turns away from them. His desire for God Almighty increases and his trust and reliance on Him grows stronger. His perception of receiving things from the people changes into receiving them from God Almighty at their hands. His perception and judgment (**'aql**), which are common to all the people, become more balanced and his analytical wisdom becomes endorsed by God Almighty, while another depth of wisdom will be added to his understanding.

O poor miserable man in need of the people. O you who created a deity out of them and associated them with God Almighty. Beware never to die in that state. Should that happen, God Almighty will never open His door to your soul, nor will He look at it, for He will be angry at every polytheist who entrusted his needs to anyone besides Himself. First retreat from your mind, desire, and carnal self (**nafs**), next from the people, then from the world, then from hereafter, and finally from anything other than God Almighty Himself. If you want to be alone with your Lord, be free from your own existence, manipulations and hallucinations.

O insolent one, you sit in your hermitage, though your heart and thoughts go to people's homes. You sit in your hut anticipating that they will come to find you and bring you their gifts. The truth is that you miss their insanity and raving. Truly your life is wasted. You have created an image for yourself which has no meaning. Do not set yourself up to do something for which God Almighty did not qualify you or prepare you for. Otherwise, neither you nor the entire creation could carry that load. When God Almighty wants you for something, He will prepare you for it. However, if you do not have a true inner essence and a heart which is free from everything besides God Almighty, your mere seclusion (**khalwa**) will be of no benefit.

O mighty God, make me earn the benefits of what I am saying, and make them benefit from these words and whatever they understand from them.

"Our Lord, grant us the benefits of a good deed in this world, the reward of a good deed in the hereafter, and protect us eternally from the sufferings of hell-fire."

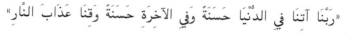

«رَبَّنَا آتِنَا فِي الدُّنْيَا حَسَنَةً وَفِي الآخِرَةِ حَسَنَةً وَقِنَا عَذَابَ النَّارِ»

❀ ❀ ❀ ❀ ❀

Chapter 21

Turning One's Attention Away from the World

The world is a veil from the hereafter. The hereafter is a veil from the Lord and Cherisher of the world and the hereafter. Any created being is a veil from the Creator. Whatever you are attracted to is a veil because of your participation in it. Be not fascinated by the creation, the world, or anything besides God Almighty. Remain thus with an unwavering steadfastness until you reach the door of His proximity, making great strides on the feet of your innermost being and true asceticism, and renouncing anything other than Him. Be denuded from any attachment, bewildered in Him an, being powerless, cry for His help. Implore Him for His support, and carefully contemplate on His preexistent knowledge (**sābiqa**) and decree about you.

Only when your heart and innermost being reach Him and stand before Him, when He raises you nigh unto His proximity, and awards you your station, He then resuscitates your being with the gift of His peace and security, entrusting you with the duty to serve the hearts of others. He grants you the commanding authority over them and makes you the physician in charge of healing such hearts. Only then may you look back towards the people and the world. Your gestures then will be a blessing and kindness towards them, benevolently taking the riches from their hands and redistributing it amongst the poor and needy, including receiving your lawful share. That will be an act of worship, devotion, and blessings for everyone.

The world cannot harm a person who acts in such a correct way. He will be safe from its peculiarities and his share will be purified from the stench of the world's turbidity and sorrows. Deputyship (**wilāya**) has clear signs on the faces of God's friends.

Only those of true discernment can perceive them. Their marks communicate, not their tongues. Let he who desires true success strive towards attaining it with his whole being and wealth and sparing nothing for God's sake. Let him free his heart from the people and the world, just as one pulls a hair from the dough or a bowl of yogurt. Like that, he needs to extricate himself from the hereafter and similarly from anything besides God Almighty.

In that state, each share will be reverently handed to its rightful owner. When one reaches God's door, he will receive his shares from both the world and the hereafter. He will find both of them standing at his feet to pay their homage and to serve him. You should never touch your shares from the world or the hereafter when they are sitting and you are standing. Take them only once you are seated at the door of the King and Master while both are standing on the feet of their servitude, holding your share on a platter over their heads.

This is their custom when serving one who is waiting at God's door. On the other hand, they truly rebuke and humiliate one who awaits at their door. Take your share from them only when you are in a state where your wealth and strength are in God Almighty. The true seekers are satisfied to be bankrupt in this world, and nothing can satisfy them in the hereafter but His proximity. They ask God Almighty for nothing other than Himself. They understood that the distribution of the wealth in this world is already divided, so they abandoned asking for it. They realized that the stations in the hereafter and the bliss in paradise are also allotted, so again they refrained from asking or working for them. They seek nothing except the effulgent light of God's countenance. Even when they enter paradise, they do not open their eyes except to the light of His divine effulgent countenance.

Acquire disinterest in the world and uniqueness of purpose. One whose heart is not disinterested and devoid of the people or mundane forces (**asbāb**) cannot travel the path of the prophets, the sincere ones in their love for God Almighty and the righteous ones, unless he contents himself with little from this world and surrenders the balance of his fate to the hands of divine decree. Do not endanger yourself by desiring much, for that will destroy you, though when plenitude comes from God's hand without your choice, you will be protected.

Al-Hassan Al-Basri, God bless his soul, said: *"Admonish* *people with your knowledge and actions."* O ye preachers, admonish people by purifying your innermost being and heart. Do not advise them by adorning your outer appearance, while hiding insolence and filth. The Almighty Lord inscribed 'Faith' in the hearts of the believers before creating them. This is called pre-existent knowledge (**sābiqa**) and one's deeds should not falter because of it or relying on it. Instead, knowing that, one should strive hard to expose himself to the currents of God's bounty, exert effort to acquire perfect faith and certitude and an unwavering determination remain at His door.

As long as our hearts strive to acquire true faith, perhaps God Almighty will grant it to us without our earning it and with little effort on our part. God Almighty describes Himself with attributes which He accepts to be His. Do you not feel ashamed to merely discuss them, confuse their connotation or refute them? You have not even learned the least knowledge which the blessed companions of the Prophet, upon whom be peace, and their successors practiced before you.

Our Lord [عَزَّ وَجَلَّ] has clearly stated about Himself that He is the sovereign Lord of the divine throne (**'Arsh**). This is exactly how He said it. Accept it as it is without ascription of human characteristics to it (**tashbīh**), or denying the functions of His divine attributes (**ta'atil**) and even without the thought of an embodiment based on human perception of things (**tajsïm**).

O God, grant us Thy Grace. Help us to achieve success and avoid inventions.

"Our Lord, grant us the benefits of a good deed in this world, the reward of a good deed in the hereafter, and protect us eternally from the sufferings of hell-fire."

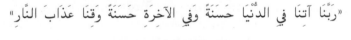

Chapter 22

Extract the Love of the World from Your Heart

Someone asked: *"How do I get the love of the world out of my heart?"*

Our shaikh [رَضِیَ ٱللّٰهُ عَنْهُ] replied: Look at the world. Examine carefully how unsparingly it stirs and turns its patrons and children upside down. See how it tricks them, fools and amuses itself with them, lures them to run after it, and raises their status until they preside over each other. Further on, see how it lets them have control over people's needs and parades its treasures and wonders before their eyes. Once they feel secure and rejoice about their high-ranking position in this world with all the comforts and service it offers them, suddenly the world will strike back at them, deceive them, tie them up and then throw them down from that height to fall and crush their heads, to be shattered into pieces to their destruction. Meanwhile the world will stand beside satan and together they will laugh at them.

This is what the world did to many sultans, kings and rich people amongst the children of Adam, upon whom be peace, and it will continue to do so until the day of reckoning. Thus, with such implements, it will exalt then abase, bring someone forward then push him back, enrich him, impoverish him, lure him to its side, then slaughter him. In fact, only the rarest of mankind will evade its plots, overcome it and never let it conquer him, and only the select few will be helped against it and are protected from its evils. These are the rare ones. One who truly knows the world, one who has experienced it and become vigilant to its cunning and tricks will be saved from its evils.

O questioner. If you look at the defects of the world with the eyes of your heart, you will be able to extract it easily from your heart, but if you see it with your physical eyes, you will be attracted to its glitters and become distracted from discovering its faults. You will not be able to free your heart from it or renounce it. You will become its prey, and it will kill you as it did others.

Wage war against your carnal self (**nafs**) to keep it under control until it becomes content. Once it consents, it will realize the imperfections of this world and naturally renounce it. The sign of its satisfaction is its acceptance and consent to benefit from the wisdom of the heart and the call of one's innermost being. It has to obey them in every respect: do what they command and abstain from what they forbid, be content with what they give and be patient with their restrictions. Once it becomes truly content (**mutma'inna**) it will emerge as part of the innermost heart and find solace therein. It will see the heart crowned with piety and adorned with the garment of proximity.

O ye people! You must have faith and believe in the truth told to you, and ascertain its source. You must stop accusing the true believers of lying. Stop arguing with them. Refrain from challenging their authority, for they are truly kings in this world as well as in the hereafter. Once they attained God's proximity, they also won everything else along with Him. God Almighty has filled their hearts and enriched them with His proximity, comfort and peace in Him, His effulgent lights, and the wealth of His divine favors. These elite amongst God's creations do not care about who has the world in his hand or who is accumulating its treasures. In fact, they do not look at the inception of things but rather at their consequences and disappearance. They place the supreme reality of God Almighty before the eyes of their innermost being. They do not worship Him out of fear of destruction nor in any hope for powers. He created them just for Himself, to remain in His company, "**...and He creates what you do not know of.**" "**He truly does whatever He wills.**"

"وَيَخْلُقُ مَالَا تَعْلَمُونْ" - "فَعَّالٌ لِمَا يُرِيدُ"

A hypocrite lies if he speaks, fails his promise, and betrays his trust. Whoever can be free from these qualities which are described by the Prophet, upon whom be peace, will be free from hypocrisy. In fact, these characteristics are a testing stone and the basis of discerning between a believer and a hypocrite. Thus, use this testing stone, look into this mirror and see the face of your heart. Find out, are you truly a believer or a hypocrite? Are you a monotheist or a polytheist? The world is a fatal attraction and a field of deceptions except for what is taken from it with a good intention to benefit one's life in the hereafter. When one's conduct in this world is carried with a good intention, the world becomes an integral part of the hereafter.

Credit God's favors to Him alone by thanking Him for them. Show your gratitude by clear expressions of it. Gratitude to God Almighty is two things: first, to use His favors in His service and to comfort the needy; and second, to acknowledge through them the One Who bestowed them and to show gratitude to their Grantor, who is the True Sovereign Lord, God Almighty.

Someone, God bless his soul, once said: *"Whatever may engross your thoughts away from God Almighty is ominous."* Meaning, should practicing His remembrance (**zikr**) distract you from focusing on Him, it will become ominous. Your prayers, fasting, pilgrimage to Mecca or any good deed, should they shift your focus away from the True Doer become ominous. If His favors distract you from focusing on Him, they will all turn ominous.

Truly you have met His favors with ingratitude and utter disobedience by turning towards someone else for your needs, and by giving intellectual reasons for every so-called worldly success. Lies and hypocrisy are now ingrained in all of your motions and stillness, form and essence, night and day. Your enemy satan has tricked you and glamorized falsehood and evil doings in your eyes and made them look normal and acceptable. You lie even during your regular prayers. You say: "God is the Greatest," (**Allāhu Akbar**), but you lie, because your heart worships another god.

Anything you call upon is a god. Anything you depend on is your god. Anything you fear is your god. Anyone you implore is your god. Look at yourself. Your heart does not agree with your tongue, and your actions are in conflict with your words. Say: "**Allāhu Akbar**" one thousand times in your heart before you say it even once with your tongue. Are you not ashamed of yourself to say: "There is no god other than Allāh," (**lā-ilāha il-Allāh**), when in truth you worship one thousand deities besides Him? Repent to Him from all your lies.

As for you, O teacher of the prescribed knowledge. Having soothed your mind with wearing the title of '**ālim**, you have memorized the textbook without acting upon it. What benefits can you draw from that? If you dare to say about yourself: "I am a man of knowledge," you would be lying. How can you be comfortable with preaching to others what you yourself do not practice? God Almighty has said: "**Why do you say things which you do not act upon?**"

«لِمَا تَقُولُونَ مَالا تَفْعَلُونْ»

Be warned! You command people to speak the truth, but you lie. You preach to them the worship of one God, while you practice polytheism. You command them to be sincere, while you are an affected hypocrite. You command them to abstain from sinful actions, when you yourself commit them. Truly, shame has disappeared from your eyes. If only you had even an atom of faith, you would be shy before God Almighty. The Prophet, upon whom be peace, said: "**Shyness is a branch of faith.**"

«الحَيَاءُ مِنَ الإِيْمَانْ»

Truly you have no faith, certitude or trustworthiness. You have betrayed knowledge and can no longer be trusted. God Almighty has ordered your name to be inscribed as "Traitor!" I know of no cure for your illness other than true repentance and perseverance in that. One who attains the correct state of belief in God Almighty and His decree will naturally surrender all his interests to Him and attribute to no one else any share in sustaining them.

O man, make no associates with God Almighty out of people or material effects, for they will bind you to their restrictions. However, once a true believer attains a true state of faith and places his entire trust in God Almighty alone, He will shelter and protect him from adversities in every instance. Only then may the believer rise from the state of true faith (**īmān**) to enter the realms of unwavering certitude (**yaqïn**). Then comes the trust of deputyship (**badal**), after that will dawn the state of invisible guardianship (**ghaibiyya**), and perhaps at the end he will become a pillar of inner and outer knowledge, a leader amongst mankind (**qutb**).

God Almighty will be proud of him in that state before all the creations, the human beings, the jinns, the angels and the luminous souls. He will exalt him, bring him nigh unto Himself, raise the status of his appointments and make him a leader of His creations. He will enrich him, strengthen him, love him, and make him a beloved of His creations. The basis of all of that, from its inception, is to believe in God Almighty and His messengers and to attest to the truth of their message. First is **Islām**, then comes **ïmān**, then acting according to God's Book and adherence to the norms of the **sharïʻa** of His Messenger, upon whom be peace.

Next is sincerity in one's deeds and actions together with a heart filled with glorification of God's Oneness (**tawḥïd**), when one's faith is perfected. A true believer is devoid of himself, oblivious of his own deeds or of anything besides God Almighty. He becomes detached from his performances. In a long struggle, being on God's side, he carries on his striving against his carnal self, mind, desire, and associating with the creations until God Almighty guides him unto His path. God Almighty has said: "**And those who struggle for Our sake, We surely shall guide them unto our path**."

«وَالَّذِيْنَ جَاهَدُوا فِيْنَا لَنَهْدِيَنَّهُمْ سُبُلَنَا»

O ye people! Become detached from all things and be solely content with His management of all affairs. God Almighty will leave those who agree to that to the hands of divine decree (**qadar**) and when they consent to His will, He will then raise them and cherish them from the fountain of His divine omnipotence (**qudra**). Blessed is he who consents to God's decree, awaits the doings of the Doer, acts in compliance with His decree, walks the path fulfilling His commands, and does not deny the blessings contained within one's destiny. The signs indicating His blessings are the mercy of being near unto Him, sole satisfaction in Him, and being free from any need of His creation. Once the heart of the true servant reaches the proximity of His Lord, Cherisher and Sustainer, He will bestow upon him the satisfaction of being wealthy in Him alone. He will raise him nigh unto Himself, establish him in his rank, appoint him to his duty, and say unto him: "**Be assured that on this day your rank is rightly high in Our presence and your trust is safe**."

«إِنَّكَ الْيَوْمَ لَدَيْنَا مَكِيْنٌ أَمِيْنٌ»

Then God Almighty will appoint him to be His viceregent over His kingdom, just as He appointed Egypt's sire Joseph, upon whom be peace, and commissioned him to rule over that kingdom, its palaces, subjects and resources, and made him its treasury minister as the trustee of God's vault. Such is the heart of man, once it becomes genuinely true, purified from everything and dedicated to no one besides God Almighty. Once it is filled with truth, clarity and nobility, God Almighty will make him influential over the hearts of the people. He will grant him an exalted rank and establish his station throughout His kingdom, both in this world as well as the hereafter, to become the cornerstone, the pillar, and the focus (**ka'ba**) of seekers and travelers on the path.

Now, the way to such success is true knowledge and an active commitment to the prescribed norms of religion. Do not get used to being out of work, being lazy or falling short in fulfilling God's commands, for He will afflict you with trials as a punishment. The Prophet, upon whom be peace, said: "**If the servant neglects his prescribed duties, God Almighty will try him with worries and stress as a punishment**."

«إِذَا قَصَّرَ الْعَبْدُ فِى الْعَمَلِ ابْتَلاهُ اللهُ عَزَّ وَجَلَّ بِالْهَمِّ»

It means, He will inflict him with burdens that do not belong to his share; that is, the misconduct of one's children, harm caused by the family, business losses, disobedience of one's children, arguments with one's wife. Wherever he turns there will be problems as a consequence of one's neglecting one's basic obligations (**farā'idh**) towards God Almighty and concentrating one's focus upon the success of his relationships with people and advancement in this world. God Almighty has said: "**What would God gain by your punishment, if only you were grateful and had faith. Nay, it is God that recognizes (all good), and knows all things**."

«مَايَفْعَلُ اللهُ بِعَذَابِكُمْ إِنْ شَكَرْتُمْ وَآمَنْتُمْ»

It is incorrect as well as impermissible for one to excuse himself by arguing that the consequences of something he failed to do is God's will and decree. He alone disposes of everything and He alone has command over all things. "**He is not to be questioned about what He does, though they are subject to His questioning**."

«لايُسْأَلُ عَمَّا يَفْعَلُ وَهُمْ يُسْأَلُونْ»

O man, how long will your selfish concerns about satisfying your mind, desire (**nafs**) and family keep you from serving the

Almighty Lord? Someone, God bless his soul, once said: *"Once your child learns how to pick pebbles and collect them then you may shift the focus of your duties away from him and concern yourself with your duties towards your Lord."* He meant that once your child understands that pebbles are useful for something and are worth something, he would have learned how to labor and earn for himself. Therefore waste not your life striving for him, for he no longer needs you.

Teach your children a craft and become free to pursue your servitude and worship of your Lord, for your family and children can be of no avail to you and are no excuse on the day of questioning. Teach yourself, family and children how to be content with little, then all together focus on fulfilling your Lord's commands. Should it be written in your destiny to have wealth, then it will come to you in its own time as decreed by God Almighty, and you will clearly understand that it is His gift. You will then become free from associating the Source with the creations. On the other hand, should the divine decree ordain otherwise, your unattachment to the world, abstinence and contentment will be your satisfaction and wealth.

For a believer who possesses such contentment, should he be in need of something from this world, he will enter and stand before his Lord on the feet of his needs. Humble, imploring and repenting, he will ask His Lord to grant His favors. Should God Almighty satisfy his wishes, this will increase his gratitude and thankfulness, but should he be denied his request, he will agree with such denial and exercise patience with God's decree without ever objecting or arguing against His will.

Such a believer does not nurture affectation, hypocrisy, hidden intentions, or utilize his religion as an instrument to become wealthy, as you do, O hypocrite. In fact, affectation, hypocrisy and sinful actions are the direct causes that bring about poverty, humiliation and rejection when asking at God's door. A hypocrite and a deceitful person earns his livelihood through religious claims and by wearing the garb of righteous people, without any qualifications. He repeats their words and wears their garb, but does not practice their actions. He claims to belong to their lineage, but that also is not true.

O man, your proclamation of "**lā ilāha il-Allāh,**" (*There is no god other than Allāh*), is just a claim, and reliance upon Him, trust in Him and renunciation of everything other than Him is the only proof of such a claim. O liars, speak the truth. O slaves who have run away from your Lord, return to Him. Seek with your hearts the gate of God's proximity, make peace with Him and truly apologize to Him.

Child, once you attain the state of pure faith, you take your lawful share from the world in full accordance with the laws of **shari'a**. Once you rise to the station of deputyship, you receive your share from God's own hand, with their testimony, meaning the testimony of the Qur'ān and the leading example (**sunnah**) of the Prophet, upon whom be peace. However, at the station of deputyship and the pillar (**qutb**), you take your share by God's doing and entrust all matters back unto Him.

Child, do you not feel ashamed of yourself? You had better cry for your sake. You have been deprived from the blessings of making the right decision or attaining success. Do you not feel ashamed of yourself for being obedient one day then disobedient the next? Sincerely devoted for today, then polytheistic on the next? The Prophet, upon whom be peace, said: **"One whose earnings were equal for two days is defrauded, while one whose earnings of yesterday were better than the morrow is deprived."**

"مَنِ اسْتَوَى يَوْمَاهُ فَهُوَ مَغْبُونٌ - وَمَنْ كَانَ أَمْسُهُ خَيْراً مِنْ يَوْمِهِ فَهُوَ مَحْرُومٌ"

Child, nothing would happen if it were dependent on you. Although you cannot succeed by yourself alone, you still must make the effort. Strive, and the bounty of your Lord [عَزَّ وَجَلَّ] will surely come. Just move your arms and feet while swimming in this ocean and let the currents and waves carry you along and deliver you to the shore.

Prayers come from you and the answer comes from God. The efforts come from you and the success comes from Him. Abstinence comes from you and the protection comes from Him. Be truthful with your heart and He will show you the gate of His proximity. There you will find the hand of His mercy extended towards you, and His kindness, generosity and love yearning for you. This is the ultimate goal of the true believers.

O slaves of your mind, desires (**nafs**) karma, passions, lust and satan. What can I do with people such as you? Herein, I have nothing but reality within reality, truth within truth, a kernel within the core, clarity within clarity, severing one attachment and connecting another. That is, sever all attachments to anything besides God Almighty and to connect oneself exclusively to Him. I refuse to accept anything from you.

O ye hypocrites, impostors and liars. I do not shy away from your masks. How could I shy away from you when you do not shy away from your own Lord and Sustainer, and instead act before Him with belligerence, impudence and contempt? You take lightly your being under His gaze, in His presence and in that of His angels in charge of you in this world. I have a truthfulness which is as sharp as a sword and with it I cut off the head of every infidel, reprobate, hypocrite and liar who does not repent and return to his Lord on the feet of repentance and remorse.

Someone, God bless his soul, once said: *"Truth is the sword of God Almighty on earth. Whatever its sharp edge falls on, it severs."*

O ye people! Accept what I am telling you. I am only advising and warning you. I am only calling upon you for your own sake. I am dead to you and your world, but alive in God's presence. He who believes me in this fellowship (**suhba**) will benefit and succeed, and one who belies me and lies while in my company will be chastised and deprived of benefits, now and later.

One of the leading first steps to know God Almighty is to refrain from disputing His truth, arguing about His decree or objecting to His will. Instead, one must consent and find satisfaction in His management of all affairs. That is why **Mālik Ibn Dinār**, God bless his soul, once said to some of his disciples: *"If you want to acquire true knowledge of God Almighty, then consent to His management and planning. Make not your mind and desire, passion, karma or will associates to Him."*

O ye people of healthy body, and weak in duty. What a great loss you have incurred with your Lord. If only you let your hearts look and see what they missed, you will be filled with regret and sorrow. Wake up!

Hear me O ye people! Soon you are going to face death. Therefore, now is the time to cry for yourselves, before others stand and cry at your graves. You have created a multitude of sins which are crowded at the exit of a dark outcome that is awaiting you. Your hearts are diseased with love for this world and attachment to it. Its cure is to abstain from it all and discard it, then aim at reaching the proximity of your Lord. The safety of your religion is your capital, and your good deeds are its profits. Stop asking for what oppresses you and content yourselves with what suffices you. A wise man rejoices at nothing. His lawful earnings (**ḥalāl**) are accountable and unlawful earnings (**ḥarām**) are punishable. Most of you have forgotten about the end and the reckoning.

Child, if some worldly substance comes to you and you find that your heart is disgusted by it, then immediately discard it. However, you do not even have a heart. You are a mixture of mind, desire (**nafs**), karma and passions. Go to every length to search for and find those who have hearts. Remain in their company so you may acquire a heart. You need a wise **shaikh** who lives and acts in accordance with God's rulings (**ḥukum**). He will teach you, train you and advise you.

O you who have sold everything for nothing, bought what is worthless and paid everything for it. You have bought the world and paid the hereafter as the price. You have sold the hereafter and acquired the world for that price. You are the product of confusion within confusion, nonsense within nonsense, and ignorance within ignorance. You eat like cattle without discrimination, consideration or examination of what you eat. You eat without placing the proper intention: "In the Name of God", (**bismillāh**), without being commanded to eat, and without the pangs of hunger. A true believer eats what is permissible and in accordance with the laws of **shari'a**. An intimate friend of God Almighty (**wali**) will in his own heart be ordered to eat or not to eat. A deputy representative (**badal**) has no such concerns as he acts within the overwhelming presence of His Lord, being totally absorbed and annihilated therein. Thus, the intimate friend of God Almighty strictly fulfills the commands as required. The choices of the deputy representative are stripped away from him, while he observes all the rules of the divine laws. As to one who has utterly annihilated himself and his ego and extinguished their attachment to the creations, he complies with the boundaries of the divine commands (**shari'a**), then cries out in the ocean of divine omnipotence for God's help. One moment he surges up by a wave, then down by another. One moment he emerges on the shore, in the next a clamor draws him back into the deep of the ocean. His state becomes like that of the companions of the cave (**ahlul-kahf**) concerning whom God Almighty has said: "**And We turn them towards the right and the left**."

They were asleep and had no active brain to use, no power of planning and no senses. Both inwardly and outwardly they had closed their eyes, resting in the abode of divine gentleness, kindness and proximity to God Almighty. Likewise, one who is brought nigh unto his Lord will definitely close the eyes of his heart to see no one but his Lord. He looks at no one but his Lord, sees nothing but through Him and hearkens to no one but Him.

Our Lord, make us die to everything besides Thee, and let us exist only in Thee.

«رَبَّنَا آتِنَا فِي الدُّنْيَا حَسَنَةً وَفِي الآخِرَةِ حَسَنَةً وَقِنَا عَذَابَ النَّارِ»

"Our Lord, grant us the benefits of a good deed in this world, the reward of a good deed in the hereafter, and protect us eternally from the sufferings of hell-fire."

❋ ❋ ❋ ❋ ❋

Chapter 23

Polishing One's Heart from Corrosion

The Prophet, upon whom be peace, said: **"These hearts are subject to corrosion; to polish them, one should regularly read the Qur'ān, remember death and join the circles of zikr."**

«إِنَّ هذه ٱلقُلُوبَ لَتَصْدَأُ، وَإِنَّ جَلَاءَهَا قِرَاءَةُ القُرْآنِ
وَذِكْرُ المَوْتِ وَحُضُورُ مَجَالِسَ الذِّكْرِ»

One's heart can become corroded. Should one adopt the solutions prescribed by the Prophet, upon whom be peace, his heart will be protected; otherwise, it will turn black. It will darken because it is veiled from the light. It will be blackened because of his love for the world, his possessiveness and attachment to the world, and its being bereft of any shyness or fear of God Almighty. Once the love of the world controls the heart of a person, his shyness from the observation of God Almighty dissipates as he amasses from the world whatever he can, whether it is permissible (**halāl**) or forbidden (**harām**). He loses his sense of descernment, drops his veil of shyness from his Lord and becomes inured to being fully observed by Him.

O ye people! Accept what our Prophet taught, and polish your hearts with the solution that he prescribed. If one of you has an illness and his doctor prescribes a specific medicine for it, he will have no peace until he procures the prescription and uses it. Thus, observe and contemplate the way of your Lord, both in public and in private. Hold Him in your mind's eye as though you were seeing Him, but if you cannot see Him, always know that He is seeing you.

One who incessantly invokes God Almighty in his heart truly remembers Him (**zākir**), but one who disdains to constantly invoke God in his heart is not remembering Him. The tongue is the servant of the heart and naturally follows it. Frequent the circles of the righteous ones and strive to heed their advice. When the heart does not regularly hear good advice, it becomes blind. True repentance is to revere and glorify God's commands under all conditions. That is why someone, God bless his soul, once said: *"In a few words: Grace is to revere God's commands and to have compassion towards His creations."* One who fails to glorify God's commands and have compassion towards His creation is distant from his Lord.

Once God Almighty revealed to Moses, upon whom be peace: **"Have mercy towards others, so I may show you mercy, for I am the merciful Lord. For one who exhibits mercy, I will show him mercy and admit him into My paradise."** Thus, blessed are the merciful and compassionate.

O ye people! You wasted your life arguing over who ate what, who drank what, what style of clothing each person wore, and how much wealth each one amassed. What a waste. If one wishes for success in his life, let him patiently control his mind and his desire. Let him deprive his carnal self (**nafs**) from the unlawful, the dubious, and all forms of passion. Let him exercise patience and, with steadfastness, obey God's commands, fulfill his obligatory duties, abstain from what is forbidden, and consent to the divine decree.

True believers exercised patience with their Lord and could not bear to be away from Him. They maintained patience in adversity for His sake, and by His decree. They were patient in order to attain His company. They pleaded with Him for permission to reach His proximity. They abandoned the abode of their carnal self (**nafs**), mind and desire, passions, karma and habits. They took the law of **shari'a** for a companion as they walked on the straight path to their Lord. On their way, they faced tremendous trials and plagues, difficulties and stress, disasters, grief, hunger and thirst, deprivation, humiliation and abuses. Yet they did not waver from their determination to walk this road or keeping their focus on the ultimate goal. They walked with certitude, without breaking the rhythm of their march. They continued to advance on their path until they reached the full realization of their own heart and being.

O ye people! Strive hard towards meeting your Lord and shy

from Him now and before meeting Him tomorrow. A believer will shy first from God Almighty, then from His creation, with the exception of something which is offensive to God's chosen way of life (**deen**) for mankind, His religion. In that case, it will not be permissible to be shy. If you recognize an act which is offensive to God's religion, then it is lawful to be forward and unstinting in establishing God's rules and in abiding by His command. God Almighty has said: "**Do not let compassion move you in favor of their case when it comes to God's religion.**"

«وَلَا تَأْخُذْكُمْ بِهِمَا رَأَفَةٌ فِى دِيْنِ اللّٰه»

To one who truly follows God's Messenger, upon whom be peace, the Prophet will happily hand over his own coat of mail and helmet. He will adorn him with his own sword, beautify him with his exalted qualities, behavior and moral conduct, and honor him with one of his own mantles. In fact, God's blessed Messenger will greatly rejoice when meeting one of his followers. He will praise God Almighty for granting him such a blessed gift, and he will make him his representative amongst his followers, a deputy and a clarion call to the door of God Almighty.

God's blessed Messenger was himself once the caller and guide. When God Almighty took him back, He appointed some of his followers to represent him and be his viceregents (**khulafā'**). These are rare people; only one out of a million reaches that state. They guide the people and bear patiently with them while constantly admonishing them. They will even smile in the faces of the hypocrites and insolent people, and will even trick them in every possible way to liberate them from their entanglements and carry them back to their Lord. That is why someone, God bless his soul, once said: *"Only a true knower of God Almighty ('**ārif**) would smile in the face of an insolent sinner."* He shows no sign of what he truly knows about the other person, though he can see the scattered ruins of that person's religion, the darkness covering his heart, his rancor and turbidity. All that happens while the sinners and hypocrites both think that their qualities go undiscovered and cannot be recognized. Nay, they have no dignity, nor are they veiled to his sight. He is surely capable of recognizing them in one glance, one word and one gesture. He, no doubt, knows them in his innermost heart as well as with his physical senses.

O poor unfortunate ones, do you think you can hide yourselves while in front of the true and righteous friends, the gnostic and wise servants of God Almighty? When will you stop wasting your life in nothingness? O ye lost people! Seek and find someone who can guide you back onto the path of the hereafter. God is the Greatest. I call upon God's glorious name (**Allāhu Akbar**). O you dead at heart, O polytheists who attribute power to worldly subjects. O ye idol worshipers. O you who worship the idols of your own will and strength, worldly titles and riches, the kings of the land and their final destinations. These are veils from God Almighty. Anyone who sees harm or benefit as coming from other than God Almighty is not His worshiper, but a slave of the idol that he seeks and to which he attributes power. Such a person dwells today in the fire of disgust and separation, and tomorrow he will inhabit the hell-fire of **jahannam**. Only the pious ones, the monotheists, the sincere ones and the penitents will be saved from the fire of hell.

O ye people! Repent with your hearts before you do so with your tongue. True repentance is to radically alter the course of one's state of being. You reform the state of your mind and desire, passion, satan and connection to your evil companions. When you repent, you reverse your condition and begin to heal the illnesses of your hearing, sight, tongue, heart and all your senses. You cleanse your food and water to avoid the sufferings associated with suspicious and unlawful food and drink. Repentance helps you to be pious and lead a righteous life in focusing your entire intention on your Lord. It abolishes the common habits and replaces them with devotion and worship. It eradicates your sins and disobedience and it helps you obey your Lord. Then you will recognize the state of the ultimate truth (**haqïqa**), and correctly observe the divine laws of **sharï'a**, and they will witness to that, because: "Any 'truth' (**haqïqa**)which is not supported by the laws of **sharï'a** is atheism."

«كُلُّ حَقِيْقَة لَا تَشْهَدُ بِهَا الشَّرِيْعَةُ فَهِيَ زِنْدَقَة»

When you reach that state, your reprehensible thoughts and darkness of character will die away. You will attribute no power to people, but instead you will be shown that everything is exclusively under God's control. Once you understand that, you will win God's protection outwardly and inwardly, while your innermost being will be occupied with your Lord. Once you reach that state, even if the entire treasures of this world fall into your lap and become yours, even if the entire creation from the first to the last follows you, none of this can harm you, change you or turn you away from the gate of your Lord. You will be constantly with Him, solely intending Him and focusing your entire being with great reverence on His divine majesty (**Jalāl**)and beauty (**Jamāl**). When you contemplate His majesty, you are shattered, when you contemplate His beauty, you are again made whole. When you see His divine majesty, you are seized by fear, and when you see His divine beauty, you hope. You are annihilated at the sight of His majesty, and regain your existence and stability at the glorious sight of His beauty. Blessed is he who tastes this food.

Our Lord, we beseech You to sustain us with the food of Your proximity. Quench our thirst with the comfort of your presence .

"Our Lord, grant us the benefits of a good deed in this world, the reward of a good deed in the hereafter, and protect us eternally from the sufferings of hell-fire."

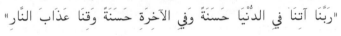

«رَبَّنَا آتِنَا فِي الدُّنْيَا حَسَنَةً وَفِي الآخِرَةِ حَسَنَةً وَقِنَا عَذَابَ النَّارِ»

Chapter 24

Abstain from Associating any Partner with God in His Rule

Do not claim a share in God's ruling and knowledge of your carnal self (**nafs**), passion and karmic nature. Fear His retribution regarding yourself and others. Someone, God bless his soul, once said: *"Agree with God Almighty concerning His creations, but do not agree with their personal opinions about God."* Whoever is condemned is condemned, and whoever is restored is restored. Learn from God's righteous and consenting servants how to agree with Him.

Knowledge was revealed to be put into action, not just for memorization or for preaching to people. Learn and act accordingly, then teach others. When you learn and duly subscribe to the knowledge you have acquired, it will speak for you. If you resolve to remain silent, then speak with the tongue of actions rather than the tongue of knowledge. That is why someone, God bless his soul, said: *"If you cannot draw benefit from observing someone, then you cannot benefit from his advice."* One whose actions conform to his knowledge can benefit himself and others.

O ye people! I only speak because God Almighty causes me to speak His will according to the state of the people present. That is why I speak. Otherwise, there would be animosity between me and you because of your state. However, I spare no expense for your sake. All my wealth is for you, nothing is left for me. If I had something, I would not deprive you of it. Between me and you there is nothing but good advice. I advise you for God's sake, not mine.

Child, consent to the divine decree, otherwise it will crush you. Willingly walk with it and follow its choices, otherwise it will cut you down. Sit submissively before it until it shows mercy and carries you on its back.

The believers commence on the path by working to earn their basic needs from the world, following the rules of **shari'a**. Once their physical bodies become debilitated and they can no longer earn for themselves, as their trust in God Almighty grows strong, that trust will become a seal of protection around their hearts and tie up their might and will. At that point their shares from this world will be brought to them blessed and rewarding, without effort or fatigue on their part. Even the garment of bliss worn in paradise by the intimate ones will be given without their will. They consent to God's choices in that too, as they did in accepting their share in the world, God Almighty delivers to them their shares in the world and in the hereafter, for He is just towards His servants.

Child, your reward is relative to your efforts. The farther you carry your heart away from anything besides God Almighty, the closer you will be to Him. Be dead to yourself and the creation and you will have lifted the veils of separation between you and your Lord.

(Someone asked: *"How do I die?"* Our Shaikh [رَضِىَ ٱللّٰهُ عَنْهُ] replied): Cease following your mind, desire, carnal self (**nafs**), passions, karma, and common habits. Abstain from seeking the people, desiring what they have or asking them for alms. Give up on them, and stop associating them with God's will in the giving or withholding. Ask nothing from anyone besides God Almighty. Let all your deeds be done for God's sake and for the pleasure of His divine countenance, not for the sake of reward or favor. Accept His management, judgment and doing. When you do so, you will be dead to yourself, but alive in Him. Your heart will become His abode. He turns it as He pleases, and your heart will be transferred to the **Ka'aba** of His proximity. You will hold fast to its covering cloth (**sitra**), always remembering Him, praising Him, and forgetting about anything else. Today, the key to paradise is the proclamation:

"Lā ilāha il-Allāh, Muhammadur-Rasül Allāh"
(There is no god but Allāh,
Muhammad is the Messenger of Allāh)

Tomorrow, the key to paradise is to die to your carnal self and anything besides Him, while observing the boundaries of the divine laws (**shari'a**). Proximity to God Almighty is the paradise of the true believers and distance from Him is their hell. They seek no other paradise and fear no other hell.

What rancor would the fire of hell have towards them? It is the hell-fire that calls for help and runs away when it sees a believer. Then how could it not run away from those sincere ones who truly love God? What a beautiful state a believer dwells in, both in this world and the hereafter! In this world he concerns himself about nothing as long as he knows that his Lord is pleased with him. Wherever he goes, he finds his share awaiting him, and he is pleased. Wherever he turns, he sees with God's light. For him, there is no darkness. All his expressions point towards God Almighty, all his dependence is on Him, and his entire trust is in Him.

O ye people! Beware never to hurt a believer, for that is like injecting poison into one's own body and is the immediate cause of one's impoverishment and suffering as a punishment. O foolish ones, ignorant of who God Almighty is and who His intimate ones are, never, and ever try the bitter taste of backbiting them. That is a lethal poison. It will be to your own peril. Never, ever, ever and never cross this road with an evil intention towards any of the believers, for they have a Protector and a jealous Guardian Who loves them. O hypocrite. The voucher of hypocrisy is hanging like a necklace around your heart, and it is permeating your entire being, inside and out. Invoke God's Oneness and sole sovereignty with sincerity, and your illness will be cured and your fetters removed.

O ye people! How often do you violate the rules of **sharī'a**, shred to pieces the armor of your piety, unravel the garment of your beliefs, turn off the light of your faith, and make yourselves abhorred and detested by your Lord? You do it so often, with every action and move. Should one of you succeed at doing an act of obedience to God Almighty, his act will be tainted with pride, love of recognition, and seeking praises. If anyone amongst you wants to worship God Almighty, let him withdraw from people, for their observance of his act nullifies it. The Prophet, upon whom be peace, said: "**Retreats are an act of worship. Practice them, for they were one of the great endeavors of the righteous ones before you.**"

«عَلَيْكُمْ بِالْعُزْلَةِ فَإِنَّهَا عِبَادَةٌ، وَإِنَّهَا دَأْبُ الصَّالِحِيْنَ مِنْ قَبْلِكُمْ»

You must have faith first, then certitude. Let your carnal self die and exist sustained only by God Almighty, not dependent on yourself or others. Do so with full adherence to the law of **shari'a**, in a way which is pleasing to God's Messenger, upon whom be peace. Do it to the full satisfaction of the glorious Qur'an, the eternally recited, heard and read revelation. There is no truth to anyone who says otherwise. What is inscribed on the pages of the Book and the Preserved Tablet are the words of God Almighty. One end of the scroll is in His Hand and the other end is in ours. You must take refuge in God Almighty, sacrifice everything for His sake, devote your entire life to Him, and hold tight to His rope. He alone can suffice all your needs both in this world and the hereafter, protect you in life and death, and defend you in every step.

Thus, work for this arable land and disregard that sterile wasteland. Serve God's Book and it will serve you. Let God's Book hold your heart, bring it before its Lord, and help you act according to it. In fact, to comply with God's Book will feather the two wings of your heart and when they reach full plumage, your heart will be able to fly with those wings to its Lord.

O you who wear the woolen garb of a sufi. First, cloak your innermost being. Then cloak your heart, and then your carnal self (**nafs**). Only after that may you put it over your shoulders. Ascetic detachment (**zuhud**) starts from the inner, not from the outer. Once the innermost essence (**sirr**) is purified, that purity will permeate the heart, the carnal self (**nafs**), the senses, the body, the food, and the garment. The effect of the purified essence will pervade every aspect of your life. First, build the inside of your house. Once that is completed, then go out and build the door. Nothing can manifest (**zhahir**) without an essence (**batin**), nor could the creations come to existence without a Creator. No door will stand by itself in the open without a house to enter, and no lock is put on the gates of a ruin.

O ye people! O ye world without the hereafter. O ye creations who think they exist without a Creator. O man, all that you have gathered will be of no benefit to you on the day of reckoning. Instead, it will surely harm you. That merchandise which you have collected herein cannot be bartered there. Once you reach the hereafter, you will find that your collection of falsehood, hypocrisy, sins and disobedience cannot be used to defraud people in the market of the hereafter.

Ah! First, correct your own **Islām**, then stretch your hand to receive your lawful share. The word **Islām** is a derivative from the word **istislām** which means an unconditional surrender to God Almighty. That is to accept that the reigns of supreme command (**amr**) are in the hands of God Almighty Himself. You submit yourself to Him, depend totally on Him, and forget about your own will and power. Surrender everything you have to Him and spend it all on His path and in obedience to His commands. Perform your duties, surrender them to Him and then forget about them. However, now all your deeds resemble a hollow nut shell. Any deed which is void of sincerity is like a hollow nut shell, a husk without a kernel, a discarded scrap of wood, a corpse without a soul, a picture without meaning. That is the work of hypocrites.

Child, the entire creation is like a machine, and God Almighty is the Maker and Operator. He alone disposes of its affairs as He pleases. Whoever understands this will be able to extricate himself from his entanglements in it and recognize the true Operator. The search and pursuit of one's interests with the creation will become odious, repulsive, self-imposing and stressful, while cognizance and pursuit of one's benefits with the Creator will bring joy, comfort and blessings. You have drifted away from the path of your predecessors, and there is no true common lineage between you and them. You have satisfied yourself with your personal opinions and you did not possess the tolerance to have a teacher advise you, instruct you and polish your conduct. O you who have deprived yourself from the benefits of the path and excluded yourself from it! You have become a toy in the hands of the satans of men and jinns. O slave of mind and desire, passion and karmic habits! O fool, what an unfortunate one you are. Now that you are dumbstruck, wake up and cry out for God's help. Get back to Him and walk on the feet of regret, sorrow and apologies. Let Him free you from the hands of your enemies and rescue you from the uproar of the ocean of your own destruction. Just reflect a little about the consequences of what you are in presently and then it will be much easier for you to discard it. For now, you are just hiding under the dark shade of the tree of slumber. Just come out from under it and you will see the sunlight by which you can recognize the road and walk the path of light again. The tree of slumber grows with the water of ignorance. The tree of vigilance is nurtured with the water of contemplation. The tree of repentance is grown with the water of regret, and the tree of love is grown with the water of consent.

Child, when you were a boy and later a young man, you might have had some excuse. However, now that you have reached nearly forty years of age or more, why do you still play boy's games? What excuses do you have? Beware not to mix with ignorant people or take them for companions, and stay not alone in secret with women or boys. Stay in the company of pious shaikhs and escape at any price from the company of ignorant young men. As a general rule, step aside from the path of the people. If any of them come to you, be to them like a physician treating a patient. Be to the people like a compassionate father with his children, and increasingly devote your life to obeying God Almighty, for obedience to God's commands is true remembrance **(zikr)**.

The Prophet, upon whom be peace, said: "**One who obeys God Almighty has remembered Him, even if his (auxiliary) prayers, fasting and reading of the Qur'ān grow less; while one who disobeys God Almighty would have forgotten about Him, even if his (supererogatory) prayers, fasting and reading of the Qur'ān increase.**"

«مَنْ أَطَاعَ اللّٰهَ عَزَّ وَجَلَّ فَقَدْ ذَكَرَهُ وَإِنْ قَلَّتْ صَلَاتُهُ وَصِيَامُهُ
وَقِرَاءَتُهُ الْقُرْآنَ، وَمَنْ عَصَاهُ فَقَدْ نَسِيَهُ وَإِنْ كَثُرَت
صَلَاتُهُ وَصِيَامُهُ وَقِرَاءَتُهُ الْقُرْآنَ »

A believer, by nature, obeys his Lord, consents to His will, and exercises patience with Him. He freely accepts his lot, sustenance, clothing, and is acquiescent with all the divine doings. But a hypocrite cares for none of that.

Child, constantly examine your state of being and question yourself concerning any false claims. You are neither truthful nor friendly. Neither are you a true lover nor a consenting servant. Neither are you a consenting soul nor a gnostic. You falsely claim to know God Almighty. Tell me, what are the signs of knowing Him? What manifestations of divine wisdom and light does your heart receive? Tell me, what are the signs of His intimate friends, His deputies and His prophets? Do you think that whoever lays claim to something will receive it without being required to submit proof thereof? Do you think that his coin is not subject to verification on the stone of truth? One of the many qualities of a true gnostic (**'ārif billāh**) of God Almighty is that he will be patient under all circumstances and agree with all of God's rulings, judgments and measures, whether they affect him, his family or the rest of God's creations.

Child, love for God Almighty cannot coexist with love for anyone else in one heart. God Almighty has said: "**God did not embody any man with two hearts**."

«مَا جَعَلَ اللّٰهُ لِرَجُلٍ مِنْ قَلْبَيْنِ فِى جَوْفِهِ»

The world and the hereafter do not mix. The Creator and the creation do not mix. Thus, discard what is perishable in order for you to attain the imperishable. Strive with your soul and wealth for God's sake so that you may attain paradise. God Almighty has said: "**Verily, Allāh has bought from the believers their person and wealth in return for the garden of paradise**."

«إِنَّ اللّٰهَ اشْتَرَى مِنَ الْمُؤْمِنِينَ أَنْفُسَهُمْ
وَأَمْوَالَهُمْ بِأَنَّ لَهُمُ الْجَنَّةَ»

Strive with ascetic detachment to expel from your heart anything beside Him so you may reach His proximity and dwell in His company, both in this world and the hereafter. O you who love the true and sovereign Lord, turn with His decree in whichever direction it turns you. Purify your heart, for it is the abode of God's proximity. Sweep it clean from everything besides Him. Then sit at the door of your heart and guard it by holding fast to the sword of glorifying God's sole sovereignty (**tawḥīd**), sincerity and truth-fulness, and open that door to no one other than Him. Let not the tiniest corner of your heart be occupied with anyone besides Him. O time wasters, this is no playground. O flakes of hollow nut shell. O husks, I have nothing but a kernel. Herein, I have loyalty without hypocrisy and truthfulness without lies. God Almighty wants piety and devout sincerity from your hearts. He does not regard your outer actions. God Almighty has said: "**It is not the meat or the blood (of your charities) that God receives, it is your piety that He appreciates**."

«لَنْ يَنَالَ اللّٰهَ لُحُومُهَا وَلَا دِمَاؤُهَا وَلٰكِنْ

يَنَالُهُ التَّقْوَى منْكُمْ»

O children of Adam, all that the world and the hereafter contain is created for you. Where is your gratitude? Where is your piety? Where is the indication of your loyalty and servitude to Him? Do not exhaust yourselves in offering deeds without soul. Actions have souls, and the soul of actions is sincerity.

❀ ❀ ❀ ❀ ❀

Chapter 25

To Have Ascetic Detachment in the World

It is related that whenever Jesus, upon whom be peace, smelled a perfumed fragrance, he would block his nose and say to his followers: "This is from the world, it will be held as a proof against you on the day of reckoning." O ye who with your words and actions pretend to have adopted a renunciate's life. You have merely put on the cloak of the ascetic, while inside you are still filled with desires, grief and sorrow for not having the pleasures of this world. You would be happier if you were to take off this mask and be frank about what desires your heart yearns for. You may like that better than your hypocrisy. When a true ascetic receives his share from this world, he wears it outwardly, while his heart remains filled with abstinence and disregard for it or anything else. Our Prophet, upon whom be peace, did say: "**There are three things from your world which I was made to like. They are perfume, women, and the delight of my eyes was placed on prayers.**"

«حُبِّبَ إِلَيَّ مِنْ دُنْيَاكُمْ ثَلَاثٌ :الطِّيبُ، وَالنِّسَاءُ،
وَجُعِلَتْ قُرَّةُ عَيْنِى فِى الصَّلَاةِ»

That is why our Prophet, upon whom be peace, was a greater renunciate than Jesus, as well as the other prophets, upon all of whom be peace. He liked women, perfume and prayers, though he had no attachment to them or anything else. They represented a share in his destiny and the decree of His Lord's preexistent knowledge, and he took his share in submission to and fulfillment of the divine command. Thus, whoever takes his share in such a manner (i.e., **zuhud** and obedience), will be in a state of worship, even if he wears the crown jewels of the entire world. O ascetics walking on the feet of ignorance. Hearken, believe and do not contradict. Understand this kind of knowledge, so that you may not refute the truth of the divine decree with your ignorance. Anyone who has not fathomed this knowledge, who suffices himself with his personal opinions and agrees with what his mind, desire (**nafs**), passion, and satan tell him is a slave of the accursed satan (**iblis**), the one without hope. He follows him and makes **iblis** his teacher and shaikh. O ignorant ones. O ye hypocrites. How unjust are your hearts. How offensive is your stench. How insane are your babbling tongues. Repent from all your sinful deeds. Cease attacking God Almighty and His intimate friends, whom He loves and Whom they love. Do not criticize them for partaking of their shares apportioned for them by God Almighty, which shares they take by command and not by desire. Their fervent and penetrating love for God Almighty and their intense yearning for Him make them renounce everything for His sake. Inwardly and outwardly, they abstain from everything except the allotted portions written in their names. They cannot escape from taking them. Their worst calamity is to indulge in this world or to become known to it, to remain immersed in its glitters, to enjoy their allotted portions and to mingle with the nonbelievers who accuse God Almighty and them of lies and falsehood.

Child, as long as you remain subject to your mind and desire (**nafs**) and passionate attachments, abstain from talking with the people. Have no words to say to anyone. Should your Lord decree something for you, He will prepare you for it. Should He will, He can make you renowned with all your family and He will establish you in that station, but it will be He Who will bring forth the demonstration of His benevolence, not you. Thus, surrender yourself, your speech and your whole being to His decree, and occupy yourself in working for Him. Be like deeds without words, sincerity without falsehood, and praise His sole sovereignty without any associations with Him. Be anonymous rather than known. Rest in the dimness of solitude rather than in the light of fame. Be an essence without a form, an inward without an outward, and abolish your own intention (**niyyah**). You speak to the Almighty Lord and point to Him (in every prayer) by saying: "**Thou art Whom we worship and Thine help we seek**."

«إِيَّاكَ نَعْبُدُ وَإِيَّاكَ نَسْتَعِينُ»

This speech is in the present tense. It is addressed to someone present herein. "Thou art Who is present herein. You Who knows me, Who is near me, Thou art the witness over all my actions and thoughts." Talk to Him with this kind of clarity of intention and in this manner during your prayers, or at any other time. That is why the Prophet, upon whom be peace, said: **"Worship God as if you were seeing Him. Even if you cannot see Him, know well that He is seeing you."**

«اَعْبُدِ اللهَ كَأَنَّكَ تَرَاهُ، فَإِنْ لَمْ تَكُنْ تَرَاهُ فَإِنَّهُ يَرَاكَ»

Child, purify your heart by taking in only lawful earnings, and by eating only permissible food. Then you will know your Lord. Make sure that every bite you eat is clean, that every piece of cloth you wear is clean. Cleanse your food, your clothing and your heart and you will become pure. Sufism is a word which is derived from the (Arabic) word **safā'**, meaning purity. O ye who emulate the wearing of woolen garment (**süf**). A sufi who lives by the true practices of the path first purifies his heart and then rises with it above anything other than his Lord. This state cannot be achieved by merely changing the raiment you wear, or by making your face yellow and emaciated, by hunching your shoulders or by joining a group of like people, who babble with stories about the righteous ones. Nor can it be achieved by moving your fingers like prayer beads, repeating the adequate praises of **tasbïh** (Subhān-Allāh), Praise be to God, and **tahlïl**, (uttering the formula: "**Lā-ilāha il-Allāh**," there is no god other than Allāh). Instead, a true ascetic state comes through truly seeking God Almighty, by renouncing the world, through freeing one's heart from attachment to the creation and by being partial to nothing but God Almighty.

It is related that someone, God bless his soul, once said: *"One night I prayed: 'O Lord. Deprive me not from what benefits me and does not offend You:." He further related: I slept that night after saying that prayer repeatedly. During my sleep I saw a dream. It was as if someone were telling me: 'And you too, disdain not from performing a deed which benefits you, and abstain from doing what causes harm to you.'"*

O ye people! Make true your lineage to your Prophet, upon whom be peace. One who correctly emulates his character is of true lineage to him. However, merely saying: "I am his follower (**ummah**)," without emulating his leading example will not benefit you. If you truly follow him in words and actions, you will be in his company in the hereafter. Have you not heard God's words saying: **"Do what the Messenger commanded you to do and abstain from what he forbade you to do."**

«وَمَا أَتَاكُمُ الرَّسُولُ فَخُذُوهُ وَمَا نَهَاكُمْ عَنْهُ فَانْتَهُوا»

Comply with what he commands you to do and abstain from what he forbids you to do. Such pursuit of obedience will bring your hearts to the proximity of your Lord in this world, as well as your souls and bodies in the hereafter. O ye ascetics, you do not know how to be true renunciates. Although you do disregard with detachment the calls of your carnal self (**nafs**) and passions, you still suffice yourselves with your own opinions. Follow and accompany the gnostic shaikhs, the learned and the workers who reach out to help people with a good word. They advise others with no selfish motive on their part. Be with them but keep your hearts with God Almighty, as they do. They seek Him and turn away from anyone else.

Child, turn your heart to your Lord before you are laid inanimate on your back. You have satisfied yourself by merely relating stories about the virtues of the righteous ones, chattering about their achievements and wishing you could attain their state. You are like one who closes his fist in the water, but as soon as he takes his hand out and opens it, there is nothing there. O fool. Mere hope is the valley of idiots. The Prophet, upon whom be peace, said: **"Beware of mere longing, for it is the valley of folly."**

«إِيَّاكُمْ وَالتَّمَنِّى فَإِنَّهُ وَادِى الحُمْقِ»

You still engage in the acts of evildoers and aspire to the stations of the righteous ones. He whose hope and anticipation for reward is greater than his fear of God Almighty is an atheist (**zindïq**), and he whose fear exceeds his hope will end in despair. Proper safety comes from balancing both hope and fear. The Prophet, upon whom be peace, said: **"If the believer's fear and hope were to be weighed, they would balance."**

«لَوْ وُزِنَ خَوْفُ المُؤْمِنِ وَرَجَاؤُهُ لاعْتَدَلَا»

Someone, God bless his soul, once said: "After Sufian Al-Thawri died, God bless his soul, I saw him in a dream and asked him: 'What did God Almighty do to you?' He replied: 'One of my feet *was put on the bridge to judgment (**sirāt**), and the other entered paradise.'"* May God's peace be upon him, He was a true jurist (**faqïh**), a true ascetic and pious one. He acquired the true knowledge and duly acted upon it. He gave his knowledge worth by acting upon it, and gave his deeds worth by being sincere in his actions (**ikhlās**). Hence, God Almighty rewarded him by satisfying his endeavors to reach His proximity, and He granted the Prophet, upon whom be peace, the acceptance of his follower. May God bless his soul, and those of all the righteous ones, and may we all be included in His mercy.

Whoever does not follow the Prophet, upon whom be peace, and does not take the laws of **sharī'a** in one hand and the Book which is revealed to him in the other hand, and does not reach God Almighty on his way, is doomed to destruction upon destruction. He becomes an instrument of deception that misleads others, and he himself goes astray. These two parameters (the Book and the law), are the guides to the ultimate truth of God Almighty. The Qur'ān is your guide to God Almighty and emulating the Prophet's leading example (**sunnah**) is the guide to the Messenger, upon whom be peace.

Our Lord, widen the distance between us and our carnal selves. **"Our Lord, grant us the benefits of a good deed in this world, the reward of a good deed in the hereafter, and protect us eternally from the sufferings of hell-fire."**

«رَبَّنَا آتِنَا فِي الدُّنْيَا حَسَنَةً وَفِي الآخِرَةِ حَسَنَةً وَقِنَا عَذَابَ النَّارِ»

✼ ✼ ✼ ✼ ✼

Chapter 26

To Conceal One's Difficulties from Others
Including Shaikh Abdul-Qadir Gilani's Daily Invocations

The Prophet, upon whom be peace, said: "**One of the treasures of the Divine Throne is the concealment of one's difficulties**."

«مِنْ كُنُوزِ العَرْشِ كتْمَانُ المَصَائِب»

O you who constantly complain about your difficulties, what benefits can your petition to the creations bring you? They have no power to harm or benefit you. Should you trust them to change your condition, as though they have a hand to open the door of God Almighty for you, that would be polytheism (**shirk**), which will only further distance you from Him, bring you under His wrath and veil Him from you. O ignorant one who professes to have knowledge. Amongst the signs of your ignorance are your asking for the wealth of the world from other than the hand of its Lord, and your asking for relief from your difficulties by complaining about them to the creations.

O unfortunate one, a vicious hunting dog can be trained to not eat the hunted bird and to deliver the animal, thus learning how to discard his karmic nature and gluttony. The falcon also can learn through training to oppose his innate nature by not eating the prey, as he did in the wild. Instead, the falcon delivers it to his master and satisfies himself with what he is left to eat. If all of that is possible, then your mind and desire (**nafs**) are more worthy of such training. Teach your carnal self and acquire this understanding before your mind and desire eat up your religious life (**deen**), rip your existence into pieces and betray the various trusts placed with it by God Almighty. The carnal self, mind and desire (**nafs**) has the believer's religion in its custody, as long as flesh and blood are entrusted to him (**amānah**). Let the carnal self (mind and desire) not walk in your company unless you have properly trained it. When it learns, understands, and becomes content, only then bring it along with you, never leave it alone, and take it wherever you go. When the carnal self (**nafs**) is content, it becomes forbearing, understanding, and accepts whatever is destined for it. It will create no differences as to the nourishment it receives, whether it be wheat bread or barley. It rises above luck and merges with it. At that point, abstaining from food becomes better than eating, as your controlled carnal self (mind and desire, **nafs**) becomes your helper to do good deeds, fulfills its rewarding duties, and prefers to satisfy the needs of others before its own. Its karma subsides as it becomes generous, open handed, detached from the world, and desirous of the hereafter and its rewards. Then in the hereafter, once you become detached from the controlled self, mind, and desire (**nafs**), and seek the company of your Guardian Lord, it will become your helper and seek His company too. It will become one with your heart and walk straight to His door. Henceforth, God's preexistent knowledge (**sābiqa**) says to it: "Eat this, for you did not eat it before and drink this, for you renounced this drink earlier." A patient in his proper mind does not eat except from the hand of his physician or by his orders. Meanwhile, he remains an adept student and accepts whatever his physician prescribes for him. He will curtail his gluttony whether the physician is present or not.

O greedy and hasty one. If all this food was created just for you, then who else could eat it other than you? Your clothing, dwellings, vehicle and wife were all created just for you. Who can take that portion away from you? What type of ignorance is this? Verily, you lack true steadfastness. You have no intelligence, no faith, and no trust in God's promise. O tough guy. If you work for a generous employer, then behave yourself. Ask not for riches or even wages from him—both will be given to you without your asking or impoliteness. Once he sees that you have renounced gluttony, greed, desire for everything you see and improper conduct, he will select you, treat you differently from your coworkers, comfort you, delight you, keep you at leisure, and appoint you as their supervisor. Thus, no one can remain in the company of the Just Lord through objection and opposition.

Instead, His proximity can be won only through good behavior, inner and outer peace and an unwavering consent to His will. Whosoever consents to the divine decree will enjoy the eternal company of God Almighty. A true gnostic (**'ārif billāh**) remains steadfastly on God's side and no one else's. He consents to His will and to no one else, and is alive in Him but dead to others.

Child, if you speak, do so with a good intention. If you remain silent, do that too with a good intention. You cannot draw any benefits whatsoever from any deed without first making the proper intention (**niyyah**). But in your case, whether you speak or remain silent, you are constantly at fault because you have not yet corrected your intention. So far, both your speech and silence have no prophetic traditions (**sunnah**).

O ye people! When trials affect your livelihood and earnings become scarce, you change to the worst. For even a single bite of food, you become most vehement. When a fraction of your benefits is deleted because of your own sins, you immediately explode and deny every other benefit you have, as though you have the power to dictate to Him and have orders for Him to fill. You say: "Do this. Do not do that. Why did You do this? It should have been like this!" Of course, you do that after having been rejected, abhorred, and denied His favors. Who do you think you are, O son of Adam? Have you forgotten that you were created from a discarded sperm? You had better become meek and humble yourself before your Lord. Without piety, your actions will not be considered gracious in the sight of your Lord, or that of His righteous servants. This world is the abode of the wisdom behind the divine decree (**hikmah**), and the hereafter is the abode of the indisputable divine power (**qudra**).

O ye people! You are under the constant watchful eyes of vigilant witnesses. They are commissioned by God Almighty to carry on their duties, but you are not even aware of it. Be wise. Open the eyes of your heart and look. If guests come to visit your house, be not the one who commences the conversation. Instead, let your words only reflect the answer to their questions. Ask nothing out of curiosity, and mind your own business.

It is obligatory (**fardh**) to constantly proclaim the indisputable sovereignty of God Almighty's Oneness (**tawhïd**). It is also mandatory (**fardh**) to seek only lawful (**halāl**) earnings. To seek to acquire the basic religious knowledge is a must. To have sincerity in one's actions is a must, and to disregard any expectations of a reward for one's deeds is a must (**fardh**). Save yourself! Escape from the insolent people and the hypocrites and join the company of the righteous ones amongst the sincere believers. Should you be confused and unable to differentiate between the righteous and the hypocrite, then stand up in the night, offer two **rak'āt** in prayers to God Almighty and ask: "O Lord, O my Cherisher and Sustainer, guide me to meet the righteous amongst Your creation. Guide me towards the one who can lead me to You, who can nourish me with your food and your drink, who enlightens the eyes of my clarity with the light of Your proximity, and who will tell me about what he eyewitnessed, not what was related to him in the traditions." Such true friends of God Almighty ate from the food of God's favors, drank from the water of His presence, and witnessed with their own eyes the door of His proximity. They were not fully satisfied with just hearing reports about Him. Rather, they strove, struggled, exercised patience and journeyed a great distance away from themselves and from the entire creation until they reached their destination. They then became acquainted with the truth. Once they reached the proximity of their Lord, He refined their conduct, polished their mannerism, and unveiled to them the undiminishing wealth of wisdom and true knowledge. He showed them His kingdom and made them fully realize that there is no one in the heavens or the earth besides Him, no giver other than Him, no one who deprives besides Him. No one can move any object whatsoever, or make it inanimate other than Him. There is no bestower or judge other than Him, no exalter or abaser other than Him, no subjugator or subduer other than Him, and no conqueror besides Him. He shows that to the eyes of their hearts and innermost beings. Consequently nothing in this world will be of any value or carry any weight in their eyes.

O Lord. We implore Thee to show us what Thou has showed them, and grant us pardon and well being. **"Our Lord, grant us the benefits of a good deed in this world, the reward of a good deed in the hereafter, and protect us eternally from the sufferings of hell-fire."**

«رَبَّنَا آتِنَا فِي الدُّنْيَا حَسَنَةً وَفِي الآخِرَةِ حَسَنَةً وَقِنَا عَذَابَ النَّارِ»

O ye people! Repent from disregarding the virtues of piety. Piety is a remedy, ignoring it is a disease. Repent to your Lord, for repentance is the cure of the illness of sin. One day, the Prophet, upon whom be peace, told his companions: "**Shall I tell you about your illnesses and its remedy**?" **They replied: Indeed O Messenger of Allāh. He said: Your illness is your sins and your remedy is repentance**."

«أَلاَ أُعَلِّمُكُمْ مَا دَائِكُمْ وَمَا دَوَائِكُمْ؟ فَقَالُوا بَلَى

يَارَسُولَ آللّهِ ، فَقَالَ:دَائِكُمُ الذُّنُوبُ وَدَوَائِكُمُ التَّوبَةُ»

Repentance (**tawba**) is the wedding celebration of faith. To regularly join the study circles of remembrance (**zikr**) and to obey God's commands cure one's faith. Repent with the tongue of true faith, and you will achieve success. Speak with the tongue of sincerity and constantly proclaim the indisputable sovereignty of God Almighty (**tawhïd**) and you will succeed. Strengthen yourself with your faith and make it your defense when visited by trials and adversities from your Lord.

(*At the beginning of every discourse, our Shaikh, God be pleased with him, would start with the invocation*): "**All praises and praising are due solely to Allāh, Lord, Cherisher and Sustainer of the universes**."

«الْحَمْدُ لِلَّهِ رَبِّ العالَمِينَ »

(*He repeated that prayer three times, stopping for a moment of contemplation after each invocation, then continued*): "All praises are due to God Almighty: praises to equal the number of His creations, to measure the weight of His Divine Throne, to meet His pleasure, to equal the number of His infinite words, to extend to the heights of His knowledge, to comprise all that He wills, creates, discards, originates, and restores to life again. Lord of what is unseen and what is manifest, the Merciful and Compassionate, the King, the Holy, the Almighty and Wise. I bear witness that there is no god other than Allāh alone, no associate has He. His is the dominion of the heavens and the earth, and to Him all praises are due. He gives life and causes death, while He is the ever living Who does not die. In His hand are all the treasures of wealth. He has power over all things, and unto Him everything is destined. I bear witness that there is no god other than Allāh, and I bear witness that Muhammad is His servant and Messenger. He sent him with the decree of ultimate guidance and the religion of truth. '**To proclaim it over all religions even though the polytheists may detest it.**'

"لِيُظْهِرَهُ عَلَى الدِّيْنِ كُلِّهِ وَلَوْ كَرِهَ الْمُشْرِكُونَ"

Our Lord, grant Thy utmost blessings upon Muhammad
and the family of Muhammad. Protect the leader of the country
and its nation, the guardian and the subjects. Our Lord, bring
unity and harmony amongst their hearts, and repel any evil that
any one of them may cause the other. Our Lord, you know what
thoughts we hide, please correct them. You know our needs,
please fulfill them. You know our sins, please forgive them. You
know our imperfections, please veil them. Our Lord, let us not be
seen where Thou hast forbade us to be. Find us not absent from
where Thou hast commanded us to be. Make us not forget Thy
remembrance, and make us not forget about Thy subtlety and
skill (**makr**). Let us need to seek none but You, and make us not
amongst the heedless. Inspire our guidance. Guard us from the
evil of our mind and desire, make us fully occupied in Thy service
and in none other than Thee, and cut off any disturbances that
might ever separate us from Thee. Our Lord, inspire us to be
constantly immersed in Thy remembrance, to be grateful to Thee,
and to properly engage in offering our devotion to Thee."

(Then he would turn his head towards his right side and say):
"There is no god other than Allāh. Whatever Allāh wills will be. We
have no will or power except by God Almighty, Allāh, the Most
Exalted, the Most Magnificent." *(Again, he would turn his face
forward and repeat the proclamation, then turn it to his left, and
repeat the same. He would then continue):* "Our Lord, do not put
us to test or expose our hidden secrets, do not charge us for our
misconduct. Make us not live in heedlessness and take us not
back to You in a sudden seizure."

**"Our Lord, condemn us not if we forget or fall into error.
Our Lord, pardon us and do not require us to suffer the
consequences of our wrongdoings, as those before us had to
do. Our Lord, lay not upon us a greater burden than we have
strength to bear. Expiate our sins, grant us Thy forgiveness,
and have mercy upon us, for Thou art surely our Protector.
Lord , grant us victory over the infidels and the disbelievers."**

"رَبَّنَا لَا تُؤَاخِذْنَا إِنْ نَسِينَا أَوْ أَخْطَأْنَا رَبَّنَا وَلَا تَحْمِلْ عَلَيْنَا
إِصْراً كَمَا حَمَلْتَهُ عَلَى الَّذِينَ مِنْ قَبْلِنَا رَبَّنَا وَلَا تُحَمِّلْنَا

مَا لَا طَاقَةَ لَنَا بِهِ وَاعْفُ عَنَّا وَاغْفِرْ لَنَا وَارْحَمْنَا أَنْتَ مَوْلَانَا
فَانْصُرْنَا عَلَى القَوْمِ الكَافِرِينَ»

(After these prayers, our Shaikh would sail into his talks
armed with revelations from the unseen with what God Almighty
had opened his heart. He spoke without any written preparation or
unnecessary words. Occasionally, he would have learned a saying
of God's Messenger, upon whom be peace, a proverb of virtue, or a
story about a wise man that someone in the audience related to him.
He then commenced his talk with that subject in order to share its
blessings and furthermore, he built his discourse on it.)

Chapter 27

Do not Lie

Be wise, do not lie. You say: "I fear God," when in fact you fear someone else. Fear not a jinn, a human being, or even an angel. Fear not anything, whether a rational being or a silent animal. Be not afraid of the sufferings of this world, of those in the hereafter. Instead, fear only God Almighty, Who has the indisputable power and will to inflict punishment. An intelligent person will fear no critic as long as he remains on God's side. He becomes deaf to anything beside God's speech. He sees the entire creation as powerless, infirm, and needy. He is a true believer and such are those like him. They are the possessors of knowledge (**'ulamā'**) from whom one can draw true benefits. Such teachers, who are well acquainted with the revealed laws and the real meaning of **Islām**, are like physicians to the religion. They have the knowledge and experience to correct any fracture of the connection to one's religion (**deen**).

O you, who have fractured the connection to your religion, come forward before such physicians, and let them treat your impairments. The One Who created the illness has also created the cure. He is best to know what is appropriate. Never accuse your Lord [عَزَّ وَجَلَّ] of being unjust. Your carnal self (**nafs**), mind and desire are the ones to blame, and let the accusations come from someone else. Say to your carnal self: The gift is for one who obeys, and the stick is for one who disobeys. When God Almighty intends the welfare of a servant, He will strip away his worldly possessions from him. Then, should the servant consent with patience and gratitude, God Almighty will raise him, comfort him, shower him with His bounty and fully satisfy him.

Our Lord, we implore You to grant us Thy proximity without trials or adversities. Shelter us with Thy kindness in whatever Thou hast destined and decreed for us. Protect us from the actions of the evildoers and shield us from the immoral conspiracies of the envious one. Be Thou our Guardian. Protect us as Thee intended and as Thou please. We ask for Thy pardon, and we implore Thee to bestow upon us a healthy religious life in this world and in the hereafter. Help us to do good and to have true devotion and sincerity in our actions. Amen.

A man visited **Abu Yazïd Al-Bistāmi**, God bless his soul, and kept looking right and left somewhat anxiously. Abu Yazid asked him: "Is there anything you need?" The man replied: "I am looking for a clean place to perform my prayers." Abu Yazid replied: "Cleanse your heart first, then pray wherever you want." No one can expose affectation better than the sincere ones, as they were once plunged into it, then freed themselves from it. In fact, affectation is a common hurdle on the path of the believers, and they have no way out but to cross over it. Affectation, self-admiration and hypocrisy are a few of the arrows that satan shoots at the heart.

O ye people! Accept what you are told by the true gnostic shaikhs and learn from them how to walk on the path leading to the true and sovereign Lord, for they have travelled it. Ask them about the different types of diseases of the carnal self, mind and desire, passions, and karmic habits that one may encounter on the path, for they had to undergo their own sufferings with them. They too experienced their dangers and consequences. Only after arduous struggle were they able to extricate themselves from them, overcome them, capture them and have mastery over them.

Let not your carnal self be inflated by the pride satan blows into your mind. Do not retreat when the arrows of your mind and desire strike you, for they are only satan's arrows, as he has no access to you except through your **nafs**. The satans of jinns have no access to you except through human satans, which are the mind, the desire and evil companions. So, cry out for salvation and ask God to help you conquer these enemies, for He will rescue you. Once you reach Him, discover what He has and receive it from Him, then return to your children and the people to take them back to Him. Say to them: "Bring all your family to me." The prophet Joseph, upon whom be peace, when he won the kingdom and its treasures, said to his brethren: "**Bring all your family to me**."

«ائْتُونِى بِأَهْلِكُمْ أَجْمَعِينَ»

A truly deprived person is one who loses his connection with God Almighty and misses being in His proximity, both in this world and in the hereafter. God Almighty has said in one of His Books: "**O son of Adam. If you miss My Presence, you would have missed everything.**"

«يَاآبْنَ آدَمَ إِنْ فُتُّكَ فَاتَكَ كُلُّ شَىءٍ»

How could you not miss realizing God Almighty when you are constantly turning away from Him and from the believers amongst His creation. You hurt them with your words and actions, thus objecting to them inwardly and outwardly. The Prophet, upon whom be peace, said: "**To hurt a believer is greater in God's sight than demolishing the sacred Ka'aba and the oft-frequented house of worship fifteen times.**"

«أَذِيَّةُ المُؤمِنِ أَعْظَمُ عِنْدَ اللهِ مِنْ نَقْضِ الْكَعْبَة
وَالْبَيْتِ المَعْمُورِ خَمْسَ عَشْرَةَ مَرَّةً»

Listen, O unfortunate one. Woe to you who keeps injuring those who need only God Almighty (**fuqarā'**). They are the believers in Him and are worthy of His nearness; as they truly know Him and trust in Him. What a fool you are. Don't you realize that soon you will be dead, and that you will be dragged from your home, laid on your back? Even your money, which is your pride for now, will be looted and can no further benefit or assist you.

Chapter 28

To Love in God Almighty

The Prophet, upon whom be peace, related that a man came to him and said: "Truly I love you in God Almighty." The Prophet replied: "Then take adversities for a garment, and wear poverty for a cloak."

«عَنِ النّبِيِّ صلىَّ ٱللّهُ عَلَيْهِ وَسَلَّمَ أَنّهُ جَاءَ إِلَيْهِ رَجُلٌ

فَقَالَ لَهُ: إِنِّي أُحِبُّكَ فِى ٱللّهِ عَزَّ وَجَلَّ فَقَالَ لَهُ:

إِتَّخِذ البَلَاءَ جِلْبَابًا، إِتَّخِذ الفَقْرَ جِلْبَابًا»

In a way, he was saying to that man, if you want to be like me, you must emulate my example, because consent is the primary condition of love. **Abu Bakr Al-Siddïq** [رَضِيَ ٱللّهُ عَنْهُ], God be forever pleased with him, when he proved his love for God's Messenger, upon whom be peace, spent all his wealth on the path to serve his beloved. He emulated his character and shared his poverty until he was left with only a woolen wrap strapped around him for a covering. He consented with the Messenger outwardly and inwardly, secretly and publicly. While you, O liar! You claim to love the righteous ones, yet you selfishly hide your dinār and pennies. Still, you want to be in their company. Think about it. This is clearly false love. A true lover never hides a thing from his beloved; instead, he gives him preference over himself in everything. Poverty never parted from the Prophet, upon whom be peace. That is why he said: **"Poverty flows to one who loves me faster than the rapids of a waterfall."**

«اَلفَقْرُ أَسْرَعُ إِلَى مَنْ يُحِبُّنِى مِنَ سَيْلِ المَاءِ إِلَى مُنْتَهَاهُ»

'Āisha, God be forever pleased with her, said: *"Life remained tight while God's Apostle, upon whom be peace, dwelled amongst us. When God Almighty took him to Himself, the world profusely* *poured its wealth into our hands."* Thus, in order to love the Messenger, one needs to emulate his poverty, and to love God Almighty, one needs to be steadfast and patient in the face of adversities.

Someone, God bless his soul, once said: *"Loyalty is subject to trials."* It is thus so that none can through lies, hypocrisy or affectation ever claim to possess the ultimate love for God Almighty. O man, refrain from your false claims and lies. Expose not your head to their dangers. If you come here, be then truthful, otherwise, do not follow us. Do not glamorize your coin in front of the money changer. He will not only refuse to accept your counterfeit, but surely he will expose you to shame. Do not endear the snake or the lion to you, for they will surely kill you. If you are 'Eve,' then go near the serpent. Only if you have strength, then go near the lion. To be on God's path, you need truthfulness and the guiding light of knowledge. Through it, the effulgent light of gnosis rises high in the hearts of the true believers, the truthful and true friends of God Almighty. Its radiance will never set, night or day.

Child, do not dwell in the company of the hypocrites, who are the subject of God's wrath. Be wise and do not go near the majority of people, for they are wolves wearing human masks. Hold to the mirror of common sense, look therein and ask God Almighty to let you see and recognize your own state and theirs. I have experienced the creations and the Creator, and I have found that evil comes from the creation, goodness from the Creator.

Our Lord, protect us from their evil and grant me the undiminishing wealth of Thy goodness, both in this world and in the hereafter. O ye people! I am not seeking you for my own benefit, but rather yours. My work is to twist and reweave your own ropes and tie up their broken ends. I do not take anything from you except for your benefit not mine. I have my own share, which suffices me. I only labor and trust in God Almighty for my earnings. I do not await what you bring me, as that pretentious hypocrite does. He has forgotten about his Lord, and depends on you and on what you bring him. I am the testing stone which verifies the nature of the people of this earth. Thus, be wise and do not come here and expose your profanities before me, for I know you well. I know your best from your worst as a result of God's preparing me and by His grace. If you want to succeed, then be like hot iron on my anvil. Let me hammer your brain, carnal self, mind and desire (**nafs**), passions, karma, satan, enemies and evil companions. Seek the help of your Lord to conquer them.

Victorious is the one who exercises patience in struggling with them; defeated is the one who is subjugated to them. The plagues are many, but their abode is one. The illnesses are many, though their physician is one. O ye who are sick! Put yourselves in the hands of the physician. Do not accuse him of wrongdoing, when in fact he is administering your treatment. He is more compassionate towards you than you are to yourselves. Serve him and stand guard always in readiness, awaiting his commands. If you do not oppose his instructions, you will recover completely and receive the undiminishing wealth of both this world and the hereafter. The true believers have adopted the restraints of silence, decline, languor and bewilderment. Once they achieve that state and remain thus, should it be God's will, He will cause them to speak in the same way He will make inanimate objects and the stones speak on the day of reckoning. The believers utter nothing unless He makes them utter it. They take nothing they are not given, and reach out for nothing unless they are made to do so. Their hearts join the ranks of the angels, about whom God Almighty has said: "**They never disobey God's commands, and act only by His orders.**"

«لَا يَعْصُونَ ٱللَّهَ مَا أَمَرَهُمْ وَيَفْعَلُونَ مَا يُؤْمَرُونَ»

They join the ranks of the angels and furthermore, rise above that station to know and realize their Lord and Cherisher. At that station, even the angels will accompany them to draw benefits from the knowledge and wisdom which pour into such pure hearts. Their hearts are guarded from all the afflictions that befall their bodies, senses and carnal selves. If you want to reach their station, then you must first correctly implement the state of true **Islām** in your life. Then abstain from sinful actions, whether your indulgence is private or public, cure them by the fear of wrongdoing (**wara'**), then become disinterested from even the permissible and lawful in this world. Suffice yourself with God's favors alone. Having attained that, then become detached even from seeking His favors and seek satisfaction solely in His proximity. If you can truly realize satisfaction in His proximity alone, He will shower you with His bounty, return your original share, and let you experience the undiminishing wealth of the gates of His kindness, mercy, and ultimate favors. In this case, He limits the comforts of this world, then expands them to a term. This endowment is reserved for the elite and rare amongst His intimate friends (**awliyā'**) and the most sincere ones in their love for Him (**siddïqïn**), because of His knowledge of their exalted piety, for they occupy themselves in nothing but Him.

Regarding most of the **awliyā'** and **siddïqïn**, the comforts of this world remain withheld from them, for He loves to see them free from anything but Him, and, most definitely, He loves to see them regularly coming before Him and asking for their needs. In their case, He knows well that should He grant them the properties of this world, they will fall short in serving Him and become occupied in serving them. These are the majority, and the elite are the rare and exceptional. Rarer still is the category of our Prophet, upon whom be peace. Amongst the endowments offered to him was the wealth of the entire world but that did not concern him, or prevent him from serving his Lord. He declined his share with the most perfect renunciation and abstinence. Even when the keys to the coffers of worldly treasures were presented to him, he again declined and prayed: "**O my Lord, grant me the life of the meek and humble ones, the death of the meek and humble ones and join me with them on the day of gathering.**"

"رَبِّ أَحْيِنِي مِسْكِينًا وَأَمِتْنِي مِسْكِينًا وَاحْشُرْنِي مَعَ الْمَسَاكِين "

Ascetic detachment (**zuhd**) is a special favor from God Almighty, otherwise no one is ever capable of renouncing his share. A true believer throws the weight of concerns off his shoulders and takes a complete respite from eagerness, greed or haste. He renounces the material world with his heart, abstains from it with his innermost essence, and solely occupies himself with that which he is commanded to do. He correctly understands that his share will not be lost, thus he does not need to ask for it. His share has to run after him and humbly request acceptance.

Child, first you need faith to guide you on the path to your Lord [عَزَّ وَجَلَّ]. Then you need certitude to set your course and strengthen your determination. At the beginning, you need to be immersed and absorbed in spiritual love (**hamayān**), at the end you need strong faith (**imān**). In contrast is the road to Mecca, about which someone said: "The road to Mecca needs faith first and then to be immersed and absorbed in spiritual love." But in truth, this road which I am pointing at, requires **hamayān** and **imān**, both at the beginning and at the end.

It is related that when **Sufian Al-Thawri**, God bless his soul, first entered the path of seeking knowledge, he tied a pouch carrying five hundred dinārs on his waistband. Out of it, he would spend for his daily needs, and pay for his learning. Occasionally, he would tap his pouch and say: "If it were not for you, these people would have pushed us around as they pleased." However, once he had acquired true faith and knowledge, and had known God Almighty [عَزَّ وَجَلَّ], he gave everything he had to the poor and needy in one day, then said: *"Even if the skies were made of iron that does not rain, and the earth from rocks that do not sprout forth, should I have any concerns about my daily bread, I would be a disbeliever."*

For now, you must work to earn your livelihood utilizing practical means (**asbāb**) until your faith grows. Once your faith in your Lord [عَزَّ وَجَلَّ] becomes stronger, only then move away from the cause towards the Causal Being Himself (**Musabbib**) [عَزَّ وَجَلَّ]. Even the prophets, upon all of whom be peace, had to work to earn their livelihood. In the beginning, before they became God's prophets, they used practical means. Then as God's prophets, they placed total trust in God Almighty and combined working for their livelihood with trust in Him. The work is **sharī'a**, and trust in God Almighty is **haqīqa**.

O deprived one of God's grace. Disdain not from working with your own hands to earn your livelihood, and depend not on what people give you. Do not seek their bounty. You will have denied the favors granted to you by the divine decree. This will cause you humiliation, and your Lord [عَزَّ وَجَلَّ] will abhor, dispel and distance you from Him.

In fact, to disdain from working for your livelihood and to strive after what people can do for you in itself is a punishment from God Almighty. When God stripped the prophet Solomon [عليه السلام] of his kingdom, one of the trials he was put through was to beg for his livelihood. When God Almighty tightened his means, He drove him out of his kingdom, and limited his resources until he had to beg the people for his food. The immediate cause of that humiliation and deprivation came from Solomon's

[عليه السَّلام] housing a woman who worshiped a statue in his palace for forty days. Thus, he was put through this punishment for an equal amount of time, day for day.

True believers can find no relief from their stress, no easing of their burdens, no comfort for their eyes, and no solace from their trials until they meet their Lord [عَزَّ وَجَلَّ] Meeting Him is two-fold: First, they meet Him in this world with their hearts and innermost being, which is extremely rare; then, they meet Him in the hereafter and see Him with their physical eyes. Before that, their lives consisted of trials and tribulations.

(Following that discourse, our shaikh [رَضِيَ اللّهُ عَنْهُ] *spoke about the nafs, and added):* Deprive your carnal self from all pleasures and intoxicants. Give it clean food without impurities. Clean food is the permissible (**halāl**), and impure food is the for-bidden (**harām**). Feed your **nafs** what is lawful to protect it from going wild, or becoming arrogant or foolish.

Our Lord, teach us about You, so we may know You. Amen.

Chapter 29

Never Humiliate Yourself to a Rich Man because of His Wealth

The Prophet, upon whom be peace, said: "**Whosoever thrives on ingratiating himself with a rich person, asking for what he possesses, will lose two-thirds of his religion.**"

«مَنْ تَرَعْرَعَ لغَنِيٍّ طَلَبًا لِمَا فِى يَدَيْهِ ذَهَبَ ثُلُثَا دِيْنه»

Listen, O ye hypocrites! This awesome loss awaits one who humbles himself before rich people. Therefore, what do you think will become of one who prays to them, fasts for them, journeys on a pilgrimage to them, and kisses their doorsteps? O you who associate others with your Lord [عَزَّ وَجَلَّ] and depend on them. You have no idea of who God is or what His messenger brought. Acknowledge your sins and submit to God Almighty in **Islām**. Repent and be sincere in your repentance so that your faith may be healed, your certitude may grow, and your profession of belief in God's Oneness (**tawḥīd**) may bloom, scented with perfume, while its fragrance rises to the Divine throne!

Child, once your faith grows and is properly trained, when its tree grows up high, God Almighty will enrich you and eliminate your dependence on yourself or the creation. He will satisfy all your needs and set you free from dependency upon what you earn or even the efforts to earn them. Your Lord [عَزَّ وَجَلَّ] will satisfy the hunger of your carnal self, mind and desires (**nafs**), heart (**qalb**), and innermost being (**sirr**). He will set you at His door and replace your poverty with the undiminishing wealth of His remembrance, His nearness, and the peace and comfort of His presence. Once you reach that state, you will no longer be concerned about who gathers what in this world or what anyone does. You will not care then in whose hand the world is. In fact, when you see someone who possesses riches in this world, you will feel compassion towards him, though by looking at him you will also experience constraint and darkness. O you who profess to have knowledge but keep asking for the wealth of the world from its children, humiliating yourself before them. Knowing you as such, truly you are one of those whom God Almighty has left astray. The blessings of your knowledge have gone, its kernel has gone, and a few flakes of husk are all that remain.

As for you who profess to worship your Lord [عَزَّ وَجَلَّ]. Your hearts worship the people, fear them, and implore them for your needs. Outwardly you appear to worship God Almighty, but inwardly you worship none but the creations. All you care about and ask for are their material possessions, their pennies, dinārs, and similar wealth, all of which will end in ruins. You keep hoping for their blessings and praises. You fear their wrath and blame. You fear that they might deprive you and you hope for their generosity. Your manners, deception, and soft speech occur only at their doors.

O ludicrous one, you are nothing but a buffoon, a polytheist, a hypocrite, a pretender, a profiteer, and an atheist. O fool, before whom do you think you are pretending grandeur? Is it before Him: **"Who knows the betrayal of a glance of an eye and Who knows what the hearts conceal?"**

"يَعْلَمُ خَائِنَةَ الأَعْيُنِ وَمَا تُخْفِى الصُّدُورُ"

O poor unfortunate one. You stand in prayers and say: **"Allāhu Akbar**, God is the greatest," but you lie because, in your heart, the people are greater to you than God Almighty. Repent unto Him, and be sure that none of your deeds are offered for other than His sake, and not for the sake of the world or even heaven. Be one of those who seek only His countenance. Give the Lordship (**rubūbiyya**) its due rights and do not work for the sake of receiving praises or compliments. Do not make offerings for the sake of reward or in fear of deprivation. O fool, your lot will neither increase nor decrease. Whatever good (**khair**) or bad (**sharr**) your destiny has for you will surely come to pass. Thus, be not concerned about what God Almighty has already decreed. Focus your attention on serving your Lord [عَزَّ وَجَلَّ], control your attachments, reduce your hopes, lessen your expectations, and recognize that your death is surely coming soon. Only then can you safely cross the bridge (**sirāt**). Always remember that you must, under all circumstances, comply with the laws of **sharī'a**.

O ye people! Do you not understand the benefits of complying with the laws of **sharī'a**? At present, you fail to properly comply with them outwardly and inwardly. You follow your carnal self, mind and desire (**nafs**), passion, and lust, heedlessly deceiving yourselves about God's forbearance. Day after day He lifts and extends His warnings. Unless you heed and repent, in the end, the punishment will descend upon you from every direction. O man. At the end He will seize you, and pour punishment over your head. Then comes death, and you will be lowered into your grave, to be laid therein. You alone will experience its tightness, darkness and sufferings. These shall be your companions until the day of resurrection. On that day, you shall be resurrected and driven to join the great gathering (**Yaomul-Hashr**). On that day, you will be questioned about each atom's weight of your actions and deeds, and you will be asked about the actions of each hour and about every minute detail.

You are stones without souls, statues without life, as powerless and worthless as weathered pieces of skin, useful only for burning in the fire. Your worship has no sincerity and, because of that, has no soul. That is why both you and your act of worship are worthy of no better destination than hell-fire. Frankly, you need not even bother if your deeds are void of sincerity. That is a total waste. You are like the group of people described in God's Book as: "**laboring in vain**." You work hard in this world, but without sincerity, only to stand in hell in the hereafter unless you repent and ask for God's forgiveness before death comes.

Return to your Lord[عَزَّ وَجَلَّ] now! Renew your **Islām**. Repent truthfully and sincerely before death comes, for on that day, the gate of repentance shall be closed and you will no longer be able to enter therein. Go back with your heart to Him now, lest He decide to close the gate of His bounty to you. Further, He might cast you as prey to your own carnal self, mind and desire (**nafs**), your own will, strength and worldly possessions, withdrawing His blessings from them all.

O fool, are you not ashamed of yourself before Him? You have made your money a god, your pennies your main concern, and you have completely forgotten about your Lord [عَزَّ وَجَلَّ]. Soon you shall discover what end awaits you.

Child, regard your jobs and money as the share of your dependents. Work for their sake and in accordance with the law of **shari'a**, and let your heart trust in God Almighty alone. Ask that your sustenance and theirs come from Him, not through your dependence on your job and income. In that case, He will provide for your needs and for theirs at your hands while He will grant unto your heart the blessings of His abundant favors, His proximity and His peace. He will take away your family's dependence on your person, suffice you in Him and enrich them as He pleases. At that point, it will be said to your heart: "This is for you and that is for your family."

Now, how can you reach what I have described when you spend your entire life equating yourself and others with God Almighty, veiled from Him, and banished from the company of His near ones? You never seem to have enough of the pleasures of this world or of gathering its wealth. Shut the door of your heart to anyone but your Lord [عَزَّ وَجَلَّ] . Forbid anyone else from entering. Let them permanently despair of ever entering there. Instead, make your heart the abode of the remembrance of God Almighty. Repent time and time again from your own wrongdoings. Show constant regret for your claim of independence and misbehavior. Cry hard for what you have done in aggression against your own soul. Comfort the needy with a little of your money. Do not be stingy, for soon you will part with it. A believer with unwavering certitude, determination and absolute clarity about the One Who inherits everything in the world and in the hereafter, is never stingy.

It is related that Jesus son of Mary, [عليهما السَّلام], once said to satan: "Whom do you love most amongst the creation?"

Satan replied: "A believer with avaricious qualities."

"And whom do you hate most?"Jesus [عليه السَّلام], continued.

Satan replied: "A sinner who is generous."

Jesus asked: "Why is that?"

Satan retorted: "Because I hope that the stingy believer will fall into the sin of disobedience through his avarice, and I fear that the generosity and good heart of the sinner may erase his sins."

O man, let your business in the world serve your basic needs. Earning your livelihood lawfully is ordained by the **shari'a**.

The purpose of your lawful earnings is to satisfy your needs and to let you use them to obey your Lord [عَزَّ وَجَلَّ]. Upon observation, one finds instead that you use what you earn to help you indulge in the sin of disobedience. Once you are financially comfortable, you become delinquent in your prayers and sharing through good deeds, and you delay in your payment of alms (**zakāt**). These are the signs of a sinner, not an obedient servant. Your earnings then become like the plunder of a highway robber. Death will soon come. On that day the believer will rejoice while the disbeliever and the hypocrite will be in agony. The Prophet, upon whom be peace, said: "**When a believer dies, he will wish that he had never been in this world for even an hour, in consideration of the bounty and blessings his Lord has reserved for him**."

«إِذَا مَاتَ الْمُؤْمِنُ يَتَمَنَّى أَنَّهُ مَا كَانَ فِى الدُّنْيَا وَلاَ سَاعَةً لِمَا يَرَى مِنْ كَرَامَةِ اللهِ عَزَّ وَجَلَّ لَهُ»

Where is the one amongst you who is steadfast in his repentance? Where is the one who is ashamed of himself before his Lord [عَزَّ وَجَلَّ], who is aware that God Almighty is observing his every move and thought? Where is the one who publicly and privately disdains forbidden acts? Where are those who lower the eyelids of their eyes and of their hearts, who look away when confronted by what is not lawful to see? The Prophet, upon whom be peace, said: "**Yes, the eyes commit adultery when they look at what is forbidden**."

«إِنَّ الْعَيْنَيْنِ تَزْنِيَانِ وَزِنَاهُمَا النَّظَرُ إِلَى الْمُحَرَّمَاتِ»

How often do your eyes commit adultery, gazing at what is not lawful for them to look at amongst women and boys? Do you not hear the words of God Almighty saying: "**Command the believers to lower their gazes and guard their modesty**."

«قُلْ لِلْمُؤْمِنِينَ يَغُضُّوا مِنْ أَبْصَارِهِمْ»

O poor man. O you who are needy. Be patient with your poverty. Worldly poverty always has an end. The Prophet, upon whom be peace, once said to his wife 'Aisha, may God be pleased with her: "**O 'Aisha, swallow patiently the bitter taste of this world and await the sweet bliss of the hereafter**."

«يَا عَائِشَةُ تَجَرَّعِى مَرَارَةَ الدُّنْيَا لِنَعِيمِ الآخِرَةِ»

Child, you never know what your name will be in the hereafter. You never know whether it will be written as 'miserable' or 'happy.' It is understood that God Almighty has kept that as His secret and preexistent knowledge. However, despite your lack of such knowledge, you should never abandon the fear of wrongdoing. Do not say: "It is written," then become disloyal or break the rules of **shari'a**. Instead, do what He commanded you to do, and be not concerned about what has been ordained. That is something hidden, and neither you nor anyone else has access to it. That knowledge is part of the unseen (**ghaib**).

The true believers have folded and discarded the sleeping bag of this world and stood long nights in the presence of their Lord [عَزَّ وَجَلَّ]. They enrolled in His service and joined the multitude of His servants. They take from the world their basic provisions and do not indulge in its pleasures. They train their bodies to remain in a constant state of worship. Guarding their modesty from satan's treachery and plotting, they follow the commands of their Lord [عَزَّ وَجَلَّ] and emulate the leading practice of their Prophet, upon whom be peace. In fact, everything they do is done with that determination and with the strength of detachment. Our Lord, make us one with them and let us share in their blessings. Amen.

Child, as long as the love of the world dwells in your heart, you will not experience even an iota of what the righteous have attained. The eyes of your heart will not open as long as you keep toiling amongst the people, equating them with God Almighty as providers. Say nothing until you truly renounce the world and its creation. Be steadfast in your efforts and you will see what others cannot see, when you break through the veils of the ordinary. If you discard what you anticipate, you will receive what you cannot foresee. If you practice piety and fear of wrongdoing, privately and publicly, depending solely on God Almighty, He will provide you with access to the unexpected. Once you renounce, He will give; once you discard, He will endow. At the beginning, discard everything for His sake and at the end receive everything from His hand. At the beginning, instruct your heart to discard the world and its pleasures, and at the end you will receive your share. The first state is that of the pious ones, and the second state is that of the representatives (**abdāl**) who have achieved true obedience to their Lord [عَزَّ وَجَلَّ].

O impostor, hypocrite, and polytheist. Do not compete with the righteous over what they have received from their Lord and what you are commanded to renounce. These are rare people. Do not desire what they have attained, for you have no power to affect it. They broke through the veils of ordinary habits, while you still hold on tightly. That is why their barriers were lifted, while you remain behind the veils. The pious woke to pray at night, while you slept. They fasted while you ate, they felt fear when you thought you were at peace, and they knew peace when you were afraid. They spent freely on God's path, while you begrudged giving charity. They worked to serve their Lord, while you worked for someone else. They continued seeking Him, while you sought someone else. They surrendered everything, while you withheld and fought Him.

Hence, the true believers were satisfied with His judgment. They restrained their tongues from complaining about their difficulties, but you did not. They patiently bore the bitter taste of adversity, and therefore the bitter became sweet. The knives of the divine decree cut through their flesh and they did not care, nor did they feel pain. They were floating in an ecstasy of wonderment, subdued by the sight of Him Who holds the power of destiny in His hand.

People feel at peace with the righteous, for they cause harm to no one. It is said that the truly righteous (**abrār**) are those who never hurt a soul, or even the tiniest of ants, which are barely visible to the naked eye. They pursue their connection with their Lord by fulfilling His commands. They act with good conduct with people, and they hold to the good ties of mercy and compassion with their families. This is why they live in heavenly bliss, both in this world and the hereafter. In the world they are blessed with God's proximity, and in the hereafter they dwell in the bliss of paradise, seeing their Lord, being close to Him, listening to His words and wearing His gifts. Are there any similarities between you and such people? It will be better for you to occupy yourself with repenting from your sins, your belligerence, your impoliteness, and your arrogance towards your Lord [عَزَّ وَجَلَّ].

O fool, be shy of God Almighty and not of His creation. He is the one who existed in eternity before any other existence became His creation. How is it then, that you are shy with the temporal, yet belligerent with the Primal Lord? He is the Generous One, and everyone else is miserly. He is the Rich One, and everyone else is poor. He endeavors to give, while others strive to deprive. Present Him with all your needs, for He alone has the power and wealth to fulfill them. Find Him through His work. Find Him where He displays His craft. Be steadfast in observing the rules of **shari'a** and remain pious in His presence without fail. If you are steadfast in that state of piety, He will lead you to Himself, where you will be occupied in serving Him, instead of serving what He created. Find Him, ask for Him. Begin by detaching from the world and the hereafter, for your preordained share will not pass you by. Discarding everything except Him will purify your heart from its burdens. However, if your heart does not point you towards Him, you will live like brainless cattle. Wake up! Discard this world and join the company of the wise, those whose hearts have led them to God Almighty. Learn wisdom from them. Then, with that wisdom, know yourself and your Lord.

Alas! Your life is being wasted, but you are unaware of it. How long will you maintain this obstinacy about the hereafter and run after the world?

O fool! What has been allotted as your food, no one else will eat. Likewise no one else shall sit in your place in paradise or in hell. Truly, heedlessness has captured you, and passion and lust have imprisoned you. You care for nothing but your food, drink, sexual life, sleep, and attaining your personal goals. Your worries are the worries of the nonbelievers, the pretenders, and the hypocrites. Your greed is never satisfied, whether it is for lawful or unlawful food. Your heart cares not a bit whether or not you have a religion by which to live.

O poor indigent one, cry for yourself. When your own child dies, you act as though the world has come to an end; but when your religious life (**deen**) dies, you do not care at all or cry for it. Even the guardian angels in charge of you are crying for your sake when they see the great loss you have incurred. Truly you have no brain. If you had one, you would have cried over the loss of your religion. You have capital, but you make no effort to use it. Your brain and modesty are your capital, but you do not know how to barter with them properly. A knowledge which you do not act upon, a brain which you do not put to use, and a life without benefit—these are like a vacant house, a hidden treasure, and food which goes to waste before it is eaten. Even if you do not recognize the state that you have fallen into, I do. I hold the mirror of **sharï'a**, which represents the manifest decree (**al-Hukmu-zhāhir**). I also carry the mirror of knowing God Almighty, which is the inner knowledge (**al-'ilmul-bātin**).

So wake up from your slumber, wash your face with the water of wakefulness, and see for yourself. What are you? Are you a Muslim or a reprobate? Are you a believer or a hypocrite? Are you a monotheist or a polytheist? Are you affected or sincere? Do you consent with or oppose God Almighty? Are you happy with Him, or discontent? God Almighty does not care whether you are content or discontent. The losses or benefits are yours. Glory to Him, the Generous, the Forbearing, the Benevolent Lord [عَزَّ وَجَلَّ]. Everything is under the umbrella of His kindness and bounty. If not for His kindness, we all would have perished. If He were to confront each of us for every act we do, we all would perish.

Child, look at yourself. You consider it a favor to God Almighty when you worship Him. Then, despite your being easily distracted during prayers, by pride, falsehood, and hypocrisy, you still dare to ask for a highranking station. You ask Him to shower His blessings upon you, while you continuously challenge His righteous servants in spite of your own moral decay. Why do you have to mention them, or let alone claim to know them? O runaway slave. O fugitive. O deviate from the circle of the righteous and those who believe in God's Oneness among this nation (**ummah**).

O poor unfortunate one, cry for your losses, so that He may turn to you. Reflect upon your calamity, and put on the garb of a mourning, so perhaps He may come to comfort you. You are separated by veils from Him, but you do not know it.

A righteous man, God bless his soul, once said: *"Woe to the unfortunate who are veiled and not even aware of it."*

O fool, what kind of heart do you have? What do you understand? To whom are you complaining? For whose help do you cry? With whom do you sleep? When you fall into difficulties, whom do you trust? Talk to me. I know your lies and hypocrisy. To me, you and all creations are like mites. I know the truthful ones amongst you, and those I humbly serve. Should it be the wish of a true believer, he may bring me to the marketplace and sell me. He may even lease my labor to someone else and keep the profits. Should it be his wish, he may even own my clothing and anything else I have. He may even order me around or turn me into his own laborer. I will let him do that. But as for you, you have no truthfulness, no belief in God's Oneness, nor faith in Him. What Shall I do with you? Shall I patch you into a crack and bury you? Nay, you are like defective lumber, good for nothing but the blazing fire.

O ye people, the world will one day vanish, and life in it will come to an end. The hereafter is ever near. Knowing that, you still do not care. Your main concerns are still with the world and what you can get from it. Truly, you are the real enemies of God's favors. When He tries you with adversities, you cry aloud when He tries you with ease and comfort, you keep it secret. If you hide God's favors and show no gratitude for them, He will strip them from you. It is told that the Prophet, upon whom be peace, said: "**When God Almighty bestows a favor upon a servant, He likes to see him wear it.**"

«إِذَا أَنْعَمَ اللهُ عَزَّ وَجَلَّ عَلَى عَبْدِهِ نِعْمَةً أَحَبَّ أَنْ تُرَى عَلَيْهِ»

The true believers have concentrated their worries and made them all one. They cast out all material things from their hearts and replaced them with One thing unlike others. They freed their worship from pride, falsehood, hypocrisy, and affectation, and established in their place a true state of worship of their Lord [عَزَّ وَجَلَّ].

Yet you remained slaves of the creation, slaves of affectation, falsehood, and hypocrisy, slaves of people, passion, luck, and praises. Only those amongst you whom God Almighty willed to realize a true state of worship will attain it. These are rare and unique ones. Some of you worship the world, would love it to be permanent, and fear that it will perish; another group worships the people, fears them, and implores them. Others worship paradise and yearn for its comforts, but do not beseech its Creator [عَزَّ وَجَلَّ]. Some worship the fire of hell and fear it, but do not fear its Creator. Who are these created beings? What is paradise? What is hell-fire or anything besides Him? God Almighty has said: "**They were commanded to worship Allāh alone, to offer their devotions sincerely to Him and never to deny their religious covenant.**"

«وَمَا أُمِرُوا إِلاَّ لِيَعْبُدُوا اللهَ مُخْلِصِينَ لَهُ الدِّينَ حُنَفَاءَ»

Those who have true gnosis and knowledge of God Almighty worship Him for His sake alone, not for any other purposes. They offer due reverence to His Lordship (**rubūbiyyah**), and perform their worship (**'ubūdiyyah**) with its due rights. They worship Him in compliance with His command and because they truly love Him, nothing else. They solicit only Him and discard everything for His sake. By contrast, you are forms without souls. You live in the outer form, and they live within the essence. You are like statues, and they are the embodiment of inner truth. You are loud spectacles, while they are hidden secrets. These true treasures of God Almighty are the men of the prophets [عليهم السلام] and their servants. They walk beside them, right, left, front and behind. They eat and drink the leftovers from the prophets' plates, and they act according to the knowledge they acquired from them. That is why they are worthy of being their inheritors. The Prophet, upon whom be peace, said: "**The people of knowledge are the heirs of the prophets**."

«العُلَمَاءُ وَرَثَةُ الأَنْبِيَاءِ»

Once they act according to that which the prophets [عليهم السلام] taught, they become their viceregents, inheritors, and representatives. O fool, alas! Don't come here to bring up the letter of the law alone. Comply with it! A case without evidence does not merit investigation. Like that, knowledge without actions brings no benefit. The Prophet, upon whom be peace, said: "**Knowledge calls for actions. If actions do not respond, then knowledge will depart**."

«يَهْتِفُ العلمُ بالعَمَل فَإِنْ أَجَابَهُ وَإِلاَّ آرْتَحَلَ»

The blessings will depart, but the chaff will remain. The husk will be there, but the kernel will be gone. O ye who have neglected to act upon the knowledge you have learned. Some of you are so skillful in memorizing and reciting an entire collection of poetry with its meticulous expressions, flawless elegance, eloquence, and style; yet you still do not possess enough diligence or sincerity to act accordingly. If only your heart would learn proper conduct (**adab**), your entire body would follow suit. The heart is the king of the body. When the king is good, the subjects will learn goodness. Knowledge is the shell; actions are its kernel. The shell is kept to preserve the kernel, and the kernel is kept to preserve the oil; but what can be done with an empty nutshell? If the kernel has no oil, what can it be used for? Like that, knowledge will depart when one's actions do not conform to it. What benefits can you attain if you merely study and memorize what you do not act upon?

O man of knowledge, if you wish to gather the undiminishing wealth of this world and the hereafter, then act according to what you have learned and teach it to others. O rich man, if you want to acquire the benefits of this world and the hereafter, then comfort the poor and the needy with some of your money. The Prophet, upon whom be peace, said: **"People are God's dependents. The ones He loves most are those who care about His dependents and benefit them the most."**

All praises and glory are owed to Him Who makes some people need others. He knows the wisdom of doing so. O rich man, how can you run away from me? The charity I collect from you is for your own benefit. My true wealth comes from God Almighty and He alone enriches me. You will see the day when He shall make you need my help.

Ibrahïm Ibn Adham, God bless his soul, when he saw little patience on a poor person's face, would pray: *"Our Lord, extend Thy benevolence and generosity to us in the world, but make us not attached to it. Our Lord, do not veil its comforts from us or make us desire them. Make us not perish running after them. O our Lord, show us Thy mercy and kindness in whatever judgment and destiny Thou wilt for us. Amen."*

❋ ❋ ❋ ❋ ❋

Chapter 30

Acknowledge God's Favors with Gratitude

Blessed is he who shows gratitude towards God's favors, who acknowledges them as His blessings, who ascribes all success to Him and who discounts himself, his material means and will from any power to effect such attainment. A wise person does not credit himself with the success of his labor, nor does he under any circumstances anticipate any reward for it from God.

O unfortunate one, you worship God Almighty without true knowledge, you practice abstinence without fathoming it, and you take your share from this world without understanding. You are encumbered with veils upon veils, which is the result of your being utterly despised and repudiated. You do not differentiate between good and evil, neither do you care whether things belong to you or to others, nor do you know your true friends from your enemies. This is the result of your ignorance of God's decree and your disdaining to serve the gnostic shaikhs, the shaikhs of actions and knowledge whose function it is to guide you to your Lord [عَزَّ وَجَلَّ].

First, you proclaim the testimony, there is no god other than Allāh (**lā ilāha il-Allāh**). This must be followed by action in order to reach your Lord [عَزَّ وَجَلَّ]. No one who ever reached that state did so except through true knowledge, renouncing the world and abstaining from it, both inwardly and outwardly.

The seeker on the path of asceticism casts the world away from himself, but the fully realized ascetic extracts the world completely from his heart. With such beings, abstinence becomes a fully ingrained habit which is intermingled within their bodies and souls. The fiery temper of their karmic habits becomes extinguished, their passions are defeated, their souls are appeased and no evil could possibly rise again from their carnal selves (mind and desire).

Child, asceticism is not a trade you can engage in, nor is it something you can pick up with one hand and throw away with the other. Asceticism is a step by step development. The first step is to look straight at the world and see the nature of its reality. See it as it was seen by all of God's prophets and messengers (upon all of whom be peace), and as seen by God's intimate friends (**awliyā'**) and representatives (**abdāl**), who are present in every age. You can see the world in its reality only by following in the footsteps of your predecessors on the path with words and actions. Once you emulate their example, you will see what they perceived. Once you follow their example with words and actions, body and soul, in knowledge and practice, publicly and privately; once you fast the way they fast; pray as they pray; partake your share from this world the way they do; renounce what they renounce; and love them with all your heart, then God Almighty will grant you a light through which you can see your own reality and that of others.

He will make you see your own blemishes and deficiencies and those of others as well. You will be able to detach yourself from your own carnal self, its karmic desires (**nafs**) and the entire world. Once that state is achieved, then the resplendent light of His proximity will dawn upon your heart, and you will become a believer who has true faith, certitude and determination. You will become a gnostic and a wise man who has the true knowledge to see things as they are in their real form and essence. You will see the world with the same clarity as seen by those ascetics and renunciates who preceded you on the path. You will see it as ugly-looking and deformed. This is how the world is seen by such people, while in the eyes of the patrons and kings of this world, it looks like a young bride with sparkling beauty. The true ones see the world as despicable and discarded. They burn its hair, scorn its robe, scratch its face, and take their share from the world forcibly and in spite of it, while remaining wholly engaged and immersed in the realms of the hereafter.

Child, if you can grow true ascetic detachment in the world (**zuhud**), then do so by first abstaining from making your own choices. Become free from attachment to the creation. Fear them not, nor ever implore them for anything. Scrutinize carefully everything your desire suggests to you, and do nothing it suggests until a decree comes from your Lord [عَزَّ وَجَلَّ]. You will recognize

His decree for you either through an inspiration to your heart or a dream, or by finding yourself despising and avoiding that which desire has suggested to you. Even if your personal emotions are calm about the matter, the main point of recognition is in the heart. If the heart is peaceful and quiescent concerning it, you may take that as evidence of God's will. Otherwise it will be a catastrophe.

You can have no peace unless, your carnal self, mind, desire, karma, passions and anything other than your Lord [عَزَّ وَجَلَّ] die away. Only then will you be alive in His proximity. First is death to the carnal self, then comes the resurrection. Next, if it be His will, He will broaden your existence. He may even return you to the people to serve their real interests and bring them back to the door of their Lord [عَزَّ وَجَلَّ]. You will turn only to the world or the hereafter to reach and receive your share from them. You will acquire a new might which will help you to endure the stress of dealing with people, and to guide them away from their heedlessness, and help them fulfill God's commands in that respect. However, should you not wish to do so, you will find that remaining in His proximity is the perfect satisfaction and freedom from everything else. You can never find satisfaction in the creations once you have realized the Creator [عَزَّ وَجَلَّ], Who created everything before they ever existed, and Who Himself existed in eternity before anything was created, the One Who shaped every form, and Who will be there after everything is annihilated.

O ye people! Your sins are pouring like heavy rain, so counter them by repenting with every breath. O unfortunate one, you are futile, wild, lewd, lustful and a trespasser. Look around you at the defaced graves and talk to its people with the tongue of true faith; they will surely tell you about their conditions.

Child, you profess to represent God's will and claim to be carrying the staff of His representatives. Despite all that falsehood, I let you indulge in your claim without quarreling with you or defaming you in public. O ye people! I swear by God Almighty that you shall be questioned about my admonishing you here today. I will testify to your falsehood and cut off the heels of the hypocrites and the liars in words and actions amongst you. I have repeatedly probed many shaikhs and questioned them with the criterion of truth before I was accredited with such right of investigation.

O ye people of this earth. O ye dough kneaders. Your actions have no salt. Come here and take all the salt you need. O ye salt buyers, come forward. O ye hypocrites. Your dough has no salt. It is unleavened. It needs the yeast of knowledge and the salt of sincerity. O you hypocrite. You are imbued with hypocrisy. Your hypocrisy will soon become the fire which will burn you. Dispel this nonsense from your heart, and you will be saved. Once the heart acquires true sincerity, the body will follow it and both will become free. The heart is the shepherd of the body. Once the heart follows the path of righteousness, the body will follow suit. Once the heart and the body turn to honesty and uprightness, the believer's growth will have reached its goal, and he becomes the shepherd of his family, neighbors and town. His station rises in relation to the strength of faith he acquires and his nearness to his guardian Lord [عَزَّ وَجَلَّ].

O ye people! Have good conduct with God Almighty as you are always in His company, and beware of His swift retribution. Follow His judgment (**hukum**), for He, in His infinite wisdom and preexistent knowledge (**sābiqa**), has assigned to each one of you the duty of following His commands. Act according to His rulings and fulfill their terms. Once you obey His commands, they will then take you by the hand and bring you before the Master for Whom you have worked. There you can draw benefits from a knowledge which you could not otherwise have gained. There you will be with Him by His knowledge, and with His creations by His judgment (**hukum**). Nevertheless, you have not yet complied with the first duty of prescribing to His commands, though you keep asking for the second part, which is to be with His creation and be their teacher.

Nay, listen. Once you establish a strong foothold on the first step and are confirmed there, then call for the second station. You have not yet recognized the student, how could you then meet the teacher? Be wise, and relinquish your demands. First acquire knowledge, then practice it with devout sincerity. The Prophet, upon whom be peace, said: "**Learn first, then renounce.**"

$$ تَـفَرَّغْ ثُـمَّ اعْـتَـزِلْ $$

A believer is one who first acquired the obligatory knowledge before he withdrew to his privacy to worship his Lord [عَزَّ وَجَلَّ]. He experienced the creations and detested them, but when he experienced his Lord [عَزَّ وَجَلَّ], he loved Him, sought His company and asked to serve Him. The people came after him, but he ran away from them and sought someone else. He renounced them and had desire for someone else. He understood well that the creation has no power to produce harm or benefit, good or evil, and if any of that is done through them, it will all be done by God Almighty Himself and no one else. Such a believer also recognized that being distant from the people is more beneficial than mingling with them. Thus, he went back to the source and stepped away from the branch. He understood that the branches may be many, but the trunk of the tree is one, so he held tight to it. He looked into the mirror of reflection and contemplation and realized that waiting at one door is better than waiting at many doors. Thus, he stood by God's door and held firmly to its knob.

A believer of true faith, certitude and sincerity is a wise person because he is given the best of understandings, and that is why he steps aside and declines the world.

Chapter 31

The Good Type
and the Bad Type of Anger

After some talk, our shaikh ارضی آللهُ عَنْهُ *said:* If anger is dictated by love for God Almighty, then it may be praiseworthy, but should it be caused by anything else, then anger is blameworthy. A believer holds fast in support of God's cause, but not for own. He defends God's message, not his personal gains. He may even become extremely angry if someone breaks the laws of God Almighty, as a tiger becomes angry should someone dare to pull away his hunted food. For the sake of such a believer, even God Almighty Himself will be angry towards one who upsets His servant, as He will be pleased with one who makes His servant happy.

O man, do not pretend that your anger is for God's sake, when in fact it is for your own. That will make you a hypocrite, besides other things. What belongs to God Almighty will grow, last and be fulfilled, but anything else will be subject to change and ultimately vanish. Whatever you do, do it without personal desires **(nafs)**, passions, or satanic qualities. Dispel all of that, and do nothing if it is not for His sake and in compliance with His command. Do not act except by sure command from God Almighty, which can be determined either by the revealed laws of **shari'a**, or by inspiration to your heart, which must not counter the revealed laws.

Renounce yourself, the creation, and the whole world, and He will then relieve you from their burdens. Yearn for the peace, joy and comfort of His proximity alone. In fact, there is no peace or tranquility except in His presence, and no comfort other than with Him. This can be achieved only after cleansing yourself and becoming free from the encumbrances and stresses of your mind, desires, passions and self-centered existence. Join the company of the true believers and you will be strengthened by their strength. You will see what they see, and God Almighty will be proud of your attainment, as He is proud of theirs. The Sovereign King will speak of you amidst His high ranking subjects. Purify your heart from anything other than Him and you will see everything through Him. You will see Him as the all-pervading Sovereignty, and through Him you will see His work toward His creation. Just as you would not come before worldly kings with dirty clothing, how dare you attempt to come before God Almighty, King of all kings, when your heart is filled with impurities!

You are like a large urn filled with dirty sediments. What can be done with you? Turn your urn upside down, throw away its contents, then wash it clean. Only then may you be fit to enter before kings. Your heart is filled with sins, fear of the people, feebleness and complaisance towards them, as well as love of the world and its glitters—all of which is just a speck of the impurities contained in your heart. Say nothing unless your carnal self, mind and desires (**nafs**) die and are carried on the coffin of your truthfulness. At that point, it will be of no importance whether you mix with the people or not. Remain silent as long as your awareness is saturated with their presence and finds in them something to gain. Do not even extend your hand for them to kiss. Say nothing unless you become seized with the awe of His proximity. Then you will be preoccupied and unconcerned about them or their kissing of your hand, their gifts or lack of them, and their praises or blame. Once your repentance is true, your faith will become true and it will grow.

In fact, according to the people of sunnah, the Prophet, upon whom be peace, taught that one's faith may increase or decrease. It grows with obedience and diminishes with disobedience. This is a general rule that concerns the majority of the people. As to the elite (**khawās**), their faith increases when their hearts become free of the people, and diminishes when they become attached to them again. Their faith grows when they hearken to their Lord [عَزَّ وَجَلَّ], but diminishes when they hearken to other than Him. They trust in Him, depend on Him, become pious by Him, lean on Him, fear Him, and rely only on Him, return to Him for all their needs, glorify His divine Oneness, and depend solely on His guidance. Thus, they become charmed and captivated by the One Who has no associate. In their hearts they glorify His Oneness, and outwardly they comfort the people. Even if someone transgresses against them out of ignorance, they do not reply in kind. God Almighty spoke of them saying: **"And when the ignorant ones address them, their reply is 'Peace.'"**

«وَإِذَا خَاطَبَهُمُ الجَاهِلُونَ قَالُوا سَلَامًا»

You must control yourself. Be silent and forbearing towards the transgressions of an ignorant person when the bullish karmic nature of his mind, desire (**nafs**) and passion rise up. However, should he commit a sin against God Almighty, then speak out, for it becomes unlawful to resort to silence in such a case. Your speech then becomes an act of worship, whereas should you refrain from pointing out the truth, that in itself would become a sin. If you can enjoin the right and forbid the wrong, then fail not to do so, for an auspicious gate has opened before you to enter. Take advantage of that opportunity.

Jesus, upon whom be peace, would feed on the grasses of the desert , drink the water of its pools, and rest in caves and ruins. When he slept, he used a stone or his forearm for a pillow. Such is the example for a believer, who should be preparing himself to meet his Lord [عَزَّ وَجَلَّ]with the same resoluteness. Should he still have a share in this world, it will surely come to him. It will suit his outer form, satisfy the basic needs of his carnal self (**nafs**), while his heart remains unwavering with its Lord [عَزَّ وَجَلَّ].

The heart of a believer once seized by ascetic detachment is not changed by his success in the world or taking his share from it. If a believer loves the world and its people or indulges himself in its desires and pleasures, he will not be able to bear being distant from them even for a moment. Day and night, he will be preoccupied in serving them, and certainly fail to worship his Lord [عَزَّ وَجَلَّ] , or take refuge in His company, remember Him or even obey His commands. That is why God Almighty will let him see his own faults in order for him to repent and regret the days he spent in emptiness. Then, through the instructions of the revealed Book, the leading example of the Prophet, upon whom be peace, and the explanations of the gnostic shaikhs, God Almighty will let him see the deficiencies in this world, and his ascetic detachment will naturally grow. Every time he looks at one deficiency, he discovers many more, and subsequently realizes that this world is perishable. Being temporary and short lived, its pleasures are momentary, its beauty is ever withering, its character is ferocious, its claws kill, and its words are poisonous. Often it divorces its lovers, has no ethics, honor or promise and, in fact, to erect a foundation on it is like trying to build a house on water.

Such a believer chooses not to take the world as an abode for his heart, or as a house for himself. He rises one more station, whereby his faith, certitude and determination become stronger. He then realizes his Lord [عَزَّ وَجَلَّ] and then chooses not to make the hereafter an abode for his heart either. Instead, he chooses proximity to his Lord and Master to be his final destination, both in the world and in the hereafter, and he makes it the resting place for his heart and innermost being to dwell therein. At that point, even if he were to build the entire world or a thousand houses therein, that would be not impede his own progress, for he would be building for others, not for himself. He subscribes to God's commands in doing anything, and consents to His judgment and decree. His Sovereign Lord will appoint him to serve the people and to comfort them. He works day and night cooking and baking for others, and does not eat even a single bite from it. A special food will be reserved for him from which no one else can partake. He breaks his fast when his own food arrives, yet remains fasting and hungry when feeding others. An ascetic is fasting from food and water most of the time, and a gnostic is always fasting, but without his own knowledge of it. He is kept on a special diet and never eats except from the hand of his own physician. His illness is distance from his beloved, and his medicine is His proximity. The ascetic fasts during the daylight hours, but a gnostic fasts day and night. He never breaks his fast until he meets his Lord [عَزَّ وَجَلَّ]. He practices a life of perpetual fast and is constantly feverish. His heart is always fasting and his innermost secret being is constantly feverish. He has understood that his total recovery will come when he meets his Lord and remains in His proximity.

Child, if you want to succeed in your life, then free your heart from the people and remove them from it. Fear them not, ask them for nothing, search for no delight or peace in their company and be not pacified by their presence. Have aversion for them all and run away from them. Feel disgusted and nauseated by them as though they were a decaying cadaver. Once you can do that, then you will be able to find peace in the invocations and remembrance of God Almighty (**zikr**), and you will feel disturbed if anyone else is mentioned.

Chapter 32

Fulfill the Divine Command

After some talk, our shaikh [ارَضِىَ آللهُ عَـنْـهُ] *said:* Fulfill what is commanded. Abstain from what is forbídden. Exercise patience when facing adversities, and seek God's proximity through added devotions (**nawāfil**). Then you will be called a vigilant worker who strives for success, while depending on the help of his Lord [عَزَّ وَجَلَّ]. Do so without pretense and with a steady endeavor to attain His pleasure, and He will use you.

Ask Him and humble yourself before Him. Implore Him so that He may provide you with the real tools (**asbāb**) of devotion. Hence, should He intend you for something, He will prepare you for it. His command is that you hasten, and success will come from Him. What is manifest is His command, and what is hidden is its success. Forbiddance of wrongdoing is the manifest order (**zāhir**), and within that order (**bātin**) is a hidden protection from evil consequences. With His help, you acquire determination. By His guardianship and protection, your abstinence matures, and by His infallible power, you succeed at exercising patience.

O ye people! When you come here, use your intellect and insight, and have steadfastness, good intention, certitude and determination. Remove from your heart any accusations against me and have only good thoughts towards me. Only then may you reap the benefit of what I say and understand the inner meanings. O you who persecute me. When tomorrow comes, you will discover in what I am immersed. Do not contend with me, otherwise your heart will be defeated and you will be forced to retreat. The weights of this world are on my head, the hereafter weighs on my heart, and God Almighty weighs on my innermost being. Thus, do I have a helper amongst you? Is there someone here who knows how to come forward and endanger his own head?

All praises are due to God Almighty and by His grace I need the help of no one but Him [عَزَّ وَجَلَّ]. Be wise and behave yourselves properly with the true servants of God Almighty, for they are the removers of obstacles. They are the instruments of God's providence to the people and the land. They are God's deputies on this earth and its protection. Because of them, the earth is saved from destruction. What do you think your affectation, hypocrisy and polytheism could rescue? O ye hypocrites. O enemies of God Almighty and His Messenger, upon whom be peace. O ye logs for the hell-fire.

O beloved Lord, turn to me and to them and accept our repentance. Our Lord, wake me and wake them. Have mercy upon me and upon them. Free our hearts and bodies and make them serve only you. If we are not able to do that, then let our physical forms serve the needs of our families in their worldly affairs. Let our desire be for the hereafter, and our hearts and innermost beings be solely for You. Amen.

Child, nothing can come from you if you are the doer. Nothing comes from you, though you must be present. Remain steadfast at the gate of the work site until you are hired. You and success (**tawfiq**) are like that: You are the worker, success is the one who hires you, and God is the Owner. He commanded you to hasten to obey His commands, and He will guarantee your success.

O unfortunate one, you have entangled yourself in the rope of fear and dependence on other people. Remove these shackles from the feet of your mind and desire (**nafs**) and discover how naturally your carnal self will hasten to serve its Lord and Cherisher [عَزَّ وَجَلَّ]. It becomes peaceful and content (**mutma'in-na**) in His presence. Make your carnal self become detached from any desire for this world, its pleasures, women or anything else therein. Should any of these things be written in your destiny, they will come on their own accord, without your will or asking. At that point, God Almighty will call you an ascetic. He will look at you with His divine benevolence and you will not miss even the tiniest bit of your share in this world. However, as long as you depend on your own will, power and material possessions, then nothing will come your way from the treasury of the hidden wealth.

There is a proverb which says: *"While there is something still in your pocket, nothing else would come from the hidden treasure."*

Our Lord, we take refuge in You from ever depending on our own resources or living in hallucination, attached to our passions or karmic habits. We take refuge in You from all evil under all circumstances.

"Our Lord, grant us the benefits of a good deed in this world, the reward of a good deed in the hereafter, and protect us eternally from the sufferings of hell-fire."

«رَبَّنَا آتِنَا فِي الدُّنْيَا حَسَنَةً وَفِي الآخِرَةِ حَسَنَةً وَقِنَا عَذَابَ النَّارِ»

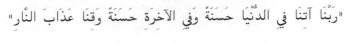

الْحَمْدُ لله رَبِّ الْعَالَمِين

Chapter 33

Seeing God Almighty
on the Day of Reckoning

He who meets someone who loves God Almighty has indeed seen
one who has seen God Almighty with his heart and stood before
Him with his innermost being. Our Lord [عَزَّ وَجَلَّ] exists, and can
be seen. The Prophet, upon whom be peace, said: **"You shall
certainly see your Lord (as clearly) as you see the sun and the
moon."**

«سَتَرَوْنَ رَبَّكُمْ كَمَا تَرَوْنَ الشَّمْسَ وَالقَمَرَ لاَ تُضَامُوْنَ فِى رُؤْيَتِه»

God can be seen today with the inner eyes of one's heart, and
tomorrow with the physical eyes. **"There is nothing like unto
Him, and He is the All-Hearing, the All-Seeing Lord."**

«لَيْسَ كَمِثْلِه شَئٌ وَهُوَ السَّمِيْعُ البَصِيْرُ»

Those who love Him can find satisfaction and pleasure in
Him, and none else. They seek His help and refuse the help of
anyone else. The bitter taste of poverty in this world becomes
sweet to them. In this world they have poverty, contentment and
bliss. Poverty is their wealth, sickness is their bliss, and bewilderment is their comfort. They are near when distant, and happy in
their hard work. So blessed be ye who are the patient and
contented ones, who have won their inner struggle against the
carnal self (**nafs**), mind, desires and passions.

O ye people! Agree with Him and consent to what He does
unto you and unto others. Make no pretense of having wisdom
and knowledge before one who is wiser than you. God Almighty
has said: **"God knows everything, and you do not."**

«وَاللَّهُ يَعْلَمُ وَأَنْتُمْ لاَ تَعْلَمُوْنَ»

Stand before Him bankrupt of your wisdom and knowledge

('**aql**) ready to receive the gift of His knowledge. Remain puzzled and make no demands. Be puzzled about Him, so you may receive knowledge of Him. First, there is uncertainty , then clarity, then knowledge. First, there is intention, then attainment. First there is will, then fulfillment.

Listen carefully and act accordingly, for I am only reweaving your loose ropes and tying up their broken ends. I have no concerns other than your concerns, I have no burden other than your burdens. I am like a free bird. Wherever I land, I pick up something. The problem is in you, who have anchored yourselves to heavy rocks. You have impaired your own freedom. O prisoners of mind and desire, who are unable to break away from your passions.

Our Lord, have mercy upon me and upon them.

Chapter 34

Dispelling Arrogance

After some talk, our shaikh [رَضِيَ ٱللّٰهُ عَنْهُ] *said:* The work of God's servants is to exert their utmost to comfort the people. His servants are the true benefactors and laborers of love, robbing from here and giving there. They spirit away gifts from God's benevolence and mercy and grant them unreservedly to the poor, the meek and the destitute. They pay the debts of the indigent ones who are cramped in the constraints of indebtedness and have no means to repay what they owe. These are the true kings of the world, not the rulers and sultans who steal from the people but give nothing back. God's servants offer what they have and patiently await what is to come. They take only from God's hand, not from the hands of the creations. What their physical bodies earn goes to the people, but what their hearts earn will be theirs. They spend what they have to please God Almighty, not for the satisfaction of personal goals, praises or recognition by the people.

O man, dispel your arrogance towards God Almighty and His creations. Arrogance is one of the qualities of the tyrants who will be thrown face down into the hell-fire. If you incur God's displeasure and anger, you are arrogant. If you do not answer the call to prayer when the muezzin calls, you are arrogant towards God Almighty Himself. If you be unjust to any one of His creations, you are arrogant towards God Almighty Himself. So, repent unto Him. Be truthful and sincere in your repentance before He justifies your destruction at the hands of the weakest ones amongst His creatures, just as He did to Nimrod and other such kings. When they showed arrogance towards Him, He brought them humiliation after might and suffering after comfort. He caused them to die after having experienced the joy of living in this world.

O ye people! Show some piety. Polytheism can be manifested outwardly as well as inwardly. The outer form of it is to worship idols, but the hidden one (**shirk**) is to depend on the people or even to consider them capable of causing either harm or benefit. Among the people, there may be one who is extremely wealthy, but wealth neither affects him, nor is he attached to it. He controls it, and it does not control him. It loves him, and he has no love for it. It runs after him, and he never runs after it. He uses it, and it does not use him. He disposes of his wealth as he pleases, and that does not weaken him. Such a one has indeed made his heart truly worthy of God Almighty. The wealth of the whole world has no power to spoil such a heart. Subsequently, he disposes of it, and it has no power to distract him from his focus. That is why the Prophet, upon whom be peace said: "**Blessed is good wealth when in the hands of a righteous man.**"

" نِعْمَ ٱلْمَالُ الصَّالِحُ لِلرَّجُلِ الصَّالِحِ "

He also said: "**There is no benefit in this world except for one who says: 'Blessed is good wealth**, etc.'" He pointed out that such a righteous servant of God Almighty is one who regularly distributes his money with his own hands for charitable and other constructive causes. Keep the world at your reach to serve God's dependents, but dispel it from your heart, for you will incur no loss. Let the comfort and glitters of this world not deceive you, for soon you will depart from it, and the world itself will follow suit.

Child, do not dismiss what I say to follow your own opinion, for you will go astray. Whoever contents himself with his own opinion will stray from the path, experience humiliation and be at fault. If you stubbornly stick to your personal opinion, you will be deprived from guidance and protection, because you did not seek them, or ever sought a way to receive them. You say: "I do not need the opinion of the gnostic shaikhs," though you claim to have knowledge. Then where is the action? What is the evidence of your claim? Where is the proof? Your claim to have knowledge can only be verified when coupled with actions, sincerity, patience in adversity, and when you are constant, without anxiety, and do not complain to people. You are blind. How can you claim to have sight? You have poor understanding, then how can you claim to have clarity? Repent from your false pretenses and seek the help of God Almighty alone and none else. Avoid everyone and seek the

Creator of everyone. The plight of one who lost or he who won, of one who died or he who became a king are not your concern. Just correct your carnal self until it becomes content and recognizes its Lord [عَزَّ وَجَلَّ]. Only when you reach that state, may you then look at others. Seek the road of consenting to His purpose. Seek His companionship in this world and in the hereafter, and hold onto piety and impartiality. Confine yourself to Him only. Forget the good deeds you perform and accept no titles or credit for them. Adorn yourself with nothing but abiding by what is permissible and abstaining from the forbidden, for He then has established you in that duty. O man and woman, blessed is he amongst you who possesses even an atom of sincerity, an atom of piety, an atom of patience and gratitude. However, I find you bankrupt from such claims.

Chapter 35

Giving Reverence Only to God

After some talk, our **shaikh** [رَضِيَ اللّهُ عَنْهُ] said: Woe to you, O arrogant ones, your devotions and prayers are not meant for earthly gain. Instead, they should ascend to the heavens. God Almighty said: "**Unto Him ascend all words of purity, and He exalts each deed of righteousness.**"

«إِلَيْهِ يَصْعَدُ الكَلِمُ الطَيِّبُ وَالعَمَلُ الصَالِحُ يَرْفَعُهُ»

Our Lord [عَزَّ وَجَلَّ] is firmly established on the Divine Throne of authority, He alone has dominion over the creation, His knowledge encompasses everything, and He is the originator of all marvels. There are seven verses[1] (**āyāt**) revealed in the **Qur'ān** which emphasize these meanings. I cannot erase or ignore them to satisfy your ignorance and volatility. You raise your sword against me, but that does not frighten me. You try to lure me with your money, but I do not desire it. I fear God Almighty and none else. I ask only from Him, and no one else. I worship Him, and no one else. I work for Him, and for no one else. He is my Sustainer and Cherisher, and no one else. Everything belongs to God. The servant and his personal belongings are God's property.

During this discourse, our shaikh [رَضِيَ اللّهُ عَنْهُ] *mentioned that over five hundred people have embraced* **Islām** *at his hands, and over twenty thousand Muslims have repented from their sins. He added:* These honors (**karāmāt**) are the blessings (**barakāt**) of our Prophet, upon whom be peace. God Almighty said: "**He alone knows the unseen. He does not let anyone be acquainted with His mysteries—except an apostle whom He has chosen.**"

«عَالِمُ الغَيْبِ فَلاَ يُظْهِرُ عَلَى غَيْبِهِ أَحَدًا

إِلاَّ مَنِ ارْتَضَى مِنْ رَسُولٍ»

He alone knows the mysteries of the unseen. Seek His proximity, so that you may see Him and find what He has hidden for you. Move your heart away from your family, wealth, town, wife and children, and bid farewell to them all. Walk with your innermost being (**sirr**) towards His door. Once you reach His door, then be not distracted by His servants, His sovereignty or His kingdom. If you are offered a plate of delicious food, do not eat from it. If you are offered a place to rest, do not enter. If you are offered a wife in marriage, do not consent. Do not accept anything until you come before Him [عَزَّ وَجَلَّ] just as you are, disheveled and fatigued, with your garment covered with dust from the journey. Let Him be the One who changes your condition, satisfies your hunger, and quenches your thirst. He will be the comforter of your bewilderment, the One who relieves your grief, dispels your fatigue, grants you His protection and annihilates your fears. His proximity will become your wealth, and His gaze upon you will become your food, water and clothing.

Thus, do not befriend the creation. What is the meaning of the phrase 'To befriend the creation (**tawallil-khalq**)?'[2]

«تَوَلَّى الخَلْقَ»

It means to elevate them to a state of reverence. It means to fear them, to place one's hope in them, to implore them, to feel at ease in their presence, and to trust them. This is what in truth befriending the creation means.

"Our Lord, grant us the benefits of a good deed in this world, the reward of a good deed in the hereafter, and protect us eternally from the sufferings of hell-fire."

«رَبَّنَا آتِنَا فِي الدُّنْيَا حَسَنَةً وَفِي الآخِرَةِ حَسَنَةً وَقِنَا عَذَابَ النَّارِ»

❀ ❀ ❀ ❀ ❀

---

1) Al-Fātiha , Chapter 1.
2) Tawallil-khalq: From the root of the Arabic word wilāya; trust, entrust, appointment.

وَٱللَّهُ وَلِيُّ ٱلتَّوْفِيقِ

GOD IS THE GUARDIAN OF SUCCESS

GLOSSARY

'Azza wa Jalla: [عَزَّ وَجَلَّ] Lord of Majesty & Glory
'Abd: Servant
'Ainul-yaqïn: Absolute certainty; death
'Aisha [رَضِيَ ٱللَّهُ عَنْهَا]: Wife of the Prophet, upon whom be peace
'Alïm: The All-Knowing Lord; Omniscient; a man of knowledge
'Ãlim: Doctor of religious studies
'Aliyyïn: Heavenly paradise; uppermost station
'Aql: Power of understanding; brain
'Awãm: Laymen; common people
'Ãrif billãh: One who knows God Almighty
'Ãrif: Gnostic
'Ãrifïn: Plural of 'Ãrif
'Ilm: Knowledge
'Ilmu-zhãhir: Outer, manifest knowledge
'Ilmul-bãṯin: Inner, hidden knowledge
'Isma: Protection from wrongdoing
'Ubüdiyya: Enslavery
'Ulamã': Luminaries; men of knowledge, see 'ãlim
'Uqül: Fathom; power of understanding; plural of 'aql
Abdãl: Deputies; representatives
Abdullãh: Servant of God
Abraham: The prophet of God, upon whom be peace
Abrãr: Righteous devoted servants; true ones
Adab: Proper conduct
Ahlul-kahf: Companions of the cave
Aḥsani takwïn: The best of creation
Ajyãd: Good ones
Al-ḥukmu-zhãhir: Outer judgment
Al-'ilmul-bãṯin: Inner knowledge
Al-Lowhul-Maḥfüz: The Preserved Tablets; the book in which the preexistent knowledge, and divine decree is written

Allāhu Akbar: God is the greatest
Amal: Hope; aspiration
Amāna: Trust
Amïr: Commander; prince; leader
Ammāra-bi-sü': The untamed carnal self; commands wrongdoing
Amr: Command
Ar-Rafïq Al-A'lā: God Almighty; The Upper Companion
Arbāb: Deities; worldly patrons
Asbāb: Direct causes; rope; created forces, tool
Asfār: Books
Awliyā: Intimate friends of God Almighty; representatives
Azal: Infinity
Āsiya: Wife of pharaoh
Badal: Deputy; representative
Baqā': Eternal existence
Bātin: Inner; hidden
Birr: Devoted; dutiful; devotion
Bismillāh: In the Name of God
Deen: Religion; way of life
Dinār: Unit of money
Du'ā: Supplication; prayer
Dunyā: Lower world
Fanā': Non-existence; annihilation
Faqïh: One who understands religious jurisprudence
Faraj: Relief; divine help
Farā'idh: Obligatory performances of religious rites
Fardh: Obligatory, religious duty incumbent upon every Muslim
Farïdha: Single religious obligation
Fikr: Inner contemplation
Fiqh: Religious jurisprudence
Fuqarā': The meek; the poor ones; the true devoted ones
Ghaib: Unseen
Ghaibiyya: Knowledge of the unseen
Hāal: State; changing conditions; spiritual attainment
Halāl: Permissible
Hamayān: To be immersed and absorbed
Haqïqa: Infinite truth
Haqq: The true Lord; right

Harām: Forbidden; impermissible
Hazz: Fortune; luck; lot; share
Hawul: Might; power
Hikmah: Wisdom; judgment
Himmah: Will; determination
Hubbu-nufūs: Passionate tendencies of the carnal self; love for one's self
Hudhūr: Presence; being there
Hukmul-bāṭin: Inner judgment; hidden knowledge; knowledge of the unseen
Hukum: Judgment; decree; the sphere of the world of creation
Iblis: Attribute of satan, the one without hope
Iftaqarat: State of emptiness; poor; wealthy, without needs
Ihkāmul-hukum: Establishment of the divine laws
Ikhlās: Sincerity
Ilhām: Inspiration
Imām: Example; title of the Muslim community leader; the person who leads prayers in the Mosque
Imān: Faith
Iqān: To have certitude
Islām: Submission to God's will; religion of Islām
Istislām: Unconditional surrender
Jahannam: Hell-fire
Jayyideen: Good ones; well behaved
Jāhil: Ignorant
Jihād: Inner and outer struggle
Jihādu-nafs: Struggle to subdue one's carnal self; inner struggle
Jinn(s): Creation invisible to mankind, made of fire which does not have smoke; one jinni; plural, jinn
Ka'ba: God's House in Mecca; the focal point of prayers
Karāma: Blessings, by the grace of
Karma: Inherent nature
Kāfir: Disbeliever; reprobate
Khair: Good; welfare; divine benevolence
Khalïfa: Viceregent; successor; caliph
Khalq: Creation
Khalwa: Spiritual retreat
Khawās: Intimate friends; elite
Khulafā': Plural of Khalïfa; caliphs

Kitāb: Book; The Holy Qur'ān
Kufr: Disbelief; ingratitude; atheism
Ladunnï: Knowledge from God's own
Lailatul-Qadr: Night of Power; eve of the 27th day of the month of Ramadān; the night the Holy Qur'ān was revealed
Lā ilāha il Allāh, Muḥammadur-Rasül Allāh: The proclamation of faith: there is no God but Allāh, Muhammad is the Messenger of Allāh
Lisānul-ḥāl: Prevalent expressions; words of reality; language expressing current prevailing conditions
Li-Wajhillāh: For God's pleasure; a deed without expectation of reward
Luṭf: Subtle kindness, **Latïf**: the Kind One
Ma'rifa: Gnosis; knowledge of God Almighty
Ma'aṣiya: Sin; disobedience
Maḥārïb: Niches; prayer center in a mosque where the Imām stands to lead prayers; point of retreat; recess
Maḥbüb: Beloved; beloved of God Almighty
Maḥjüb: Veiled from God's grace
Maqām: Station; permanent status
Mawālï: Followers
Mazhab: Religious school of thought
Mecca: The center of the world; The city of the Ka'ba (the house of God; The city of pilgrams
Mi'rāj: Nocturnal journey; ascension
Mu'min: Believer
Muḥibb: Lover; seeker of God Almighty
Munājāt: Inner spiritual conversation; supplication
Muqri': Qur'ān reading teacher; one who recites the Qur'ān
Murād: Intent; one who is sought
Murïd: Seeker
Musabbïb: Causal Being; Provider
Mushāhada: Looking straight at Him; face to face; witnessing
Muslim: Surrendered one; one who submits himself to God Almighty; one who follows the religion of Islām
Mutma'inna: Peaceful; content; trusting
Muwaḥḥid: One who believes in God's oneness; monotheist; one who celebrates God's Oneness
Muwaḥḥidün: Plural of muwaḥḥid
Müqin: One who has certitude; see yaqïn

Nafl: Supererogatory prayers; extra devotion
Nafs: Carnal self; mind and desire; passion; Plural: anfus; nufüs
Nafs-ul-mutma'inna: Peaceful soul; trusting and content self
Nahi: Forbidding what is evil
Nawãfil: Plural of nafl
Niyya: Intention
Noor: God's attribute; effulgent light
Qadar: Divine decree; destiny; measure
Qadã' wa qadar: Fate and divine decree
Qalam: Pen; The primal pen of decree
Qalb: Heart
Qawm: People of the faith; the righteous ones; the common people
Qiyãma: The day of resurrection; first death
Qudrah: Power; divine power
Qur'ãn: The Book of Revelations which brought the final message to the humans and the jinns; revealed to the Prophet Muhammad, upon whom be peace
Qurb: Proximity to God Almighty; nigh, close; near
Qutb: Pillar; pivot; pole; center
Rabb: Cherisher and Sustainer; Lord
Rabbãnï: Spiritual dependence; devotee; godly
Rahma: Mercy; compassion
Rak'ãt: Grouping of prayers
Ramadãn: The 9th. lunar month; month of obligatory fasting in Islãm
Rubübiyya: Divinity; Lordship; Sovereignty
Rüh: Soul
Rühãniyyün: People of the upper echelon of spiritual quest; spiritualists; devotees
Sabab: Direct cause, created cause; instrument of
Sabr: Patience
Sadaqa: Charity; favor
Safar: Book, plural asfãr; journey
Salawãt: Blessings
Salãm: Peace; regards; greetings
Salãma: Safety
Salãt: Prayers; obligatory daily prayers
Sãbiqa: preexistent knowledge; foreknowledge; antecedent

knowledge

Sāhib: Companion; accompanying on the road

Sālihïn: Righteous ones; ones who reformed themselves

Shafā'a: Interceding authority; accepted intercession

Shaikh: Teacher of religious precepts; guide; gnostic; man of knowledge; old man

Shaikhul-'ilm: Teacher of inner knowledge

Shaikhul-hukum: Teacher of religious norms

Sharï'a: Revealed laws; God's laws; divine laws

Sharr: Evil, bad

Shirk: Associating partners to God Almighty; polytheism

Shukr: Gratitude; thankfulness

Siddïq: One who is sincere in his love for God Almighty

Siddiqïn: Plural of siddïq

Siddiqün: See Siddiqïn

Simāt: Characteristics; qualities

Sirāt: Straight Path; road; crossing; bridge

Sirr: Secret; innermost being

Subhān-Allāh: Praise be to God

Sufism: An Islāmic spiritual school of thought

Suhba: Fellowship; companionship; travelling companion

Sunnah: To follow the leading example of the Prophet Muhammad, upon whom be peace

Süf: Wool; woolen garment

Süfi: See süfism

Ta'atïl: Denying God all attributes

Tābi'ïn: Followers; those who emulate the prophetic sunnah and the practices of the companions

Tajsïm: Embodiment; magnification

Takalluf: Mannerism; ostentation; affectation; pretense

Takwïn: Originating; creating; original form of man

Tarïqa: Path; a method of a shaikh; good manners

Tarubat yadāk: To become wealthy; without any need

Tarubat: Dust-covered

Tashbïh: Ascribing human characteristics to God Almighty

Tawakkul: Trust in God Almighty: reliance

Tawba: Repentance

Tawfïq: Success; blessings

Tawhïd: Believing in God's Oneness; monotheism

Tā'a: Obedience

Thākir: One who remembers God's Almighty; see zikr
Turāb: Dust; dirt; earth
Turuq: See tarïqa
Ulul-'ilm: Those who possess true knowledge
Umma: Nation; followers of the Prophet, upon whom be peace
Uns: Comfort; intimacy
Uns-billāh: To enjoy peace in God
Wahdāniyya: God's Oneness; God's Unity
Wahï: Revelation; inspiration; the archangel Gabriel, upon whom be peace
Walï: Trustee; representative; intimate friend
Wara': Reverence and fear of wrongdoing; to fear God Almighty
Wārithïn: Inheritors; heirs of the message
Wilāya: Empower; appointment of guardianship
Wujüd: Existence
Yaomul-Hashr: The day of gathering; the coming together of the creation for judgment
Yaqïn: Certitude; death
Zakāt: Due-alms; charity
Zamān: Time; epoque; period
Zāhid: Ascetic
Zhāhir: Manifest
Zhāhira: Manifestation; phenomenon
Zikr: Remembrance of God Almighty
Zindïq: Reprobate; atheist; free thinker
Zuhhād: Ascetics; renunciates
Zuhd: Ascetic detachment